women & history

VOICES OF EARLY MODERN ENGLAND

◆

Edited by Valerie Frith

IRWIN
PUBLISHING

This edition published 1997 by Irwin Publishing
1800 Steeles Ave. West,
Concord, ON
L4K 2P3
First published by Coach House Press 1995
Printed in Canada

Illuminated Texts, A Series Edited by Valerie Frith

Published with the assistance of the Canada Council,
the Ontario Arts Council, the Department of
Canadian Heritage and the Ontario Publishing Centre.

Canadian Cataloguing in Publication Data
Main entry under title:
Women & history: voices of early modern England
ISBN 0-7725-2398-3
1. Women - England - History - Modern period, 1600-   Sources.
2. English literature - Women authors.
I. Frith, Valerie. I. Title: Women and history.

HQ1593.W65 1997   305.42'09032   C97-930153-X

To the historians who made a place for women in English history, especially Alice Clark, Dorothy George, Ivy Pinchbeck, Eileen Power and, of course, Catharine Macaulay.

CONTENTS

INTRODUCTION

The two centuries encompassed by this anthology transformed England, in many ways. In 1600, Elizabeth I, the last of the Tudors, had three years left in her forty-five-year reign as the Virgin Queen. Shakespeare's home, the Globe Theatre, where he would wear the hats of actor, dramaturge and shareholder, had opened the year before. London, then, as always, was a very large city by European standards, and by the standard of England itself, which had no other cities to speak of at all, it was vast. 'The mart of many nations' since time immemorial, London attracted those seeking a fresh start or a last chance, many of whom returned, disappointed, to their parishes. They returned with awe-inspiring tales of London, so that even those who had never visited the metropolis knew that England was one country but two worlds.

London owed its cosmopolitan flavour to its status as a trading centre, certainly, but also to its position as a Protestant capital, a thriving centre of an otherwise beleaguered faith. The English took their responsibility for the survival of Protestantism very seriously. Here we have a geographically, culturally and economically divided society: London and the provinces. This same society is intensely hierarchical, divided vertically into easily identifiable classes. Yet this was very much a united society of Protestants, holding the fort against the Pope, more commonly known by incendiary and vituperative phrases like The Whore of Babylon, phrases that seem shocking to our supposedly unshockable twentieth-century eyes.

Because the English defined themselves in contrast to 'Papists', everything associated with 'popery' was self-evidently evil. France and Spain, obviously, were evil. Spanish lace and leather, French porcelain and silver, though, were not. (Their perfidy might be argued by some of the 'hotter sort' of Protestant, but seldom by those who actually constituted the English market for such goods.) But other things associated more directly with the 'Romish' mentality were suspect, like Continental methods of government and the nature of Catholic conformity. Systems of taxation, military administration, even censorship of books, could be cast as 'Popish'. Literacy was regarded not as a rudimentary skill but as a Protestant virtue and a bulwark against Rome. Protestants read the Bible; Catholics didn't. Protestants could establish their own direct contact with God; Catholics relied on priests as intermediaries. Great weight was given to the priest's putative duty to discourage reading. Anything, short of murder and mayhem, that priests tried to suppress couldn't be all bad. And, as Christopher Hill engagingly demonstrated in *The Intellectual Origins of the English Revolution*, a climate of opinion that looked favourably on experimentation was well established by 1600. For many in the elite, it was Protestant to support science and especially technology. Collaborations between, for example, ships' captains and physicists might well advance England's naval ambitions in some contest yet to come between the Virgin Queen and the Whore of Babylon.

When Elizabeth died, though, the Stuart century began. With the Stuarts, England endured decades of political rivalry so dramatic— and so ridden with irresolvable historical questions—that some of the best historical minds of every generation since have devoted their lives to two questions: why Charles I lost his head in 1649 and why his son was invited to restore the monarchy eleven years later. One thing is certain: these events took their toll in human misery, as all wars do but as civil wars do in their own calamitous way. (English schoolchildren, I have been told, digest these events as, 'For about ten years, the Roundheads and the Cavaliers galloped back and forth across the country, disrupting everything, until everyone became completely sick of it.' But this hardly does justice to the constitutional upheaval that the nation endured.)

The Restoration of the Stuarts (with Charles II in 1660) proved an inadequate solution. He and his brother, James (who would succeed him as James II) were cousins of Louis XIV, a fact that might have meant less had Charles and James not been widely suspected of Catholic sympathies, or even of being covert Catholics themselves. In the 1680s, when James' Catholicism was revealed, the Stuart century reached its second climax. The King fled the country. Parliament declared the throne vacant, and at the end of 1688, William of Orange and his wife, Mary (James' thoroughly Protestant daughter), were invited to occupy it. So radical and innovative a solution did this seem—with Parliament brokering the succession to the throne—that the English themselves immediately recognized it as a revolution.*

'Never again' sometimes seems to have been the eighteenth century's motto. Certainly, 'stability' is the textbook term associated with Georgian England, in part because of the simple elegance of the architecture and material culture (furnishings and such) that it left behind. But the eighteenth century's stability was like that of volatile chemicals in perhaps only momentary equilibrium. The eighteenth century's stability was decidedly not, as the historian J. H. Plumb put it, 'adamantine inertia'.

For one thing, England was at war almost constantly under the first three Georges. And even without the heightened political tension that war brings (as all sides dispute its management),

---

* It should be noted that the word 'revolution' did not signify then what it does now. Though it might well describe dramatic change, it also connoted a return, like the revolution of a wheel.

England was deeply divided on fundamental issues—foreign policy, the national debt, trade—because England started the century deeply divided on the question of who should wear the Crown. The question of the succession created the original Whigs and Tories. These terms were coined to describe the two sides during the crisis of the 1680s, and they stuck right through the eighteenth century, although from one decade to the next the terms 'Whig' and 'Tory' carried a bewildering array of permutating connotations. Whigs and Tories were further subdivided into Court and Country, because on questions of foreign policy, for example, there was a Court position (the King's) and 'a Country interest', the interest of the landed aristocracy and squirearchy.

These terms—Whig and Tory, Court and Country—were invoked to describe the political rivalries of whatever the day, but we should understand them as types rather than as human individuals conforming to type. Lots of country gentlemen had investments in the City; some even experimented with mining and manufacturing on their estates. But, although it was often difficult to find a full-fledged Whig or Tory person, there was an identifiable Whig and Tory position virtually from day to day through every decade. These rivalries, coupled with the urgencies of an almost constant state of war, surface in the correspondence that has survived from that time, where we find that the country seemed to be lurching from crisis to crisis. Not knowing, as we do, how it all turned out in the end, the English worried and with reason. Theirs was the stability of the ship that gets through the storm by rocking from side to side.

'Trade' is the other textbook mnemonic for the eighteenth century. Indeed, I have often thought that an introductory lecture on England in the eighteenth century could focus on coffee-houses, cheap calico and Wedgwood china. For under each of these headings a host of other subjects can be introduced.

Josiah Wedgwood represents not only the steady refinement and definition of a distinctly middle-class way of life, he (along with Matthew Boulton, a button manufacturer known as the Brass Baron of Birmingham) can be cited as the discoverer of the principles of supply and demand that Adam Smith described, decades later, in *The Wealth of Nations*. Calico invites us to consider the first British Empire and the goods it brought not just to the rich but to everyone. We might look at Stubbs' paintings of young women reaping grain in improbably clean and pretty cotton dresses and sun-dappled straw hats. How accurate can these images be? The historian Neil McKendrick asked this question in *The Birth of a Consumer Society*, and he answered, in part, by asking why we should doubt Stubbs' peasants when he is famous for his perfect horses. Moreover, though pictorial evidence is woefully scarce, English women of the lower orders clearly would have been the envy of their Continental counterparts for their clothes, if for nothing else. By the end of the century, the first paper dolls (called 'fashion dolls') were on the market, for a penny, with sets of costumes and accessories for all occasions. With these cut-outs to guide her, a young woman might decide what she would do with a few yards of cotton and ribbon after her next pay-day.

Cotton, tea, tobacco and, alas, gin, mark the collapse of what is called 'sumptuary culture', which at its extreme prescribed by law who could wear certain colours and fabrics. In its more common and everyday aspect it claimed public space for the elite, that is, it claimed that 'public' meant 'for the elite', hence the English public school. Similarly, public life was 'for the elite'; only they had a demonstrable vested interest in politics, therefore only they needed to gather to discuss 'public' affairs.

Nothing illustrates the disintegration of this understanding of 'public' better than the rise of the London coffee-house. In their heyday, during the opening decades of the century, coffee-houses were known as 'the penny universities', because, for a penny, any man could take a seat, have a cup of coffee, read the papers and discuss the events of the day with his fellows. Runners who carried messages from the City to Westminster and back again would stop in at a few coffee-houses en route, to collect tips for revealing the latest rumours from the realms of high finance and recombinant parliamentary factions.

Charles II called coffee-houses 'nurseries of sedition', and he didn't know the half of it. They didn't even hit their stride until the explosion of newspapers after press censorship ended in 1695. Intensely partisan and unabashedly *ad hominem*, the political press vented its spleen and cocked its snook in weeklies, tri-weeklies and in the almost daily release of at least one new pamphlet strutting its views and reviling its opponents.

The press as we know it was born in eighteenth-century England; these were the decades when the press first claimed a freedom for itself, and an odd sort of freedom it seemed, at first, especially when 'the press' began to mean newspapers, not books, and when the power of the press suggested not the dissemination of the gospel but the invention of public opinion. The press managed to secure its own liberty in large part because it was able to put its own troubles with the authorities into the limelight whenever it felt threatened. To represent its crises as matters of universal concern, the press expounded on Liberty in general, English Liberty, that is, as enshrined in Magna Carta, or so they said. Magna Carta, like the Ancient Constitution that it was said to have affirmed, served more as folklore than as fact. It signified those Liberties of the freeborn Englishman that distinguished him from the servile wretches of France. Liberty was part of his patrimony. Its origins were traced through English history, not through theoretical convictions about human rights.

Since Liberty was English, Liberty was also Protestant, from the beginning of the two centuries encompassed by this book almost until their end. In 1800, however, the English were still coming to terms with the contrast between Liberty and Liberté. In 1788,

England celebrated the centennial of its own Glorious Revolution, which the English (though not the Scots or the Irish) liked to describe as a bloodless, constitutional affair. The following year, it began to seem as though France would become a constitutional monarchy, too, as indeed it did, falteringly, for the next couple of years until the blood began to flow from the guillotine without reference to the revolution's constitutional principles. Sympathizers who had planted Liberty trees on English soil were confused and embarrassed; members of associations that considered themselves the Friends of Liberty found themselves described as enemies of their country. And so the century known for its stability ended in a climate of uncertainty: still not sure who to blame for the loss of America; unconvinced that the anarchic developments across the Channel could be confined to France; and unable to deny the accelerating pace of social and economic change that we know as the Industrial Revolution.

For all that, some things stayed the same. The family, for example, remained the basic social and economic unit through the entire period we are studying. The household was meant to be a microcosm of the kingdom as a whole. A man's home was his castle; there, he ruled, and the law recognized him as the master of his wife and his children, as well of his servants and apprentices. He was entitled to beat them all. Men who did not resort to coercive violence could congratulate themselves on their civility and Christian forbearance. Submission to patriarchal authority enjoyed heaven's blessing as well as the state's. And, despite the unsettling incursions of industrialization, the old domestic economy survived, not only in the countryside but in the towns and even in London. Wherever the home remained a workshop, cottage industries held their own, spinning, hammering and carving against the day when the factory would make them obsolete and their wares appear crudely fashioned, as well as too expensive.

It is no accident that, in the struggle between continuity and change, the family was the repository of tradition. Buttressed by the authority of the ancients, the family continued to be regarded as beyond the fray of political life. The Athenian model of the *polis* (whence we derive 'politics'), where men went to settle 'public' issues while their family life remained outside the city walls, endured. Trade was a political matter; domestic relations were not. A man's property might be subject to the slings and arrows of political fortune (as dictated by war, taxes and colonial policy), but a married woman's property was subject to her husband.

Still, perhaps unwittingly, the eighteenth century chipped away at the patriarchal family. Organizations like the Society for the Reformation of Manners insinuated the notion that moral reform was the responsibility of society as a whole. Today, we tend to look for solutions to economic and social problems in structural remedies that can be implemented through public institutions, but this is a thoroughly modern attitude. Until the mid-nineteenth century, even intellectually sophisticated people (men and women) usually believed that the cure for society's ills lay in its moral regeneration. Hence, although the moral education of the young fell, according to tradition, within the domain of the patriarch of the household, reformers increasingly treated moral education as a 'public' concern. And, as with the emerging power of the press, this posture brought with it a new definition of 'public', a definition that endowed more and more of social life with political significance.

These new attitudes suited industrial capitalism very well. As mines, mills and factories enlisted women and children in away-from-home labour, parental supervision became a less reliable source of moral education. It fell to 'public' institutions to pick up the slack. In the nineteenth century, child labour and even married women's property would be understood as questions for parliamentary debate and legislation. Still, some historians would argue that the patriarchal family only shed its pre-industrial clothes for industrial ones, that patriarchy simply adapted to necessity without losing any ground. It is into these deep waters, with their superficial calm and their turbulent undercurrents, that we who want to restore women to all of this history must plunge.

The title of this, the first volume in the *Illuminated Texts* series, is *Women and History*. When we bring these two words, 'women' and 'history', into conjunction, the consequences are explosive. Unlike 'life and times', 'wit and wisdom' or even 'war and peace', these two words do not make a euphonious marriage. Instead, they set off a pyrotechnical display of implications and disturbing questions about the nature of history itself.

'History' is one of the most capacious words we have. It is used to describe the whole past, starting yesterday, but it is also used to describe the recorded past. In this sense, 'history' marks the distinction between the whole past (everything that ever happened) and that which has been culled from it as significant enough to be called history. To further demonstrate its elasticity, 'history' sometimes denotes the process whereby the distinction between the whole past and the past worth noting is determined, as when we say, 'History will decide ...'

History in this latter sense really stands for 'historians'. When we understand history to mean 'historians', we can say that history decides what will be history; history will select, from all of human experience, that which is worthy of our attention, that which made a difference. We don't usually say that historians 'make history'. Men on the moon 'make history'; generals, scientists and statesmen 'make history'. But historians do make history. Indeed, it is they who make history of the deeds of soldiers and statesmen, not those individuals themselves. Historians make history out of two raw materials: evidence and interpretation. Like continuity and change, evidence and interpretation are fundamental concepts that one ignores at one's peril when studying the past. But the relationship between evidence and interpretation presents a problem. It may be obvious that these are the two elements that make up history, but it is far from clear where one leaves off and the other begins. We can picture 'evidence': boxes full of documents, shelves laden with letters and diaries, reels of old newspapers on microfilm. And we can imagine the process of interpretation: the historian, trained to put the evidence in its context, reads and then explains. But does it ever happen like that? Does anyone just read and read and read and then suddenly decide, I've read enough; I'm ready to start interpreting now? What brought the historian to that box of documents in the first place? A question. And that question is itself a form of interpretation that preceded even the first encounter with the evidence. Where did that question come from? Why did the historian formulate it as he or she did?

Historians are intensely aware of these issues. They try to avoid what they call 'presentism', which means looking at the past too much through the eyes of the present. But the question that draws the historian to the box of documents in the first place was formed in the present and often reflects the present's concerns. Surely, this is nothing to apologize for. After all, such present concerns make history relevant. But we cannot deny that this relevance colours both the evidence and the interpretation; it may even distort them. So when we read history that was written fifty or a hundred years ago, we see what was then the present revealed in how history was made. History reveals its own history, that is, the time when it is written.

The word 'history', then, is problematically capacious. It encompasses and thereby confounds things that ought to be understood as distinct from one another: the past itself; what is written about the past; the process of deciding what is important from the past; the people who investigate it and then write it up. It describes change, but its evidence is awash with continuity. Still, change is easier to write about and more interesting to most readers. Change gives history a plot. But does the past have a plot? Is this appetite for narrative a curse that bedevils the relationship between evidence and interpretation? Or is history, finally, a form of literature, and is 'the real past'—out there, waiting to be discovered—finally, a myth?

When we bring 'women' into conjunction with 'history', all of our fundamental questions about the nature of history generate new questions, ones that cannot be ignored. It is possible to write history—good history—without pondering for long the historiographical issues that we have been considering. But it is not possible to write (or to read) women's history and keep these questions at bay. They perch on your shoulder, whispering in your ear, all the time.

Recognizing that women have been written out of history is the least of it. True, we are still discovering women who were celebrated for their achievements in their own time but have since disappeared from the record: artists, scientists, mathematicians, even philosophers. But restoring women to history requires more than biographical attention to the neglected few. If we want to paint women into our whole picture of a society in the past—women from all walks of life and social strata—where do we look for them and what questions will we ask of those sources? When we find sources, like trial transcripts or other legal records, where women offer accounts of their lives, how much weight do we give to the fact that men were asking the questions and recording the answers, that the face these women were presenting to the world in these accounts was the face they thought would be acceptable in an all-male forum? As Sara Mendelson points out in her chapter here, 'To extract feminine meanings from the text, we need to read against the grain.' Yet if we try to extract female experience from 'the grain' of patriarchal conventions, are we not initiating a new form of distortion, since every women's experience is suffused with and modified by her knowledge of how a woman is supposed to act? One does not look at one's own behaviour and say, 'This is my own true self and that is me trying to act like a women.' Still, Mendelson's injunction is fundamental, and it is echoed in this collection by Allyson May in her chapter on infanticide trials and by Paula Humfrey in hers on domestic servants.

Those prevailing notions of what is feminine and what is masculine—notions that are instilled in us from birth—are now known by the phrase 'gender ideology', a phrase that remains both useful and precise. 'Gender' describes what is not sex. That is, 'gender' was first taken up as a term of reference to distinguish between what is biologically determined by our female-ness or male-ness, and what is socially determined (indeed, dictated) as appropriately feminine or masculine. Having made that distinction, we must acknowledge that the distinction can be fuzzy and therefore irremediably controversial. Some feminists insist that girls and boys would act the same were they not treated differently from birth; most mothers of young children, even those who consider themselves feminists, dispute this.

Still, we need the phrase 'gender ideology' when we study women's history because it exactly describes something that we always find in the past, as well as in the present: certain standards of male and female conduct that are propagated because they are deemed instrumental to the preservation of the existing social order. It is this quality of their usefulness to the status quo that makes these standards ideological.

To attempt to separate a woman's experience from the gender ideology with which she has been imbued from birth may be a dubious undertaking. Most letters, diaries and other autobiographical accounts are illuminating for precisely the opposite reason: they show us just how enmeshed the experience and the ideology are. We know ourselves as gendered social beings. Women who campaigned for social reform also cultivated their own 'respectability'. Girls with intellectual gifts and ambitions asked their tough philosophical questions with a modest and decorous tilt of the head. In Donna Andrew's chapter here, the reports from women's debating societies recount many such moments, where radical questions are softened by feminine deportment.

Gender ideology may wisely be regarded as distinct from

women's experience in another sense, however. When we go looking for women in the past, the evidence that is most abundant is
gender ideology: images of virtuous, chaste, silent, modest, pious
women. The danger is that we will confuse this propaganda with
reality, that we will conclude that this is how women actually felt
constrained to behave. This is somewhat like concluding from pho-
tographs taken a hundred years ago that people then were stiff and
solemn, when in reality their photographers placed them in neck
braces to ensure that they remained still enough for primitive cam-
eras to register a clear image of them.

At this point, then, we must look for other, counterbalancing evidence to try to determine if, for example, the propaganda of silence
and docility was generated precisely because women were perceived
as obstreperous and unruly. Where do we look for such evidence,
and what questions should we ask of it? This anthology was conceived with these concerns in mind, as an aid to formulating better
questions and to approaching sources better prepared to read them
'against the grain'.

One winter at the University of Toronto, Barbara Todd and I had
a number of conversations about how women's history is taught. We
agreed that something often goes wrong at the beginning and then
never quite rights itself. Many people—whether students or lively-
minded readers—approach women's history having already decided
that life was either better for women in the past or it was worse. Of
those who have not decided which it was, most still believe that this
is a—perhaps *the*—fundamental question. Alas, it is not even a very
fruitful one. And using it as an organizing principle for the evidence
that one explores obscures more than it reveals. Food, housing and
taxes are certainly fundamental knowledge for the study of any period (and they each lead to compelling historical issues). Insofar as the
'better life' refers to better living conditions, it is fundamental. But
this is not how better and worse are usually meant by those whose
curiosity about women's history has been kindled. They want to

know if it would have been better to have been born back then. History tries to teach us that this is not a very good question, but the more identified we are with the subject we are studying, the harder it is to be disabused of fundamental fallacies. We are right to wonder about the origins of injustice, but we will have a better chance of finding them if we keep our eyes open and reserve judgement for awhile.

Each of the historians in *Women and History* has selected a text that tends to dissolve assumptions and surprise the reader. Each has written a few introductory pages to 'illuminate' the text by explaining why she or he found it fascinating and by suggesting what you might want to look for when you read it. The book is divided into two parts: 'The Female Community' and 'The Real and the Ideal'. In Part I, you will encounter (with Sara Mendelson) 'disorderly' women and their crimes of the tongue; servants whose stock in trade was secrets and whose own secrets sometimes caught up with them (presented by Paula Humfrey and Allyson May); and the tragic consequences of female vulnerability (as Margaret Hunt and John Beattie have explored them). All of the chapters in Part I draw their material from legal records, so these chapters also offer the reader an opportunity to assess the value and the limitations of one type of evidence.

In Part II, you will meet women coming to terms with gender ideology: coping, confronting and compromising, by turns. The bold ones—like the high-minded Margaret of Newcastle (introduced by Hilda Smith) and my underhanded namesake, Mary Frith (a.k.a. Mal Cutpurse)—take pride in their unflinching perceptions of gender ideology's edicts. But the quiet tenacity of the young widow Katherine Austen (presented by Barbara Todd) as she comes into the men's world of the family business and its legal tribulations, awakens our respect, too (though it brought her no fame) as does Phyllis Deutsch's moving account of the legendary Georgiana, Duchess of Devonshire. In Donna Andrew's chapter on women's debating societies and in Ann Shteir's on women in botany, we see how resilient gender ideology is, as women with intellectual aspirations sustain the contradictions between what they see and how they must be seen. Instead of forcing those contradictions to climax and resolution, they compromise.

Andrew's press reports of the debating societies' meetings present a somewhat daunting challenge for 'reading against the grain'. How we wish that we had verbatim accounts of the proceedings and that we did not have to rely on the ideologically jaundiced eye of a male spectator! But Andrew's is not the only chapter that leaves us hungry for more. Much of the trial testimony that appears in Part I reads like only half the story, or less. When did those wretched creatures who stand accused of infanticide (in Allyson May's chapter) decide on the course of action that led to their exposure? How many of their peers were lucky enough to escape detection altogether? At moments like these, it becomes painfully clear what historians are up against.

Historical enquiry seldom illuminates the entire landscape of another age. Usually, the surviving sources compel a studiously microscopic attention, a willingness to live with some unfathomables and a little educated guesswork. But if the canvas tends to be small, the implications for our understanding of human experience are often vast and clearly relevant to our current concerns. These illuminated texts, for example, remind us that we still know ourselves as gendered social beings. Chances are, in the future, we will, too. Whatever makes us wiser about that process should be welcome, even when new questions arise with every one that we think we have answered and even though our expectations of history may be shattered. But if this is the truth, then we still come out ahead. As John Beattie often says, 'The past is messy because life is messy.'

VALERIE FRITH

A Note on Spelling Etc.

Spelling has been modernized throughout; punctuation has been changed when necessary for clarity. Abbreviations have been spelled out and capitalization has been modernized. Any other words or phrases added or deleted for clarity's sake are indicated with brackets and ellipses. With the court records in Part I, one must deal with the fact that transcripts of court proceedings were often noted down in idiosyncratic ways. Several changes have been made here in order to facilitate reading the texts and to approximate more closely the way in which the evidence was originally given. Thus, court clerks took down depositions in the third person; here they have, whenever possible, been changed to the first person. So where the original manuscript reads 'the deponent heard Mrs Cunningham say (such and such)' the text has been altered to read 'I heard Mrs Cunningham say (such and such).' The result is closer to the way deponents must actually have reported what they had heard or seen. Certain legalistic formulas have also been altered or quietly dropped, such as the convention of writing 'the said' in front of proper names and some other nouns. There is not a great deal of punctuation in these records, and the sentences often run on endlessly. Therefore commas and full stops have sometimes been inserted. Apart from these changes, the texts are as they appear in the original, complete with grammatical errors.

The Female Community

'To shift for a cloak'

DISORDERLY WOMEN IN THE CHURCH COURTS

◆

BY SARA HELLER MENDELSON

Literary and social historians are familiar with the stereotype of the 'disorderly woman', embodied in seventeenth-century images of the scold and whore, vagrant and witch. Indeed, popular proverbs defined women as unruly by nature: 'No mischief but a woman is at bottom'; 'Women and dogs set men together by the ears.' Theology supported this negative assessment, emphasising Eve's primary role in the Fall, with its disastrous consequences for mankind. The same misogynistic view was fostered by Galenic medicine, which explained women's inferior moral qualities as a function of their cold and wet humours.

The figure of the disorderly woman permeated everyday life as well as literary and intellectual paradigms. We can see its traces in the enactment of civil and criminal laws that treated women differently from men, such as the 1624 statute that made it a felony for an unmarried woman to conceal the birth of a stillborn child. In its provisions for unattached females, the 1563 Statute of Artificers allowed local officials to order unmarried women between the ages of twelve and forty years into service, for whatever wages the officials thought fit. Any woman who refused could be committed to jail 'until she shall be bounden to serve ...'[1]

Women might offend against notions of good order by breaching any of the standard feminine virtues: chastity, piety, obedience and silence. But as the statutes cited above suggest, the spectre of untrammelled

Pieter Angillis, 'Covent Garden,' c.1726 (detail). Oil on copper,
Yale Center for British Art, Paul Mellon Collection.

female sexuality was a particular source of communal anxiety. (It was not an accident that the female age limits specified by the Statute of Artificers coincided with women's childbearing years.) In response to this perceived threat, authorities sought to regulate feminine behaviour by curbing women's mobility, preferably by placing them under masculine rule.

How did the stereotype of the 'disorderly woman' relate to women's actual beliefs and experiences? If we try to explore women's lives from their own point of view, we immediately confront the problem of sources, a difficulty that is particularly acute in the case of the plebeian majority. Since about ninety percent of the female population were unable to sign their names, historians have been dependent on the mediating agency of male writers and officials for most of their information about non-élite women.

One of our best hopes in reconstructing the lives of ordinary women is in the study of their testimony as witnesses in the ecclesiastical courts. Partly because canon law did not impose the same legal disabilities on women as its common-law counterparts, and partly because many types of disputes brought to the church courts were closely linked to feminine concerns, women were well represented in the ecclesiastical courts both as litigants and as witnesses. Their depositions, personal answers and responses to interrogatories are probably as near as modern readers will ever come to hearing the actual voices of ordinary seventeenth-century women.

It is important to remember, however, that women's depositions do not represent free and verbatim speech: they are not faithful narratives of a private feminine worldview recorded for future generations of social historians. Statements were framed in response to specific questions posed by church court officials. As in any legal setting, witnesses' replies often served the strategic agenda of litigants who had produced them in court. Women's words were filtered through the minds of male clerks, who might alter their significance when noting them down. Moreover, female witnesses were always on trial for their own personal reputations, since an *ad feminam* assault was a common tactic for casting doubt on a woman's veracity. Consequently, female deponents were liable to censor their own speech to accord with communal notions of feminine virtue.

All these considerations remind us that church court evidence can never be taken at face value; it must always be assessed in terms of its social and juridical context. In extracting feminine meanings from the text, we need to read against the grain. Once we penetrate beyond the code of prescriptive discourse and legal fictions, however, female testimony can be of inestimable value, for it expresses women's own sense of order and morality, identity and self-worth. In these personal narratives, we can trace some of the positive ideals that animated a rich and complex female culture.

The documents transcribed below are church court depositions selected from two suits for defamation, that is, disputes in which the plaintiff sued the defendant for speaking words that damaged the plaintiff's character or reputation in the eyes of the community. To fit the court's criteria for a valid accusation, the defamatory words had to impute an actual criminal offence to the affronted party, not just a general insult. Moreover, the words had to have been uttered in a public (or semi-public) context rather than a private one-to-one encounter.

In both suits, the alleged words were spoken in the female-dominated *milieu* of the household, where they were witnessed by women of varying social and matrimonial status, at work at their daily tasks of spinning, cleaning and cooking. In *Flood v. Tucker*, Mary Flood charged Dorothy Tucker with spreading the story that Mary, a young unmarried woman, had had an illegitimate child whom she had either aborted or killed, and that she was now pregnant with another. Tucker was also said to have remarked that Mr Wright (the supposed father of the child) was gone. It was now time for Mary Flood 'to shift for a cloak', an expression that alludes to proverbial associations with female unchastity or general immorality. 'A cloak for knavery' was a means of covering up a crime. 'A quean [whore] hath ever a cloak for the rain,' i.e. an expedient for every difficulty. Tucker thus insinuated not only that Flood had committed a felony in doing away with her first bastard child, but that she was a 'quean' or prostitute by habit and disposition. Moreover, since her partner in debauchery had fled, Flood would be forced 'to shift for a cloak', or resort to the same criminal expedient she had employed in the past.

In the second suit, *Harris v. Rowell*, William Harris charged Audrey Rowell with calling him a 'whoremaster' (a fornicator). Rowell had allegedly cited the instance of Annie Geffry, who according to Rowell had cost Harris forty pounds. Although the statement clearly refers to some form of sexual misconduct, the significance of the forty pounds is not specified. It could hint at payments made to Annie Geffrey for sexual favours, but such a large sum more likely refers to a legal bond that constrained the father of an illegitimate child to provide for its support.

In each dispute, a cascade of charges and countercharges ensued as young unmarried female witnesses were themselves challenged about their personal, financial and sexual repute. And in both *Flood v. Tucker* and *Harris v. Rowell*, stereotypical portrayals combined biases of gender with those of class, evoking contemporary double meanings associated with women's economic and moral 'worth', and of their verbal and sexual 'honesty'. By depicting the plaintiff's witnesses as disorderly women themselves, the defence tried to destroy their personal repute and their credibility in the eyes of the court.

In *Flood v. Tucker*, the plaintiff produced Katherine Mogridge, an elderly widow and respectable householder. The main testimony, however, came from Mogridge's two maidservants, Mary Bond and Mary Smith, who were in the house spinning at the time the alleged words were spoken. The defence found an easy target in the career histories of these two young women. Both were depicted by male witnesses, friends of Tucker, as embodying the stereotype of the 'masterless woman' who roams the countryside evading the discipline of a male authority figure, whether father, husband or master. Smith had in fact been brought before a justice of the peace, having been threatened with imprisonment if she did not 'procure a master' within a month's time.

In defence of these beleaguered female witnesses, the plaintiff produced others who charged the defamers of Bond and Smith with bias, as well as with moral turpitude on their own account. But a careful reading of the evidence reveals that more was at stake than charges of bias and misbehaviour on each side. In returning home to nurse her sick mother, and presumably in taking charge of the household until her mother's recovery, Mary Smith was following a common feminine pattern. Mary Bond, too, was now living at home with her father after several stints of service with the widow Mogridge. Among plebeian households, the survival of the family unit was of higher priority than a young woman's career outside the home, and daughters were often obliged to switch back and forth between periods of service whenever family crises called for their help. What was portrayed as a feckless female urge to wander was in many cases a daughter's response to the burdens of familial obligation.[2]

In *Harris v. Rowell*, the plaintiff also called upon the testimony of maidservants at work, in the kitchen of the household where the alleged conversation took place. In this case, counsel for the defence tried to undermine the credibility of Agnes (or Anne) Barons by challenging her character for financial and sexual honesty. Barons was questioned about a dispute with a former master in which an accusation of theft was aired; she was then asked about an unmarried pregnancy that had occurred four years before. Responding to interrogatories, Barons provided her own version of the dispute with her former master, Mr Done, and of her unmarried pregnancy.

Barons' conflict with her master needs to be placed in the wider social and economic context in which servants of both sexes valued their right to mobility, since it was their most powerful weapon in negotiations for better wages and working conditions, whether from the current master or a different employer. But women's labour was perceived as less 'free' than that of their male counterparts, partly because they could be compelled to serve by law. Although Barons had given her master the customary three months' notice of her intention to leave his service, he refused to part with her, and brought her before a justice of the peace in an attempt to force her to return.

Challenged by the justice, Mr Cabell, to denounce Barons for any misconduct or crime she had committed during her service, Mr Done replied that he could accuse Barons of theft, for she had given away a piece of beef, worth 18 pence, at his door. Theft of goods valued at over a shilling (12 pence) was grand larceny, a felony or capital crime in common law, making this a very serious charge. Barons was thus provoked to narrate the full history of the piece of beef (which had cost only 14 pence in the first place). Having cooked and served the beef to ten people, she had saved leftovers for the next day and given a small piece to a poor woman who was begging at the door.

Not only does the story of the beef reduce Mr Done's charge of theft to ridicule; it offers us a window into the world of communal female culture, where food and goods were freely exchanged among female friends and neighbours, and habitually bestowed in charity to the poor, especially those of their own sex. Both wives and maidservants regarded charity, like hospitality, as one of the primary duties attached to house-wifery, all the more so since they oversaw the use and distribution of household resources such as leftover food and wornout clothing.

Counsel for the defence accused Barons of sexual as well as pecuniary dishonesty, for she had borne an illegitimate child. From Barons' point of view, however, she was the honest and faithful party, having been deserted by her suitor after their betrothal, and—a crucial point in her favour—after banns had been published for their marriage. In plebeian circles, an official betrothal put the issue of chastity on an entirely different footing. Many couples regarded an engagement as a warrant to initiate sexual relations, taking pregnancy as an urgent cue for marriage. Such mores were based on mutual trust and the vigilance of informal community sanctions. In seventeenth-century society, the system generally entailed low rates of illegitimacy and high rates of bridal pregnancy. But good faith could easily be abused by the man who fled from his pregnant fiancée and the local community that protected her.

Many of the women who appear in these records were disadvantaged by a combination of gender and socio-economic class; they were further handicapped by their vulnerability to the stereotype of the disorderly woman. In fact, we can observe women invoking misogynistic images against each other in their verbal battles, especially when normal neighbourly relations between them had broken down. But defamation suits represent the dark underside of women's communal world, a world of female friends, neighbours and relations. Beyond the pathology of church court disputes, the documents also show us a female culture based on neighbourliness and mutual help, one which valued family loyalty and the sharing of scarce resources within the community. Unlike the literary or legal stereotype of the disorderly woman, this was a paradigm of order and self-identity that had grown out of women's own experience.

NOTES

1. Statutes of the Realm, 'An Acte to prevent the murthering of Bastard Children' (1624), 21 Jac. I. ch.28; Stature of Artificers (1663), 5 Eliz., ch.4.

2. In other sources such as Leonard Wheatcroft's journal, the pattern is presented in a positive light: at least one of his daughters was always kept at home to help her mother, eventually to inherit the place of housekeeper after her mother's death. Cf. L. Wheatcroft, 'Autobiography,' in *Jrnl. of Derb. Arch. and Nat. Hist. Soc.*, xxi (1899), 41-55

I
MARY FLOOD V. DOROTHY TUCKER

---

7 DECEMBER 1635

Deposition of Mary Bond, aged about 30, of the parish of Brampford Speake, Devon, where she has lived for ten years

About a month ago, Dorothy Tucker came into the house of Widow Mogridge in Brampford Speake. Speaking of Mary Flood, Dorothy Tucker said she had had one child already, and now she was with child again. Tucker also said, 'he is gone, and it is now time for her [Mary Flood] to shift for a cloak' speaking in a railing and scandalous manner. Also present at the speaking of the words were Mary Smith and Widow Mogridge. Mary Flood is a young unmarried woman, and so far as [I know], 'an honest and chaste maiden'.

MARK OF MARY BOND

Deposition of Mary Smith, aged about 22, of Brampford Speake, where she was born

Speaking of Mary Flood, Dorothy Tucker said that 'Mary had been with child once already and destroyed it'. And [that] now Mary was with child again, and the man was gone, and it was time for Mary 'to shift for a cloak'.

MARK OF MARY SMITH

11

7 MARCH 1635[/6]

Deposition of Katherine Mogridge, aged about 64, of the parish of Brampford Speake, where she has lived for 30 years

Mary Bond lived mostly in Brampford Speake these four or five years, and lived a servant in house with [me] for near about a year. Then she went away, and afterwards came again and lived with [me] as a servant for some certain time. Then about two months ago, she went out of the parish unto her father, and remains there. Mary Smith is now a servant in [my] house ... About a year ago, Mary Smith went and lived with her mother (who was then very sick), and there tarried about a quarter of a year until her mother's recovery. Afterwards a complaint was made by some of her neighbours unto a justice for not living with a master, 'and thereupon she came and lived a servant with [me] and there yet remains'. About All-Hallow-tide* last past, Dorothy Tucker came into [my] house in Brampford Speake, and into the hall of the house, where [I] was going up and down the house about [my] business. Mary Smith and Mary Bond, being [my] servants, were then both there present at spinning. Dorothy Tucker said that Mr Wright was gone away, that it was time for him, that the gap against Mary Flood's house was stopped up. [I made] some answer, Dorothy Tucker said that Mary Flood had now made a new cloak, and asked [me] if [I] did not mark that Mary Flood looked very sadly. [I] did not hear any other words, but there might have been other words spoken which [I] did not hear.

K   MARK OF KATHERINE MOGRIDGE

Interrogatory:
[I have] known Mary Bond well for four or five years.

K   MARK OF KATHERINE MOGRIDGE

* November 1st

Deposition of Edward Panie, aged about 40, of the parish of Brampford Speake, where he was born

Mary Bond has not lived in Brampford Speake for ten years, but only came to the parish five years ago. She has always been coming and going to other places in that time, and never lived in the parish more than one and a half years at one time. She is now come out of the parish again to dwell. She is a poor woman, and such a one as little credit is to be given to her sayings and depositions. Mary Smith is a poor woman, of little credit. About a year ago, she was questioned and convented before Sir Nicholas Marten, a justice of peace, for not living with a master. And then Sir Nicholas did enjoin her to procure a master within one month following, which she did then accordingly, but did not long tarry with him, by reason whereof she was again brought before a justice [of the peace]. And was threatened to be punished if she did not live with a master. And since that time she has lived in service ... [I] being a constable did carry her before the justice.

E P   MARK OF EDWARD PANIE

Deposition of John Rackett, aged about 30, of the parish of Brampford Speake, where he has lived for 20 years

Mary Bond lived in the parish only sometimes these four or five years, and never more than one year at a time. And she has used in that time to go and live from place to place, and is a poor wench. And is now gone again out of the parish, and such a one to whose depositions little credit is to be given. Mary Smith is a poor woman, one that had used to go up and down the country from place to place. She was twice questioned before a justice of the peace, and threatened to be sent unto Bridewell within these twelve months ... unless she did get herself in some service ... She is a woman of little credit or reputation.

J   MARK OF JOHN RACKETT

◆

29 APRIL 1636

Deposition of Agnes Cowse, aged about 40, of the parish of Brampford Speake, where she has lived for 20 years

John Rackett was famed to live incontinently with his wife before their marriage. She [Rackett's wife] was with child at the time of his marriage with her. John Rackett is accounted to be a great enemy to Mary Flood and one that bears her much ill will. He resorts to Dorothy Tucker's house oftentimes. [I live] in the same parish and [am] a near neighbour unto them. Jerome Upton is a very poor fellow, and one that is oftentimes overtaken with drink. About a quarter of a year ago, Dorothy Tucker being in the house of one Whiddon in Brampford Speake, she said that Mary Flood was with child, or else she [Dorothy Tucker] was never with child. Mary Flood is a young woman and unmarried and an honest maiden. The words spoken are a great disgrace to Mary Flood. Mary Bond and Mary Smith are honest people as far as [I know], and would not forswear themselves.

MARK OF AGNES COWSE

II
WILLIAM HARRIS V. AUDREY ROWELL

31 JULY 1636

Deposition of Agnes [or Anne] Barons, aged about 24, of the parish of Ilsington, Devon, where she has lived more than two years; she was born at Staverton

About Christmas last past, [I] was in the kitchen of the vicarage house of Ilsington when Audrey Rowell came in, and Humfrey Harris, son of William Harris, was at the kitchen window loading ... gravel. Audrey Rowell, seeing him out at the window, said, 'there is Humfrey Harris, he may not be as bad as his father for aught I

know.' Then she said that 'Annie Geffry had cost his father forty
pounds.' [I] demanded wherein. Audrey replied, 'there was not such
an old whoremaster more, in the country ... there was not such a
bawdy old knave in the country,' speaking in a railing, scoffing manner. Elizabeth Mills also heard the words spoken.

MARK OF *AGNES BARONS*

Response to Interrogatories:
[I have] known both parties well for two years. [I favour] both parties alike. [I] was warned by one Ford to come to the Court and
showed a paper and said it was a process, and he gave [me] twelve
pence* towards [my] charges. [I] did live in house with Mr Done
about half a year ending about Lady day last.† [I] did serve with Mr
Done ... and being willing to go from his service, did give him
warning about Christmas last to provide another servant in [my]
place against the next quarter. And at Lady day or thereabouts [I]
went from him, and dwelt with Mr Pomery in the same parish. And
then Mr Done was very much discontented with [me] because [I]
would be gone from him, and did claim a promise of longer time,
and did procure a process from Mr Cabell to call [me] before him.
And [I] went to the justice, and there Mr Done did charge [me]
that [I] had made covenant to serve him, and that he would not
release [me] of his service. And [I] then did refuse to go to his service, and denied any such promise, as [I] justly might. And then Mr
Cabell told Mr Done that he [Mr Done] had nothing to do with
[my] service, except he could charge [me] with any wrong [I] had
done in [my] service, or had stolen anything. Whereto Mr Done
answered that he would not charge [me] with anything. Yet afterwards in [the] presence of Mr Cabell, Mr Done did say to [me] that
he could charge [me] for a piece of beef which [I] gave away at his

* Twelve pence was the standard amount allowed to witnesses for their expenses in coming to testify in the ecclesiastical courts.
† Lady day, March 25th, was one of the traditional quarterly days on which servants might begin or
end a term of service.

door. And then Mr Cabell examining the matter farther, Mr Done said that [I] gave away a piece of beef at his door to a poor woman worth 18 pence. And [I] did then presently prove before the justice by him that bought the beef that the piece of beef did cost but 14 pence, and that it was boiled in [my] master's house, and that ten people had the same at dinner. And [I] gave a little of that which was left to a poor woman at the door, and some of it [I] kept in the house 'til next day. And when Mr Cabell saw how he was abused by hearing such a brabble, he was very angry with Mr Done and did bind over him and [me] to answer at the [Quarter] Sessions. And [I] was at the last Sessions at the Castle of Exeter but was not called nor questioned there, only [I] was willed to pay Mr Cabell's clerk the fees. And [I am] a single woman and unmarried. And about four years since, [I] was betrothed and had banns published in the church. And the man left [me] and refused to marry [me], after he had abused [me] and brought [me] with child.

B   MARK OF AGNES BARONS

Deposition of Elizabeth Mills, aged about 21, of the parish of Ilsington, where she has lived about a year

A little after last Christmas, Audrey Howell was in the kitchen of the vicarage house of Mr Done ...

Mills' testimony continues, echoing Agnes Barons'.

... A whoremaster means a man of dishonest and incontinent life. Also present at the hearing of the words was [my] procontest, Anne Barons.

MARK OF ELIZABETH MILLS

Response to Interrogatories:
[I have known] the parties but a little time, not even one year. [I know] the danger of an oath. [I am] a single woman and [live] by

[my] service and [do] not know what portion [my] father will
bestow with [me]. [I] was served with a process, and was paid 12
pence for [my] charges. [I have] lived a servant in house with Mr
Done a year and three quarters last past or thereabouts. Anne Barons
was lately also servant with Mr Done, and she went from his service
without his consent, and hereupon Mr Done called her before Mr
Cabell, but did not (as [I believe]) charge her with stealing anything. [I] heard that Mr Cabell did bind Anne Barons to appear at
the Sessions.

MARK OF ELIZABETH MILLS

'She at first denied it'

INFANTICIDE TRIALS AT THE OLD BAILEY

◆

BY ALLYSON N. MAY

The narratives that follow are by no means voluntary revelations of women's lives. They owe their existence to a conflict with the law, and they describe events that the principals had striven desperately to conceal. The material is drawn from reports of eighteenth-century infanticide trials held at the Old Bailey in London, and these cases reflect the experience of a particular group of women, single mothers, who were prosecuted under a singular statute.

Whereas a married woman or a man suspected of killing a child at or soon after its birth would have been charged with the common-law offence of murder, single mothers were targeted by a seventeenth-century statute: the 1624 Act to prevent the destroying and murdering of bastard children. This Act provided that a woman who concealed the death of her bastard child was presumed to have murdered it unless she could prove by at least one witness that the child had been born dead. The presumption of innocence, to the extent that it existed in the eighteenth century, was thus reversed; concealment was taken to be proof of murder, and the penalty was death. The reasoning behind the law is clearly indicated in its preamble:

> ... many lewd women that have been delivered of bastard children, to avoid their shame, and to escape

Rowlandson & Pugin, 'Old Bailey' (detail). Engraving, from *The Microcosm of London*, 1904.

punishment, do secretly bury or conceal the death of
their children, and after, if the child be found dead, the
women do allege, that the child was born dead; whereas it falleth out sometimes (although hardly it is to be
proved) that the child or children were murdered by
the women, their lewd mothers, or by their assent or
procurement.

This was a Puritan statute, as much concerned with the initial sin
of fornication as it was with the difficulty of proving the offence.
Despite changes in the moral climate, the Infanticide Act remained
on the statute books until 1803. And since the majority of those
accused of infanticide were single women, they continued to be
charged under this Act.

The value of these trial reports as a source for women's experience must be qualified at the outset. First, the total number of
indictments recorded at the Old Bailey—let alone the selection
presented here—does not inform us of the actual incidence of
infanticide in London. Trials dealt with failure to conceal. We will
never know how xmany single women successfully concealed the
murder of their infants. I suspect that some did, and that their success depended on the complicity of a friend or friends. In the
Shrewsbury case, Elizabeth Bell appears to have turned a blind eye,
accepting Shrewsbury's explanation of a miscarriage, giving her
some hot ale and sending her off to bed. Bell's conduct is severely
criticized by the court. The loyalty and silence of a friend, however,
may have enabled other women to evade the courts entirely.
Criminal law in the eighteenth century operated under a system of
private prosecution: indictments occurred only as the result of
someone's decision to prosecute. Some cases may never have been
brought to trial because of a deliberate decision not to prosecute.

Second, the defendants do not tell their own stories. The

---

* Old Bailey Sessions Papers, Hannah Butler's Case, December 1736.

reports consist of the formal indictment and the testimony of various witnesses for the prosecution, usually followed by short statements of witnesses for the defendant, who testify as to her general good character. Judge and jury interrupt throughout with questions. Although there are eighteenth-century criminal trials in which the accused made a lengthy speech to the jury in his or her own defence, women accused of infanticide do not appear to have done so. When asked, they usually limited their defence to a denial of the charge. The accused may also have referred to or held up a few scraps of child-bed linen to demonstrate that she had made provision for the arrival of the baby, and thus had not intended to conceal the birth.

In a way, the defendant's behaviour in court is appropriate to the circumstances of the crime. In the months preceding her trial, her life had depended on silence, and when that was no longer possible, denial. The accused successively denied pregnancy, birth and, finally, murder. Some of these denials seem almost comical: 'I am not married, I am only Pot-belly'd, all our Family is Pot-belly'd—and what a disgrace it is to be Pot-belly'd!'* But the situation was anything but comic for the women involved.

In these reports we rarely hear of the circumstances of the pregnancy. The trials reproduced here reveal one case of probable incest, and another in which the accused admits to three possibilities for paternity. A case not included suggests that the father was the master of the house, but we should be wary of assuming that this was the norm. Trial reports are also largely silent as to the motivation for concealing a pregnancy and killing a bastard infant at birth. The statute, however, with its reference to shame, sheds some light on the issue, and the socio-economic status of the majority of the defendants is also significant. In four of the cases, the accused is clearly identified as a servant. One historian of infanticide, R. W. Malcomson, has shown that about 70 percent of the women indicted for infanticide at the Old Bailey between 1730 and 1774 whose occupations are known were servants.[1] J.M. Beattie found similar results in a study of Surrey indictments.[2] A servant's livelihood and consequently her very life depended on her reputation. An illegitimate child could lead to the loss of a position and denial of references, leaving the unwed mother with a narrow range of options for survival.

Because we do not hear the defendant's story in her own words, we can only guess at the feelings involved throughout her ordeal. It is trite to say that the strain generated by concealing a pregnancy, delivering unaided, disposing of the dead child and attempting to carry on work as usual must have been immense. Malcolmson has emphasized the strength of will necessary to succeed at such a task, and in the case of Martha Busby we meet a young woman who did not survive the strain. Her sense of guilt is so overwhelming that she practically courts discovery. Having constantly asked her workmates if they did not hear a child crying, she was taken up when the corpse was found.

The question of guilt or innocence is itself a difficult one. Throughout the seventeenth century, women indicted for infanticide were frequently convicted and hanged. But by the mid-1720s, juries demonstrated an increasing tendency to acquit.[3] By the second half of the eighteenth century women accused of infanticide were, in effect, tried for murder (rather than concealment); convictions occurred rarely and only in cases where there were unmistakable signs of violence. Defendants at the Old Bailey began to be met with a degree of sympathy, and the reluctance to convict suggests a certain willingness to perceive the accused herself as a victim. The cases reproduced here reflect this general leniency: only the trial of Mary Shrewsbury results in a conviction. Her baby, its head cut half off, was discovered sewn up in a cloth and hidden in a closet, leaving little doubt as to the fact of murder. The circumstances in the remainder of the cases are more ambiguous.

Although the defendants themselves were relatively silent in court, women's narratives played a crucial role in most accounts of infanticide trials. Despite the existence of a few male midwives, women were generally regarded as the experts where pregnancy and birth were concerned, and their testimony provided essential evidence in these cases. Further, they appear to have been instrumental in the process that led to prosecution, frequently responsible for initiating the investigations. Infanticide trials thus reveal women in the roles of both accused and accuser: some victims of a severe, man-made law; others willing participants in its enforcement. It must be accepted that the law could not have functioned to the extent that it did without female assistance.

As a variety of witnesses—mistresses, landladies, lodgers and fellow-servants—tell their version of events to the court, the crowded, inquisitive world in which the defendants lived is revealed, a world of gossip and constant surveillance. These cases demonstrate a general lack of privacy in day-to-day living, and a particular interest in unwed mothers. In some instances women seem to have taken on the role of moral police; certainly these trials highlight the importance attached to a woman's reputation. Frequently, the tale of investigation is the tale of a hunt, and we can only imagine the terror of the cornered suspect. Some defendants were watched and questioned during a suspected pregnancy, followed to necessary houses (privies), and peered at through the key-holes of their bedrooms. In other cases suspicions do not appear to have been aroused until the actual delivery. The accused may have been heard to cry out in the night, or someone may have found bedsheets 'in an odd pickle'. Sometimes the discovery of a corpse triggered an investigation: babies were found at the bottom of necessary houses, in cupboards, in trunks and in hatboxes.

Assessing the motives of those who actively promoted prosecutions is not easy, but testimony recorded in the trials suggests a variety of reasons, ranging from malice to a genuine desire that justice be done. Hannah Spires is called a 'murdering slut' by her mistress, and the degree of venom displayed by Eleanor Turnly against Elizabeth Turner is both depressing and extraordinary. These attitudes must be contrasted, however, with the troubled testimony of Mary Williams in the case of Mary Lewis. A midwife's horror in the Scrogham case adds another dimension: 'Said I, if you have murdered your children [twins] it is a crying sin; it is a sin against the Holy Ghost, and if that is your case I should rather die than live.'

The cases reproduced here were selected to provide as broad a view as possible of the participants in and circumstances of these very sad stories. I have tended to favour cases in which the majority of witnesses were women, but I do not believe that this results in any serious distortion.

NOTES

1. R.W. Malcolmson, 'Infanticide in the Eighteenth Century', in J.S. Cockburn, ed., Crime in England, 1550-1800 (Princeton, 1977), pp.187-209, at p.202.

2. J.M. Beattie, Crime and the Courts in England, 1660-1800 (Princeton, 1986), p.114.

3. Ibid., pp.118-120.

FROM THE TRIAL TRANSCRIPTS

JANUARY 1751

Hannah Spires, spinster, was indicted on the coroner's inquisition, for the murder of her bastard child, Dec. 9.

Susannah Cooney. The prisoner lived [as a] servant with me. On the 8th of last month, about 8 o'clock in the morning, I heard the prisoner groan. She had complained of the toothache before. I thought she had it again. She lay in the yard upon the stones. I went to her; she said she was very bad. I asked her, if she was with child. She said no. I desired her to get up, she would not. Said I, if you will not go into the kitchen, go up into the one pair of stairs room and lie down on that bed. She did.

I sent the girl up to her to see if she would have any breakfast. She said she could not eat anything. After dinner I went up to her, and said, she must have something to eat or she would be worse. I made her some panado and carried it up. After that I sent the girl up, who gave her some more. And in the evening between 6 and 7 o'clock my husband and I went to a neighbour's house; when we came back, I sent the girl up to know if she would not come down. She sent word she would not come down that night. I went up, and when I came there I saw something I did not like. I thought to myself there must be a child born, I took up a corner of the bed, and under that was a child. I called her murdering slut, or something like it. She made no answer. I drove her downstairs to her own bed, which was in the kitchen.

Q. Have you had children?

S. Cooney. Yes, I have. This child seemed to be at its full growth, but I did not examine its nails, my lord.

Q. Had she made any provision for it?

S. Cooney. She did say she had things at her mother's for it.

Q. Did there appear any wounds or marks on the body?

S. Cooney. No, there did not, my lord, or any settling of blood.

John Cooney confirmed the testimony of his wife.

Sarah Bull. I live [as a] servant in this family. After my master and mistress were gone out, in the evening I went up to see how she did, and carried her some panado, she drank it. When my mistress came home she went up and made her come downstairs. Then my mistress ordered me to bring a candle, and there was a child wrapped up in two cloths, one round the head, the other round the body.

Mary Rogers. I am a midwife. About half an hour after 10 that evening I was called out of my bed to this house; there sat the prisoner in a chair by the fire. I went to look at the child; there were all things together that should come into the world. It is my opinion the child was stagnated in the birth for want of help. When I came to clean it, there were no marks of violence upon it; the child was at its full growth, nails and everything.

James Atkinson. I am an apothecary. The child was carried to Shoreditch workhouse. There I viewed the body, I found no marks of violence upon it. I apprehend the child might be suffocated either in the birth or afterwards, but I am apt to think it was born alive, because there were settlings of blood interspersed all about the body.

Q. Could it breath and yet be suffocated in the birth?

Atkinson. Yes, my lord, it might.

Elizabeth Spires. The prisoner is my husband's daughter. She had some childbed linen at my house in her box. She had been at my house about a week before. I took the things out of the box. *They were produced in court.*

Acquitted.

◆

OCTOBER 1743

Eleanor Scrogham, of St. Margaret, Westminster, spinster, was indicted, for that she on the 13th of September, in the 17th year of His Majesty's reign, being big with two male children; she on the 13th of September, the two male children, by the providence of God, privately and secretly did bring forth alive; which said two male children, by the laws of this land, are bastards. And that she, Eleanor Scrogham, not having God, &c. on the 13th of Sept. as soon as the two male bastard children were born, in and upon the two male bastard children, did make an assault. And the two male bastard children, Eleanor Scrogham feloniously, wilfully, and of her malice aforethought in both her hands did take, and the two male bastard children being alive, out of her hands into a necessary-house did cast and throw, by which casting and throwing, into the necessary-house aforesaid, and by reason of the filth and excrement therein, the two male bastard children were suffocated; of which suffocation they instantly died. And that Eleanor Scrogham, the two male bastard children did kill and murder.

She was a second time charged on the coroner's inquisition for the murder.

Diddle Webster. The prisoner was my servant, and she was out of town with me at Stanmore where I lived [when] she was taken ill, and said she believed she was nearer her time than I thought for. I sent her to town before me. When I came to town I found she had been ill: I had taxed her with being with child in the country†; she at first denied it; and then said she was; and that she was married, and had three months to go.

† *Mrs Webster was so affected she could scarce express herself for tears.*

Q. Did you know what became of the children?

Webster. Not then I did not. I asked her where her child was. She told me it was safe and alive, and that she had put it out. I asked her where. She said, she had put it to nurse at the Bull and Gate in Holborn. I enquired after it, but it was not to be found there.

Q. Was there any childbed linen provided?

Webster. I did not see any, I heard there was some.

Q. Was not she to have gone away to have lain in?

Webster. I know no more than I have said.

Jane Thomas. Mrs Webster sent for me one afternoon about a month ago. Said she, I sent for you, Madam, upon a suspicion of my maid's being brought to bed, but now she has owned it, and says the child is at the Bull and Gate in Holborn. We went there but it was not to be found. When I came back, I said to Mrs Webster, I will ask her some questions. [If] you go out of the room ... she may answer me more readily. Said I, Sweetheart, what is become of the child. Said I, I hope you have not burned your child (for I had a suspicion that she had put it under the copper). No, Madam, said she, I have not. I asked her, what she had she done with it. Said I, I hope you have not murdered it. No, Madam, said she. Said I, is the child in the vault? She said it was; that she had a desire to go to the vault, and that it dropped from her when she was there. We got the vault searched, and as God would have it, the last child came up first. I said to the man that was searching the vault (after he had taken up one child), young man, there's another child—upon my oath, I said so to him. I said to the prisoner, are they both together? Did you throw them down? She said, No, indeed, I did not. Said I, are there two children. She said, I can't tell, there was a great deal came from me, and I was in such extremity of pain that if I had had ten thousand worlds, I could not have got off the vault. And I know that when women are in such distress of pain they cannot stir to help themselves. Said I, if you have murdered your children it is a crying sin. It is a sin against the Holy Ghost, and if that is your case, I should rather die than live.

I have been a midwife 18 years.

Q. Is it usual for women to desire to go to the necessary-house when they draw near their time?

Thomas. Yes. I had a woman that I attended that stole away from me with that intent. I know the first child had never been handled by any hand to part them, because we have a particular method that we know that by, and I believe her pains were so violent that she could not go from the place. I know when women are in the birth they can neither stand nor go, I asked her why she did not call some people. She said she thought if she had a little rest she should be better.

Q. Were the children at their full growth?

Thomas. I cannot say that they were. No woman in England can swear to a month in the birth of a child. She declared, before the justice, that she had not made any childbed-linen, but that she had given her sister orders to make some, and that she was to go there to lie in.

Margaret Oldfield. I got up that night to wash about twelve o'clock, and I heard such a scream that I was frightened out of my wits. (I am a servant, and live over against Mrs Webster's.) Said I, to the washerwoman, I believe Mrs Webster's maid is in labour, and there is nobody in the house. And if somebody does not go to her assistance she will be lost. (I think it was the 13th of September.) I knocked at the door as loud as I could knock, and called with my knocking. And she screamed out at the same time, but did not come to the door. And about eight o'clock in the morning I saw her open the windows. I asked her what was the matter, that she screamed out so? She said, she was taken with the cramp, and the colic. She said, she went to bed about ten o'clock. I asked her why she did not come downstairs. She said, she could not have come downstairs for all the world. To the best of my knowledge, the screaming came out of the room where she lay, up three pair of stairs.

Q. Was it known that she was with child?

Oldfield. Yes, it was known.

Thomas Ayres. I was sent for to search Mrs Webster's vault. I searched a little while, and I found one child. Then I took off the top of the vault, and made a larger search, and found another child.

As to whose children they were, I cannot tell. They were supposed to be the children of the prisoner at the bar.

Thomas Ball. On the 14th of September I was at the examination of the prisoner; and found, by her examination, that there was a child in the vault. I fetched the last witness to help me search for it, and we found a child. When the midwife saw it, she said, there was another; and after a further search I took that up.

—— *Bennet.* The prisoner's sister lodges at my house, and I saw her make several things fit for a child. The prisoner was to lie at my house. I had a bed ready at a minute's warning.

Ann Scrogham. The prisoner is my sister-in-law. She had made provision for the child. These are the things. She was to have lain-in at Mrs Bennet's.

I made the things by the prisoner's order.

Robert Simmonds. I am a practitioner in midwifery.

Q. I would ask whether it is usual with women, when the time of childbed draws near, to have a violent inclination to go to the vault?

Simmonds. It is very common; and it is a common prognostic of an approaching birth.

Q. Is it not possible, when a woman is in that condition, for the child to fall from her?

Simmonds. Yes, to be sure.

Jury. Where did your servant lie?

Webster. In the garret.

Acquitted.

The jury found, on the coroner's inquisition, that the children were still-born.

◆

JUNE 1734

Elizabeth Turner, of Clerkenwell, was indicted for the murder of her male bastard infant, by strangling it with both her hands, April 12.

Eleanor Turnly. The prisoner was servant to Mrs Windsor, a pastry-cook, in St. John's Lane. I and Margaret Goldsmith, came to lodge there but a little before Ladyday, and then we observed the prisoner looked big, and at Easter, she looked very lank. We suspected she had been delivered, though she appeared publicly every day. And we had never heard her cry out, but then we could not think what was become of the child. In short, we thought the family was all alike, or things could not be kept so private. We watched and harkened all as ever we could. One while ... we fancied the child might be at nurse in the garret, because they were often whipping up and down stairs. But when we could find nothing, we concluded it was baked in the oven. At last Mrs Goldsmith, going into the cellar, came up, and told me and her husband, she had seen a wig-box below, and smelled

31

something. He went down, and came up again, like a dead man, and said, he put his hand in the box, and felt a child, but was so surprised, that he did not take it out. We consulted what to do, and, says I, as they have kept this thing in hugger-mugger, we won't let 'em know the child is found before we fetch for a constable. So Mr Goldsmith fetched a constable and watch, and they brought the child up, and it was all mouldy. The prisoner, at first, denied she had had a child; but in a little time owned it was her's.

Juryman. You seemed very diligent in watching the prisoner. Did you ever tax her with being with child, before the child was found.

Turnly. No, I never spoke a word to her about it, for I could not bear the sight of the creature.

Margaret and Thomas Goldsmith, deposed to the same effect.

Elizabeth Windsor. The prisoner never told me she was with child, but she said she had been ill, and had had a great deal of water come from her, and that then she was much better. When the child was first found, she denied it, but owned it afterwards.

Dinah Beaven. The child was crowded in the box and putrefied. It was at the full time. I could discern no mark of violence. [There] was a small wound on the head; but I have known such a thing happen to an honest woman's child, when it has fell from her for want of assistance.

Sarah Hawkey. When the prisoner was brought to Newgate, some of the other prisoners took her coat, for garnish money. And they found these baby things, sewed up in her coat. Here's a shirt, a cap, a stay, a forehead-cloth, and a biggin.

The jury acquitted her.

◆

APRIL 1740

Elizabeth Evans alias Evens, of Ealing, was indicted, for that she being big with a female-child, the child, she secretly, and alone (by the providence of God) did bring forth alive, and which child by the laws of this land was a bastard. And that she, not having God before her eyes, &c. as soon as the female bastard-child was born, in and upon the female bastard-child did make an assault, &c. and with both her hands, her, the bastard-child, in a certain linen handkerchief (value 1d.) did wrap and fold, by reason of which wrapping, and folding, the bastard-child was choked and strangled, of which choking and strangling it instantly died, February 9. She was a second time charged by virtue of the coroner's inquest for the murder.

Sophia Claxton. The prisoner and I lay together in the same bed. She complained of a pain in her limbs, and kept her bed for three days. I can't tell the time exactly, when this happened, but one night, I came home and went to bed, after I had been out all day, hard at work. The prisoner in the night got upright upon her knees in the bed; and I asked her, what she was doing? She told me, she was making use of the pot. In the morning I got up to go to my work, and because the prisoner had been restless all night, I innocently went to put the clothes upon the bed, to cover her. And under her gown I saw a handkerchief; and in the handkerchief I found a baby wrapped up. I asked her why she did not call for help when I asked her what she was doing. But she made me no answer at all. This was about 8 o'clock in the morning.

I did not observe whether the child had received any hurt in its body, nor can I tell whether it was at its full growth. I never heard it cry. Though I lay with her, she never informed me of her being with child, and when I found it in the handkerchief, she said nothing to me. She did not own it was her's. I know no more.

Elizabeth Holman. I am a midwife; and I was sent for about two hours after the woman was brought to bed. I examined the child, and found it at its full growth, but it was dead when I saw it, and I can't take upon me to say whether it was born alive or not. I did not observe any hurt or bruise upon it. This was in the time of the hard frost. I can't tell what day it was exactly. After I had seen the child, I asked, how she came to kill it? She said, she did not kill it; she found it dead, and therefore laid it away from her. And before she would have killed it, she would have gone a-begging with it. I desired her to tell me who was the father? She said, she could not tell who it was got it, nor where he was, for one of the men was gone twenty miles, another thirty, and another four miles off.

Elizabeth Pearce. The prisoner lived a year and a half in my house, and I never saw any harm by her in my life. She always kept good hours. But as to this fact, I did not know she was with child, nor that she was brought to bed, 'til Claxton (the first witness) came downstairs in the morning, and told me what had happened. I asked her, how she came to be so naughty? And she made me no answer at all.

The prisoner had no witnesses to call; and, in her defence, only said she did not murder it.

The jury acquitted her.

◆

JULY 1731

Martha Busby, of Fulham, was indicted for the murder of her female bastard infant, by throwing it into an house of office, the 3rd of May last.

Elizabeth Smith deposed, that the prisoner lodged in the same house with her. And she found a child in the house of office, wrapped up in a piece of an old blanket. That the child appeared to have been at its full growth, but was wasted, being supposed to have lain there several weeks.

Mary Sweatingham deposed, that about a fortnight before the child was found, she being at work with her picking of strawberries, [the accused] asked her if she did not hear a child cry [and said] she had continually the noise of a new-born child in her ears. That she [went] to [see] the prisoner in New-Prison, and asked her, why she did not make her escape? She answered, she knew herself to be guilty, and had no power.

Elizabeth Jones deposed, that she going (about a fortnight before the child was taken up) to the pond to wash a mop, and the prisoner at the same time going to wash a tin-pot, the prisoner bid her put her hand upon her belly, and feel how soft it was grown in a week's time. And she tracked her by some blood, and also that she was another woman than she had been for 10 or 11 months. That she appeared then to be very lank, though she had looked big before.

Rachel Wright deposed, that as she was gathering strawberries, the prisoner asked her the like question as she had done Mary

Sweatingham.

Elizabeth Paul, the midwife, deposed, that in her opinion the child was at its full growth.

The prisoner called several persons to [attest to] her reputation, and the fact not being proved to the satisfaction of the jury, they acquitted her.

◆

OCTOBER 1733

Mary Doe was indicted for the murder of her male bastard infant, by strangling and choking it with both her hands, on the 29th of October last.

Frances Crook, midwife. On the 30th of October, I was sent for to [attend to] the prisoner, and found she had been delivered of a child. She said, something (she knew not what) was come from her, but it was no child. I asked her, what she did with that which came from her? She said she did not know where it was. I told her it signified nothing to deny it, for I was sure she had had a child, and therefore a child I would find. Then she confessed that it was a man child; but [she] said it was born dead, and that her father took it from her, but she could not tell what he had done with it. Her father coming in I told him his daughter had been delivered—*Delivered!* says he. *Ay so she has: of a Sir-Reverence.* Those were his words, begging Your Worship's pardon. I saw so much by his behaviour towards the prisoner, and some other passages, that in short, I told him, I believed he was father to the child, as well as grandfather; and that he had done my business, and delivered her himself before I was sent for. So he went out, and I examined the prisoner. And she declared to me, that her father had lain with her, and that she never had to do with any other man but him. On the 2nd of November following, the prisoner's mother gave me a note, I suppose it was sent from her husband, who was then run away. And in this note, it was said, that the child was wrapped up in an old curtain, and laid in among some horselitter in Tom Turd's Hole (a place where the nightmen lay their soil) and there it was found. I saw no marks of violence upon it; but I believe it bled to death for want of proper help.

Joseph Sandford, surgeon, in Goodman's Fields. On the 2nd of November last a male infant (supposed to be born of the prisoner, Mary Doe) was brought to me to have my opinion, whether it had been still-born, or not. I viewed the body, and found no external marks of violence; upon which I proceeded to open the cavities of the thorax and abdomen. The lungs appeared inflated. I cut off one of the lobes, and putting it into a vessel of water, it floated. I am therefore of opinion that the infant had breathed. I likewise found that the blood vessels in general were empty, and the navel string lacerated, and not tied; for which reason, I believe, proper help was wanting, and the child might bleed to death.

Mary White. The prisoner and her father and mother lived in a room in my house for many years. Her father is a journeyman carpenter, and her mother went out a washing. The prisoner, as far as ever I saw, always behaved herself prettily and modestly, though at last, poor creature, she happened to be with child, and she was delivered in my house.

Court. Did she call for help?

M. White. I cannot say that I heard her.

Court. Do you think she was so weak that she could not, or that she was under any surprise, and her labour came so suddenly that she had not time to call for assistance?

M. White. I know nothing as to those things, but here is a waistcoat proper for a young child, which I found in a wainscot box in her room, and she said she had provided it for that purpose. And she told me her father took the child from her. Poor young creature, she's hardly sixteen; her wicked father has ruined her.

John Tindall, constable. The midwife brought me a note with directions to search for the child among some straw, by the hog-house in Tom T——d's fields, and there we found it wrapped up in a Linsey-Woolsey curtain—her father is in Reading Gaol.

Susan Glover. I have known the prisoner two or three years; I always took her for a good-natured, inoffensive, modest girl, and I was extremely startled at the news of her having had a child; I talked with her about it—she complained of her father for deluding her, and said she had indeed had a child, but that her father took it from her, and she did not see it more. There were no marks of violence on the child, and I believe it might bleed to death through her ignorance and want of proper help.

Eleanor Whitchurch. I always took her for an honest sober girl before this misfortune, and I believe the child might die for want of help.

The jury acquitted her.

◆

FEBRUARY 1793

Mary Lewis otherwise Greenwood was indicted for that she, on the 29th of January, being big with a male child, on the same day, by the providence of God, did bring forth the male child alive, and which male child, by the laws of this realm, is a bastard, and that then not having the fear of God before her eyes, on the male feloniously, wilfully and with malice aforethought did make an assault in that she a certain piece of silk ribbon (value 1d.) with both her hands about the neck of the male child did tie, twist, fix and fasten, and the male child with the same silk ribbon feloniously, wilfully and with malice afore-thought did choke and strangle, of which choking and strangling the male child then and there instantly died.

Indicted in a second count in the coroner's inquisition.

Christopher Latimer sworn. I have only the ribbon to deliver that was about the child's neck.

Mary Williams sworn. I keep the house. I live at No. 4, New Court, Little Chapel Street, Westminster, opposite the Bluecoat school. The prisoner at the bar lodged at my house. I have known her about a year and a half if not more. She came to lodge with me as a servant out of place two or three times. She came to lodge with me the last time about three months before she was brought to bed. To the best of my knowledge, she was brought to bed three weeks last Tuesday. She did not give up her lodgings all that three months, but she was away about half the time.

She was brought to bed the 29th of January. I saw her the

morning of that day. She breakfasted with me about ten o'clock, about eleven she went upstairs to her room, a one pair of stairs room. I stayed in the house all that morning. I was in the house from that time 'til it was half after three. I did not see anything more of her, only that I spoke to her about half past two, she was in her room and the door was locked. I tried it, to go in. The man, that she [told] me was her husband wanted to speak to her. His name is Thomas Lewis. He had called at half past two. On finding her locked in I called to her and asked her to come down, that her husband wanted to speak to her. She told me that she could not come. Says she, I cannot open the door, Mrs Williams. I am naked, cleaning myself. I was at the room door while I had this conversation with her. Says I, it is me, my dear, set open the door. And she answered me, Mrs Williams, I cannot, I am naked, cleaning myself. With that I went downstairs and told the man she would be down presently, he waited a few minutes, I cannot tell how many, and I heard her unlock the door and call him. And he stepped upstairs within a step or two to the top. He did not go into the room. I did not see her at that time. I don't know what passed between them. They conversed the space of five minutes, then he came downstairs and walked out.

Q. Do you know whether she had come out of the room at that time or not? — Yes, she stood at the top of the stairs to speak to him, I heard her voice speaking to him there and saw his shadow on the wall of the landing place.

Q. Do you know what became of her after the man came down? — She went into the room and I could hear the door lock, this might be about three o'clock or something after, very likely there or thereabouts. I went out at that time for the space of ten minutes or a quarter of an hour, to the best of my knowledge. When I came back she was downstairs in my apartment sitting by my fire. As near as I can guess it was about four o'clock. I found her sitting by my fire. When I came in, I asked her why she did keep herself upstairs, and she told me she was very busy sewing. I told her she could not be at sewing work because her thimble was below, and she put her left hand into her pocket and showed me another thimble. And, says she, I have got another thimble in my pocket. I went out directly then about my business. I went out with my milk, I sell milk. I came home about half after five, to the best of my knowledge, and she was sitting down at the same place then when I came back that time. And she drank tea with me about seven o'clock as usual. She called for a penny loaf and [ate] as before. There we sat and talked 'til about nine o'clock.

We had a bed in the two pair of stairs room that we had had not an opportunity to make in the course of the day. Her room was one pair, this was two pair. I told my niece to go upstairs and make that bed. Her name is Mary Williams. She went up and made the bed, and she came down as soon as she [had] made the bed and asked me to go up into the one pair of stairs room. The prisoner was present with me in the lower room in my apartment. My niece did not tell me anything, but desired me to go up into the … room. I went up myself alone and opened the room door. My niece did not go with me; she was very poorly. This room door was not locked at that time. That was the prisoner's room. And I was very much frightened to see the room all bloody all over, and I followed [the blood] to the closet in the same room, the door was not fastened in any place at all, the door had no hinges. I saw the child lay dead on the naked boards, naked without any covering nor nothing … [His] little head was in an old slipper of hers in a dark part of the closet. I returned downstairs very much frightened. I did not make any more observations on the child, and I said, what am I to do? What is this that is come to my house? And she asked me, Mrs Williams, what is the matter? I says, O you brute, you ask me what is the matter, and you know what you have been about, locking yourself upstairs all day. And she begged my pardon. She says, I beg your pardon Mrs Williams, I could not help it I miscarried. Miscarriage or not miscarriage, I should know of it. For God's sake, says she, say not a word about it to nobody and I will take it away in the morning, and have it buried, and I will go to my uncle and be there. No, says I, not a limb of it shall go out of my house in that manner. Then Mrs Gibbs came downstairs and asked what was the matter? She is a lodger of mine. I told her there was matter enough with me, that woman had told me she had miscarried, but however, says I, she has got her dead child in the cupboard. With that Mrs Gibbs answered, let me see the child; I will tell you whether it is a miscarriage or not. I took a candle and took Mrs Gibbs with me upstairs. We went together into the room and to the closet, and the prisoner Mary Lewis followed us both upstairs. Mrs Gibbs took the child up in her arms and turned its head towards the cupboard door. I could then see a ribbon about its neck. Says I to Mrs Gibbs, what is that ribbon about its neck? Undo the ribbon. Mrs Gibbs did undo it and I was present, and then the prisoner threw herself on the side of the bed and laid down. And I asked her what she put that ribbon about the neck of the child for? To draw it from me, says she. It was a slip knot and Mrs Gibbs took hold of it in one end, and undid it, it was very easily taken off. It was tight about the neck, we could not see a bit of the ribbon about the neck it was so tight … I told her to take the child downstairs and take it to the fire and rub it. I thought to bring the child to life, and gave her a little brandy to rub it with; but when I considered how many hours the infant had laid, it was impossible. We had it to the fire and tried, but it was as cold as clay. The trace of the ribbon was very visible in the neck, and the skin was a little raised with the tightness of the ribbon on one side of it. It was a man child. With that we took the child upstairs from the fire and put it where we found it, I and Mrs Gibbs, and laid it down as we found it. With that I had her put to bed. I told her to go to bed for shame of her. After I had her put to bed I locked the room door. She went to bed in the same room; I had asked her if she would take anything, and I went down for a man midwife to look at the child.

Q. Before this, had you seen any symptoms of a delivery besides the child? —Yes, it was in the pot along with the baby in the closet and an old rag of a pocket handkerchief with it.

Q. You mean the after burden? —Yes.

Q. When did you see the prisoner after this happened? — The next morning, I went upstairs and asked her if she would have something to eat, and asked her why she did not leave the child alive in some corner of the room for me, and if she had a mind to run away herself if she had left the child alive I should not care. I wish I had now, Mrs Williams, says she. Whether she meant that she wished she had left the child alive or wished that she had run away, I cannot say.

Q. How came you to forget … this [when you were] before the coroner? — I answered every thing they asked me.

Q. Did she say any thing about the birth? — She told me it was a miscarriage. I asked her whether she found the child was dead or alive with her? And she told me she believed it was alive in the birth; I went with that and acquainted the people at the office. I went first of all to a gentleman, Mr Ashmole, in Petty France and told him what had happened and he went with me to the justice's office, Queen-Square. She was in bed all this time in my house.

Q. There was no restraint upon her all this time after the child was found. Did you lock her in the next morning? — I did not; the parish people came there about ten o'clock on Wednesday and the woman from the work-house was watching her all night.

Q. You had known this woman a good while, of course you must have had a good opinion of her — I had a very good opinion of her, if she was a sister of mine I could not have a better opinion of her.

Q. Perhaps she had before this time communicated to you that she was with child? — Yes, she agreed with me to nurse her for the month. She told me the first time she came she was married and with child, and since she came to lodge with me she told me that she had an uncle in Bond Street and kept a public house, who had promised to send her three sacks of coals for her laying in and a sack of wood. And she told me that a relation had promised her all the baby linen, but she never brought none to my house. I saw her working at a bit of a shirt and a cap. I asked her whether she was doing her baby linen? She said, yes, my baby linen is at a relation's; this is nothing but to amuse me.

Q. How long was it before she was brought to bed [that you saw] her at work about this shirt? — About a month or more I had seen such a thing in her hand; but she told me her baby linen was at a relation's.

Q. From her coming to you she made no secret that she was with child? — She told me she was with child, and she told me she was married, and I was to take care of her during her laying in.

Q. That was agreed upon? — It was.

Q. What was to be done with nursing of the child? — She told me she would never suckle herself, nor no woman living should suckle her child. I was telling ... her one day [about] bringing something for the baby's use. She used to say don't you fear, I shall have every thing that I want for my baby in time. Says she, I shall not lay in 'til the latter end of February. She was going on in my debt, telling me she had a yearly income and the writings were in Mr Montague's hands. She said, she had 15 l. a year. She told me the Wednesday morning after she was delivered that she was not married.

Mary Williams sworn.

I am the niece of the former witness. I live in the same house with my aunt where Mary Lewis lodged. Thomas Lewis who the prisoner called her husband came in about half past two, on the 29th of January, and he wanted to speak with Molly, as he called her. My aunt answered him, she was upstairs ever since breakfast. My aunt told him to come in and sit down, and my aunt went upstairs and told [the accused] that Lewis wanted to speak to her. I could hear my aunt trying to go in, but the door was locked, and my aunt told her to open the door, and asked her what did she lock the door for? I heard [the accused] speaking these words: I cannot because I am cleaning myself. And my aunt came down and told Lewis that she was a cleaning herself, and would be down by and by. She was not very long in the room and I heard her come out of the door and shut the door after her, and [call] to Lewis, if you want to speak to me come up. She stood on the landing place. Lewis went up and spoke to her; he was there about five minutes. I don't know what they were saying, I did not hear that at all, but he returned downstairs and went out, and my aunt went to fetch her milk home.

And in the time that my aunt was out [the accused] came downstairs. And I was sitting with my face towards the window sewing. She came by me and sat down in the corner by the fire. I asked her what she had been doing upstairs; and why she did not come down and keep me and my child company? I have been sewing, says she, very busy about it. That was the very words. And I said, your thimble is here. She told me she had another thimble in her pocket. I said, I thought you were ill or something. No, no, says she, I was not ill. When I am ill I will let you know fast enough.

I was in the room downstairs by the fire. My aunt came home about half past five o'clock, and she drank tea with us about seven as usual. About nine o'clock at night we had a bed in the two pair of stairs not made. My aunt told me to go up and make the bed, so I did. As I was going up I saw a stain in the landing place where [the accused] stood to talk to Lewis. As I was coming down after I had made the bed, I turned into this room, and the bed was all over of the same.

Q. What kind of stain did it appear to be? — Blood. I went no farther I was so poorly. I went then downstairs and I told my aunt to go up the one pair of stairs room. What for? says my aunt to me, is the woman's coals coming? No, no, says I, go upstairs and see what is coming. And my aunt [lit] a candle and went upstairs. I did not go with her. While my aunt was gone up, the prisoner never spoke a word to me, nor I to her. My aunt returned down, there was nobody with her but herself. O God! What is this that is come to me in my house? says my aunt. And the prisoner made answer, what is the matter Mrs Williams? And my aunt said, matter enough, what have you been doing upstairs? How can you ask me what is the matter? And she said to my aunt, I beg your pardon, Mrs Williams, I could not help it, I have miscarried. My aunt answered her and said, miscarriage or not miscarriage, you should have let me [know]. She told my aunt to say nothing about it that night and she would take it away in the morning, and have it buried, and she would go to her uncle and be there. My aunt said, not a limb of it shall go out of my house in that manner. Mrs Gibbs came downstairs at this time and asked my aunt what was the matter? I fell in a fit at seeing what I did upstairs, and my aunt told Mrs Gibbs that that woman said she had miscarried upstairs. Mrs Gibbs says, let me go up and I will tell whether it is a miscarriage or no. My aunt and Mrs Gibbs went up and the prisoner followed them, and I followed her upstairs. My aunt and Mrs Gibbs went to the closet and I was at the closet door, and I saw the child laying there before they took it up. And Mrs Gibbs took hold of the child and took it up, and my aunt said, what is that ribbon about the child's neck? I saw the knot on the left side, and Mrs Gibbs undid the knot directly, for my aunt told her, and they carried the child downstairs and had it in a flannel by the fire; the child was so cold it was all in vain, and then they carried it up again and put it down in the closet where they found it, and came downstairs both of them. But my aunt put her to bed first. And we went downstairs and my aunt locked the room door after her, and my aunt went out for a doctor, but the doctor could not come that night. I looked at the child after the ribbon was taken off and the track of the ribbon was in the child's neck.

Elizabeth Gibbs sworn.

Q. We understand that you went upstairs this night to examine the room, who did you go up with? — With Mrs Williams, and I saw as fine a child as ever I set my eyes upon in the cupboard with its head in an old shoe. I put my hand on its left shoulder and I thought then that I saw its right foot wag, that made me cry out to Mrs Williams, bring me a flannel for I think it is alive now. I observed a great deal in the cupboard. I took the child up. Mrs Williams said, what is this ribbon about its neck, Mrs Gibbs? I laid hold of the ribbon at one end and off came the ribbon. I gave it a good hard pull. We carried the child downstairs in a flannel and we rubbed it by the fire. I could observe no life in it, but it was very black about the mouth. And [there] looked to be a blow on the temple. I carried it upstairs again, and I put it where I took it from as I found it was dead. I said, I will take care of the ribbon and gave it to the coroner. And I received it of Latimer now; it is a silk ribbon.

Margaret Garret sworn.

I was one of the women sent from the work house to take care of the prisoner. I searched her pockets and I found two little shirts and two little caps. The prisoner [made] them herself. I found them of my own accord.

Ann Steward sworn.

I was the other woman sent to take care of the prisoner. I was present when Margaret Garret searched the prisoner. I [saw] her find the things she has mentioned in the pockets of the prisoner. I know them to be proper things for a young child.

Francis Moseley sworn.

I know the prisoner. About ten weeks ago the prisoner lived with Mr Trevers as a chair woman. I was an assistant to Mr Trevers as an apothecary. I asked her once what time she expected to lay in? She said, in eight weeks. I asked her if she was going to stay with us in the situation of a servant? She said, she could not as she had not above eight weeks before she expected to lay in. I enquired what she meant to do with her infant? It was one afternoon while we were at tea. She said, to put it out to nurse and to procure herself a situation as wet nurse. She was only there 'til we were supplied with a constant servant. She slept in the house while she was there. There was no concealment whatever.

—— *Linn sworn.*

I am a surgeon. I live in Parliament Street. On the 30th or 31st of January I was desired by the coroner to examine the body of the child, previous to the coroner's sitting. I found an evident mark like a ligature about its neck, and a slight excoriation, as done by the ligature. I opened the body. I found the lungs had contained air, having been partially inflated. The blood vessels about the neck and heart were particularly turgid and full. I did not open the head, if the child had breathed it must have been a very short respiration. If it had breathed at all it must have been very short.

Q. Was it possible for the lungs to be inflated to such a degree without the child having some degree of breath? — I should think not.

Q. Had not the breath which it might take in the act of delivery be sufficient to inflate the lungs? — It might most assuredly.

Q. And yet the child died instantly? — It might. I went up to the prisoner and told her that I understood there was a ribbon found about the child's neck. I wished to know of her what was the reason for applying it. She said, she applied it to bring the body of the child from her. She found herself in great pain and that it stuck at the shoulders. She was pulling it for about ten minutes before she could get it away from her. The child was remarkably large, and it appeared to me that she could not have got it away without some such assistance. I am not a practitioner in midwifery. Here is a gentleman here who can speak better to that point. He is the man midwife to the parish; but that is my opinion of the matter.

Q. Now, sir, supposing this story to be true, suppose the child had been some time stuck by the way, by the shoulder, before she applied the string, might not that impediment suffocate the child? — In my opinion equally so.

Q. So that the child might be suffocated in the delivery before the application of the string? — I believe it frequently happens.

—— *Graves sworn.*

I am a man midwife employed by the parish. I saw the child, and a very large child it was, prodigious large over the shoulders, and when the child sticks so it stops the circulation between the mother and the child, and destroys the child ninety-nine out of an hundred.

Q. Was it likely it would be the case with this? — I have no manner of doubt.

Not Guilty.

Tried by the first Middlesex jury before Mr Baron Thompson.

◆

FEBRUARY 1736

Mary Shrewsbury, otherwise Threwsbury, was indicted for the murder of her male bastard child, by giving it a mortal wound with a knife in the throat, of the length of four inches and the depth of two inches, of which it instantly died, Feb. 4.

She was a second time indicted by virtue of the coroner's inquest for the murder.

Mr Boy. This accident happened, in Moorfields on Friday 7-night last. Application was made to me on suspicion of a murder. I, being overseer of the poor, went to the house, and the people told me the child was put down the vault. I put a guard in the house that night, and the next morning I brought a skilful midwife. We went upstairs, and the poor creature, the prisoner, was sitting upright in her bed, with a book in her hand, and the tears ran plentifully down her face. There were five or six people in the room. I asked them if they had searched the room. They said they had. Then I went down and searched the vault, but I found no more than what is common in such cases. Then I ordered the vault to be emptied, and there was nothing found, though the contents were well examined. I desired the midwife to go up and examine the woman again. She did not care to go without the beadle, so he went with her, and they searched the room again, and found the child in a hole in the closet. She owned what was done she did herself, and that the other woman here only emptied the pot. So the justice discharged her because the prisoner took it all on herself.

Q. Were there any marks of violence on the child?

Mr Boy. Only the head cut about half off.

Ann Palmer, midwife. The Parish Office sent for me to examine the prisoner. I found she had been delivered of a child. When I enquired what she had done with it, she would make no direct answer, but sat up in her bed crying, with a book in her hand. I could get nothing out of her, but only, that what this Eliz[abeth] Bell had done, was by her orders. I asked her what Bell had done. She would not tell me, but only desired I would be favourable. And Bell being gone away, I could not persuade her to tell me where she might be found. At last we found this Bell, and upon her examination, she said she had put nothing down the vault but the after-birth. For says she, the child she threw down there herself. I went to the prisoner again, and told her that Bell had informed us, that she (the prisoner) had put the child into the vault. She owned she did so, and begged I would be favourable in my information, telling me, it was dead when she put it down. Well, says I, I hope you have not havocked it. No, she said, she had not. Then the vault was raked, and nothing found, but the afterburthen. Still she insisted upon it, that her child was there. Upon which it was quite emptied, but no child was found. I knew there must have been one born, so I searched again. With the beadle and other women. And I took her out of bed in a blanket, and searched the bed. Behind the bed I found some rags stained &c. &c. At the feet of the bed, I found a box with more rags in the same condition. I shook them all out, but found no child. In another box I saw something that put me upon enquiring, what she had been doing in it. She told me, she had only put some clothes in it. At last we searched the closet, and in a nook which ran into the chimney, behind a small trunk, we found it, sewed up in a cloth. When I pulled it out of the hole, the prisoner swooned away. When she recovered, I asked her several questions: how she could cut her child's throat so barbarously, and how she could in her present condition have strength to sew it up? She said that the Devil had given her strength and not God. The Lord have mercy upon you, says I, and so I left her.

Q. Was the child's throat cut very much?

Palmer. It could not be cut worse, unless it's head had been cut right off.

A Witness. This Bell was the prisoner's landlady, and seeing her come down with a mop and a pail from the prisoner's room, I asked her what was the matter. She told me that Mary (the prisoner) was not well. I went up, and knocked at her door, and she told me, the key was under the door. I opened it and went in, and I asked her what she ailed: I saw spots of blood upon the floor, and I enquired how they came there. She said, she was as women are, when they are disordered, but, says she, my landlady Bell is coming to wipe them up. In the closet I saw a pan full of cloths, not very fit to be seen. What's all this Mary, says I? God bless you, says she, don't say anything, I have miscarried and was three months gone. I told her I was sorry for that, but however, I made her some hot water-gruel, and carried it to her in bed, and left her to eat it. When I was got downstairs, I endeavoured to settle myself to my work, but I was very uneasy in my mind, and (to make short of my story) I could not rest 'til I had made some farther enquiry. I asked her where she had put the miscarriage. She told me that Bell had put it down the vault. The vault was searched, but it was not there. It was found at last in a nook, that went into the chimney. I was present when 'twas pulled out, and according to my judgement 'twas at it's full growth.

Midwife. 'Twas at it's full growth. It had hair and nails perfect, and was a larger child than is common.

Eliz. Bell. I came home that night about 10 o'clock, and seeing a great deal of blood upon the floor, I asked the prisoner how it came there. She said, don't be frighted, I have miscarried, she desired me to tell no body, and begged I would carry down the pot. I got her some hot ale, and went to bed.

C. You have behaved very ill in this affair, and you deserve to be severely reprimanded. You saw all the symptoms of the woman's being delivered, and instead of making a discovery, you ran out of the way. Your proceeding was very shameful, and I am afraid you are as much concerned in this murder as the prisoner herself—Get you gone.

Prisoner. It was dark when I was delivered, and the child was dead.

Guilty. Death.

'I saw, through a large chink in the partition ...'

WHAT THE SERVANTS KNEW

◆

BY PAULA M. HUMFREY

It is a commonplace to say that domestic servants see many things but are themselves invisible. For female servants in early modern London, household work certainly offered considerable exposure to the details of others' lives. But these women were themselves exposed, highly mobile and vulnerable to the uncertainties of employment in an urban market. What a domestic knew about her master or mistress sat in a delicate balance with what she revealed about herself.

Women in domestic service were a numerically significant part of the working population in the metropolis at the end of the seventeenth and beginning of the eighteenth centuries. (In 1767, Jonas Hanway estimated that, in London, one person in thirteen was a servant. As many as 25 percent of labouring women in the capital may have been domestics.) Their work might be determined by the specialized function for which they were hired and for which a hierarchy obtained: a housemaid might aspire to become a cook; a cook would in turn defer to the ladies' maid in a family substantial enough to employ both.[1] However, the passages I have selected here reveal that domestic service for women was defined most often by the organization of particular households and by the needs of individual employers rather than by static job designations. Women often acquired positions in service in a haphazard way that did not depend

51

William Hogarth, 'Heads of Six of Hogarth's Servants' c 1750–5 (detail).
Oil on canvas, The Tate Gallery, London.

on any essential qualities of background or training. Their autobiographical comments suggest that female domestics in early modern
London tended to follow 'snakes and ladders' patterns of employment, in a sequence of jobs in households of divergent status. A
servant's fortunes often depended on how successfully she brokered
references and personal connections as well as on her set of skills.

The records of female servants' lives are fragmentary, and so reading their stories is inevitably an exercise in putting pieces together.
The depositions excerpted here reflect this. Collected from the
records of the Court of Arches, the principal court of the ecclesiastical Province of Canterbury, these passages form a collage of decla-
rations concerning domestics in different areas of the metropolis
over a period of more than forty years. Lengthy narratives about
servants, even fragments of narratives, are difficult to locate in this
source (as in others) despite the court's interest in servants as important witnesses in matrimonial and testamentary suits.[2] These statements are compelling for precisely this reason: they allow us to
glimpse the lives of non-literate women who have left us no other
record of their experience.[3]

The women who gave these depositions were called as witnesses. All were subject to the pressures of giving sworn testimony, and
all were constrained to respond to questions. This arrangement gave
deponents a formal arena in which to tell their stories, and so
allowed them to recount what they thought was important about
particular episodes in their lives. While the substance of their depositions may or may not have been literally true, what they said was
plausible to the court and duly set in the record. Moreover, many
testimonies concern information that servants probably had little
reason to lie about: their ages and origins, their previous jobs. These
women must have been keenly aware that they were giving weighty
and official testimony to a high-level court; it is vibrantly clear in
these documents that servants assessed evidence and presented
opinions, promoted their own agendas and used the opportunity for

speech-making to their perceived best advantage, just as they did in the course of the incidents they were brought to court to describe. It is therefore important to consider that the depositions were originally the transcripts of spoken words, which even when rehearsed, differ from the self-conscious, written reflections of the literate classes.

This material is an aperture into servants' worldviews. What gradually becomes clear is that, in spite of the diversity of their circumstances, they had something significant in common. Female servants' ability to manipulate what they knew and were willing to reveal about themselves and others was a real determinant of power in their lives. While their depositions describe the physical environments of their workplaces in considerable detail, the range of responsibilities for which they were paid tend to be allusively introduced. It is obvious that the women differ in age, backgrounds and employment circumstances. However, as the ideas and opinions women present in different depositions begin to overlap, it emerges that there are also strong points of connection between their experiences. It is the motifs threaded through the welter of detail that make the various forms of paid household work for women cohere into 'domestic service'. This is one way in which the consistent format of the depositions alerts us to an important subtext of the 'official' presentation of evidence. Domestic service in early modern London was defined by conditions of employment for women rather than a particular range of duties. The maid of all work in the petty tradesman's family had much in common with the Countess's chambermaid.

In the first section of depositions below, servants describe their origins and the circumstances that led them to service, and stress other kinds of work that they did or were prepared to do in addition to domestic labour. They often describe their experience of service as a series of short-term positions entailing considerable mobility. Their testimonies also suggest the importance of networks of personal connections for individual women. In the second section, the depositions emphasize the fabric of households and disclose information about working environments and the human interactions that suffused these domestics' performance of their assigned tasks. Even in the more affluent families described below, female servants worked in close contact with their employers.

A recurring issue in the Court of Arches records generally is women's adaptation to the contingencies of pregnancy and childrearing. The presence or prospect of children had an enormous impact on a servant's ability to earn money, and many depositions highlight the ways in which a woman's stature depended on her maintaining an appearance of 'virtue'. The passages in section three combine the themes introduced in earlier excerpts with servants' management of their own and their mistresses' maternity. The concluding section includes two groups of depositions. They describe in detail the complexity of domestic arrangements that is implied elsewhere in the records. These narratives strongly suggest that protecting one's own reputation while gathering knowledge about others must have been central to female servants' management of their working lives.

NOTES

1. See J.J. Hecht, *The Domestic Servant Class in Eighteenth-Century England* (1953) for a good description of the hierarchy of positions in household service

2. The best discussion of the provenance of the Court of Arches records and description of the Court and its business is found in M.D. Slatter, 'The Records of the Court of Arches', *Journal of Ecclesiastical History*, 4 (1953), p.139-53.

3. The ability to sign one's name did not necessarily reflect true literacy; it was only an indication that the signatory had 'learned her letters'.

THE SERVANTS' DEPOSITIONS

I

FEBRUARY 1692

Deposition of Elizabeth Hudson, spinster; St. James in the Fields, Middlesex; aged 20 years

About a fortnight before last Michaelmas was two years [I] lived as a servant with [a woman who] followed the trade of a pawnbroker and let out goods upon pawns and took money for the use of them ... [I] now live with [my] sister at her house at the end of Portuguese Row in Lincoln's Inn Fields ... [my] sister's husband's name is Isaac Abram and [he] keeps a brandy shop ... [I] lived with [my] sister about three months last past, and before that lived at [my] cousin Bate's, who keeps two hackney coaches at his house in Piccadilly, from about twelve months and upward, and for about a quarter of a year before [I] was servant for a widow gentlewoman in Gerard Street, and for about six weeks before that [I] lived with [the pawnbroker], and about six months before ... being sick, was boarded by [my] father at Mr Pickett's at the Bear and Staffe in Castle Street by Leicester Fields, and before [my] sickness [I] was servant in [a peer's] family for about three years and a half ... [I] usually get [my] living by going to service, but at present [I] live with [my] sister, and maintain [myself] by making shirts and other linen, and [am] worth nothing but what [my] father pleases to give [me].

SIGNATURE

◆

JANUARY 1726

*Deposition of Margaret Anderson, wife of George Anderson, porter;
Middlesex; aged 30 years*

[I] was brought up to spinning and washing ... and to service and
never followed any other employment ... [I have] lived in St.
Andrews Street by the 7 Dials above six years, and before that [I]
lodged at the Two Brewers in Castle Street by the 7 Dials above a
year ... [My] aunt Alice Sharp there kept house, and when [I] first
came to St. Andrews Street [I] lodged with [my] aunt for a year,
and after that with Richard Everson in the same house for a year
longer and from that time have been a housekeeper in the same
street ... the names of [my] father and mother were Richard and
Mary Swan and they died in [my] infancy ... [My] father was a
labourer.

MARK

*Deposition of Anna Gary, wife of John Gary; St. Anne in the Liberties;
aged 30 years*

[I] was bred up to plainwork and afterwards went to service and
thereby maintained [myself] and [am] now partly maintained by
[my] husband and partly by [my] needle and other honest labour
... [I have] lived at Mrs Lambeth's in Milk Alley by Soho Square
between 4 and 5 weeks and before that [I] lodged at George
Anderson's in St. Andrews Street by the 7 Dials about a year and
two months ... [I lived] with [Sarah Cross] as her servant at the
house of Henry Sheppard, a farrier, at Red Lion Yard, Gray's Inn
Lane, two years ... with Mr Martin at Mrs Shill's at a saddler's
shop near Somerset House in the Strand about a year and a half
... with Mr Faxby a cheesemonger in Warder Street in Old Soho
for 2 months and a half ... [I] was born at Haymarket and the

names of [my] father and mother were William Battin and Margaret Battin ... They kept a saddler's shop and died when [I] was a young girl.

MARK

Deposition of Mary Culcup, spinster; St. George Hanover Square, Middlesex; aged 25 years

[I] was born at Westminster ... the names of [my] father and mother were Owen and Susannah Culcup ... [My] father blew the bellows of the organ at the parish church of St. Margaret Westminster and was one of the parish bearers and [my] mother washed gentlemen's linen ... They are both dead and [I] have heard that [my] father was a sugar boiler and kept slaves at Barbados ... [I] was brought up to work at [my] needle and ironing 'til about five years and a half since, and from that time have lived in service ... [I] have lived as a servant with ... Mr Thomas Coach about 3 years and three quarters and first went to live with him on Easter Eve 1723 and continued to live with him in Castle Street by the 7 Dials about or more than half a year and then removed with him to Berwick Street and lived with him there about 15 months and from there [we] removed to New Bond Street and lived there about a month and from there to Cross Street by Carnaby Street near Golden Square and lived there about 8 months and from there removed to May Fair [where I now live] ... before [I] went to live with Mr Coach [I] lived with Captain Evans in Russell Court, Drury Lane, and in Maiden Lane by Covent Garden and at Hamstead for about 16 months ... at Russell Court [we] lodged at Mr Ford's, a public house ... and at Maiden Lane at Mr Brooks's, a chairman, and at Hamstead at Mr Lewis's, a gardener.

SIGNATURE

II

MAY 1696

Deposition of Anne Orran, spinster; St. Peter Cornhill, London; aged 23 years

[I am] servant to [Mary Palmer] and have been so three years and a half last past ... [I] have taken particular notice ... of the kitchen of [Martha Branch] and the dining room of Mary Palmer ... [Branch's] and [Palmer's] houses stand sloping or slanting near to each other ... [Branch's] kitchen window and Mary Palmer's dining room window are not directly opposite to each other [but are] of a near equal height of one storey high ... Palmer's dining room being over their tap house and [Branch's] kitchen over their shop which is a poulterer's shop ... Branch's kitchen window is but one small light, which [I] for [my] own satisfaction measured ... and found it not to be quite half a yard wide ... Palmer's dining room window and [Branch's] kitchen window are about two yards and a half distant according to [my] guess from each other ... There now is and there was all the month of August last past a trough or box used for a garden by [Palmer] which adjoins to [her] dining room window, and ... by [my] own measure which [I] have made lately ... the end of the box or trough which next answers [Branch's] kitchen window is within two inches of a yard or thereabouts distant from the kitchen window ... [As of] the 15th of August last past the box was full with ... things, which at that time of the year were ... thick grown and not fallen, but about three quarters of a yard high ... Laths [are] fixed to the sides and ends of the trough, which laths are about two inches broad, and about the breadth of a hand distant from each other, the window is in a manner at that time of the year covered and [I] well remember all the month of August there was two pots of greens one each side ... [of the] trough or box ... and two pots of greens ... mints and balm high grown which were on the inside of [Branch's] kitchen window ... [During] the month of August ... it was impossible for any person to see out of Mary Palmer's dining room window into [Branch's] kitchen ... [I] constantly look after [Branch's] children and [I] well remember [I] came to town with the children the 2nd day of August 1692 ... [I] constantly put [the children] to bed winter and summer between six and seven of the clock at night, and [I] always set the childrens' basket of clothes on the dresser near the kitchen window ... [The] kitchen is furnished with wooden chairs and the cradle always stands before the chairs with the head toward the kitchen window and the feet toward the fireplace, which ... is at the farther end of the kitchen about five yards distant from the window ... [My] mistress did go to bed between 6 and 7 of the clock on Thursday the 19th of August, because after [my] mistress was in bed, a neighbour's apprentice and a man and his horse were talking together, and in discourse [I] told the company ... that night was a fortnight [and that I] was merry with [my] fellow servants on Box Hill near Epsom ... [I] was in the shop and kitchen of [Branch's] house all [that] evening.

MARK

◆

OCTOBER 1668
Deposition of Sara Whitlock, spinster; St. Giles Cripplegate, London

About one of the clock in the afternoon, happening about seven months since, a difference happened between Elizabeth Harding, [my] mistress, and [her neighbour] Cornelia Hodges about some water running out of [Hodges's] sink into [Harding's] cellar ... [My mistress] was informed by [a fellow] servant that the boy that Cornelia Hodges had employed to carry the water out of the cellar was unwilling to carry all of it out ... [Harding] told [me] that she would speak herself to Cornelia Hodges about the same and [I] went into the cellar again leaving Cornelia Hodges then in a yard adjoining to both their houses and being used by them both, the same being in St. Buttolph's Aldersgate ... Immediately after [I] was got down into the cellar, [I] heard Hodges and [my] mistress talk

aloud, whereupon [I] immediately went upstairs to hear and see
what the matter was and … saw Hodges as she was standing in the
yard say to Harding as she was looking out of her kitchen window
up one pair of stairs … you are a whore and have been the undoing
of many, and kept the husbands company when their wives and
children have wanted bread … Harding was before of very good
name and fame … [but she is now] disdained and disgraced … [I]
used to go to service for [my] living and [have] lived with Harding
a little above a year and before that lived for many years at Barking,
and [I have] known Harding ever since [I] came to live with her,
and presently [there]after knew Cornelia Hodges … [I am] still servant to [Harding], but [am] not any otherwise related to her … [I]
maintain [myself] by going to service and [am] worth little and [am]
not taxed.

MARK

◆

JANUARY 1675
Deposition of Sara Oakes, spinster; St. Mary Magdalene, Bermondsey

On a day happening at the end of July or the beginning of August
last past, [I] being servant to Christiana Tatham, being in [my] mistress's washhouse in Bermondsey parish about [my] occasions [my
mistress] … happened to be there at the time (namely about ten of
the clock of the day) at which time Mrs Granger [who was]
Thomasina Flewe's daughter happened to be in her [own] washhouse which was divided only by slit deals from the washhouse of
[my] mistress, which partition had many large crevices and chinks
or crannies therein through which any person in one of the places
or washhouses might easily be seen by anyone which would look
thereinto from the other washhouse … [My mistress], seeing that
Mrs Granger was in her washhouse, told Mrs Granger of a certain
scandal which [my mistress] said was raised by [a] maid named
Anne who was then in the Granger's washhouse … [My mistress]
told Mrs Granger that Granger's maid gave out that [my mistress]

had St. Anthony's fire in her leg ... [and] the dispute or talk
between them grew very high, they looking through the crevices
or chinks of the partition one on the other ... During the talk or
dispute, [my mistress's] child who was then at the street door [was]
happening to cry ... [I] went to see what ailed her, and being
come to the street door [I] saw the maid of Mrs Granger who,
during the dispute, was in the washhouse go from her mistress's
house into the house of Thomasina Flewe, not far distant from
Granger's house on the same side of the way, and at the door [I]
stayed and saw Thomasina Flewe and her daughter's maid come out
of Flewe's house and go into Mrs Granger's house, so presently
after which their entry [I] returned to [my] mistress's washhouse
about [my] business and soon after her coming thither, Thomasina
Flewe (being come into her daughter's washhouse) there fell into a
great rage and in her rage and anger looking through a large
crevice or vacancy in the partition on [my mistress] who was then
in her washhouse ... spoke in an angry and malicious manner to
[my mistress] ... and said, you are a rotten pocky whore and you
stink as you go along the street, whereupon [my] mistress saying to
her by way of question, you will speak no more than you would
prove, Flewe replied saying, I'll say no more than I'll prove, intimat-
ing by the forceful way of speaking that [Tatham] had committed
the crime of adultery of fornication or incontinency ... [I] saw
Thomasina Flewe look through a large crevice or chink of the partition on [my mistress], then in her own washhouse when she
spoke the words and heard her speak the same being then in the
washhouse, and there was also present in the washhouse of [my]
mistress [my fellow servants] Johanna Scarlett and Mary Turner
who saw and heard the same ... [These] words are since become a
public talk and the credit and good name of [my mistress] was and
is thereby much impaired and diminished amongst her neighbours
and acquaintances ... [I] saw Thomasina Flewe when she spoke the
words aforesaid looking through a crevice of the partition ... she
wore a loose gown striped for the most part or all red and white,
she was standing when she spoke the words, stooping and having

one hand on the partition ... [My mistress] did not in any way excite Thomasina Flewe ... When Flewe had abused [her, my mistress replied,] away Mrs Flewe you are an old fool and more fit for Billingsgate than for a civil house, or words to that effect.

SIGNATURE

◆

SEPTEMBER 1697

Deposition of Frances Lamb, wife of William Lamb; St. Mary in the Savoy, Middlesex; aged 27 years

In the year 1693, [I] was servant maid to Mr Thomas, a sherriff, now a sword cutter by the Savoy Gate ... [who] lived next door to Francis Weston, a seedman, over against the May Pole in the Strand ... sometime in the latter end of the summer 1690 ... [I] was dressing [my] head one Monday morning up one pair of stairs backwards in [my] master's house ... even and next to the bedchamber of Mrs Elizabeth Weston [in the adjoining household] ... hearing Mrs Weston's voice saying, Frank don't play the fool, and hearing a man's voice saying, God I will ... it was Frank Alchin's voice [who was] then apprentice to Mr Francis Weston ... the wall which divided the bedchamber of Mrs Weston from the room where [I] was then in, being an old decayed wall of plaster and an old ragged hanging before it, with [my] fingers [I] very easily made a hole, and through the old hanging and shattered wall [I] then saw Mrs Weston in naked bed and her apprentice Frank Alchin lying upon her naked body in his clothes ... [I] saw Alchin wipe his nose which then bled, on each side of the pillow on which [Mrs Weston] lay and heard them as they lay kiss and smack each other's lip ... [I] immediately went downstairs into the shop where [my] master and Nicholas Jacques, his apprentice, were at work and there told [my] master, if he would please to go up he might see Frank the apprentice upon his mistress ... Thereupon [my] master and Nicholas Jacques and [myself] did go up, and Nicholas made the hole in the wall bigger ... and then through the hole [I] saw Betty, the then

maid servant to Elizabeth Weston, in [the] bedchamber and heard
Betty ask her mistress what made Frank ... come downstairs in such
a heat and disorder ... Mrs Weston told Betty that Frank had been
playing the fool, and Betty asked her how blood came upon the pil-
lows ... Mrs Weston said it was bleeding of [his] nose, you know he
is impudent ... [I] did soon after ... talk of what [I] had seen to several of the apprentices and servants in the neighbourhood, and they
used to laugh at Frank about lying with his mistress, and Frank in
[my] hearing said that his mistress was not the first woman he had
lain with, and that his mistress had such fine breasts and skin that
flesh and blood could not forbear her ... [Myself and my] fellow
servant Nicholas did promise Francis Alchin that [we] would not tell
his master that [we] saw him lie upon his mistress ... and [I] did not
tell Mr Weston thereof until about six months since, and [I] believe
that the apprentice boys and servants did talk of the same among
themselves ... About two or three days after ... as [I] went by the
shop, [Mrs Weston called to me] and in a threatening manner told
[me] that she had heard that [I] should report [I] saw her and [I]
replied that [I] had reported no more than what [I] saw, and [Mrs
Weston] farther said she would have [me] punished by a justice if [I]
could not swear there was not a thread betwixt her and her man.

SIGNATURE

◆

DECEMBER 1734

*Deposition of Lilieas Cameron, spinster, now working for the Rt. Hon.
Trevor Sill, Lord Viscount Spilsborough; aged 25 years*

In [April 1733, I] went to live with Lord and Lady Spilsborough as
their housekeeper and to wait upon the Lady ... in July 1733 [I]
was attending upon the Lord and Lady in the dining room of the
Lordship's house in Hanover Square [when I] heard them talk of
their intention to travel ... Lady Spilsborough about the same time
ordered [me] to get her things ready to prepare to go with them
and to prepare as many things as would serve her for four months

... and on or about the 11th day of the month ... [we] set forward
upon [our] travel and [I] accompanied them ... on the 11th day of
Sept. following [we] arrived at Brussels and there took up [our]
lodgings ... during which time the Lady Spilsborough lay and
lodged adjoining to a bedchamber wherein Mr Jeffreys lay ... about
1 of the clock of a Saturday night [I] being in [my] lodging room
which was very small and adjoining to the bedchamber saw the
Lady Spilsborough sitting undressed upon a chair and without stays
and Mr Jeffreys then sat across her lap with his face towards her in a
very indecent posture, and thereupon [I] put out [my] candle,
because [I] would not see what passed between them, the door
standing ajar very near them, and so as [I] could not shut it without
the Lady's observing the same and [I] was unwilling she should
know [I] had observed them, and [I] heard her say to Mr Jeffreys,
Lilly is asleep ... by their talking and breathing and being so very
near them and by the light of a candle which was burning in the
Lady's bed chamber [I] know they continued in that indecent posture for about or near a quarter of an hour and [I] then did believe
that he then did have carnal knowledge of her ... [The whole
group] proceeded from Brussels to Paris ... and there lodged at a
house called L'Hotel Imperial in a street called Rue Dauphine ...
and on or about the 7th day of October following at about 2 of the
clock in the morning ... Robert Goodin came to [me while I was
in my] bed and had [me] go to the Lady Spilsborough [saying] she
is crying and roaring, for my Lord has catched her and Mr Jeffries
in bed together, and thereupon [I] arose and went into the Lady's
bedchamber, and as she was going up the stairs [I] met [my
Lordship] coming down the stairs and he then speaking to [me] says
'what do you think Lilly, I have catched your Lady and Mr Jeffries
in bed together' and when [I] went into the bedchamber ... and
Lady Spilsborough who was sitting and crying upon a chair
between the bed and the door ... said, Oh Lilly I am undone ...
she had then nothing on but her bed gown and a short petticoat
and then speaking to Robin Goodin she says, 'Oh Robin, did you
ever think that my Lord would catch Mr Jeffries and I in bed

together ... [Goodin said,] Yes madam, my Lord and I have heard him go to bed to you every night from the 26th of September except last Sunday and Monday, and he then also told Lady Spilsborough that he had known Mr Jeffreys to stay with her Ladyship 'til six of [the] clock in the morning, to which she replied, It's very true Robin, you keep a very good account but he never stayed with me 'til six but one morning, he always went away at four, Oh Robin why did not you give me a hint of it when you knew my Lord had a mind to catch me, and he telling her that he dared not and that he was sworn not to discover it, she again replied, Ah Robin but you might have given me a hint of it to prevent my eternal ruin.

SIGNATURE

III

FEBRUARY 1726

Deposition of Anna King, wife of Anthony King; St. Martin in the Fields, Middlesex

About two years since [my] husband Anthony King ... who then lived as a servant with Anna Maria Drake ... told [me] that her maid was gone from her and that she wanted somebody to lie with her and desired [me] to go to her and thereupon [I] went to her at her lodging in Tavistock Street, and when [I] had been with her about two days, she hired [me] to live with her as her servant at the wages of £5 per year and 5s per week for board wages, and [I] continued to live with her from that time 'til about three days before Christmas last ... And when [I] first went to her, she was [unmarried and] big with child ... [About four days after the birth, the baby's father] desired [me] to get a nurse for the child and thereupon [I] went to ... Dorothy Brumstone, an aquaintance of [mine], at her house in or near Red Cross Street and agreed with her at 4 and 6p a week for the nursing of the child in case [my mistress] liked her ... Dorothy on the same day went to [my mistress] ... the following Sunday [the baby's father] gave [me] two shirts to make clothes for the child and [I] bought several necessaries for the child by the order of [the father, who] then gave [me] a guinea to buy the same and he also gave [me] 15s. to pay for the nursing of the child, and [I] paid the same to Dorothy Brumstone ... When Dorothy had nursed the child some weeks, [the father's] servant came to [me] and told [me] that his master desired to speak with [me] and thereupon [I] went to him in his lodging in a court in Fleet Street and he then told [me that I] must fetch the child from Dorothy Brumstone and [that] it was not proper that it should be there any longer, and [he] then sent his man to Middle Row in Holbourn ... Mrs Griffin, who was a stranger to [me], then came to him, and he then gave her some money to pay for the nursing of the child, and then [I] went with him and Mrs Griffin to the house of Dorothy Brumstone ... Mrs Griffin paid her for the nursing and then carried the child to one Mrs Hamond up two pair of stairs at a barber's shop in Little Kirby Street, Hatton Garden.

MARK

◆

JUNE 1697

Deposition of Dinah Allsop, spinster; St. Anne Westminster, Middlesex

On St. Paul's day in the month of January 1693, [I] became a servant to the right honourable Anne Countess of Macklesfield, and lived with and waited on the Countess ... until the beginning of the month of July 1696 last past, at which time [I] went away from the Countess's service ... When [I] first came into the Countess's service, she had a woman besides [me] to wait on her, and about Michaelmas 1694, [this] woman being before lately married went away, and from Michaelmas 1694 to the beginning of July 1696, Anne Countess of Macklesfield had no other maidservant to wait on her but [myself] ... In the month of June 1695, the Countess Anne, being then at Woodcott, fell very ill, and then the Countess was forced to discover to [me] that she was with child, and did then tell [me] that she had been unfortunate, and was with child, and was so ill she was afraid it would be her labour and then she said she would hasten to London, for she had all things ready there for her labour, and immediately the very same day [I] with the Countess Anne went from Woodcott to a private house in Queen Street in Piccadilly, and by the Countess's order fetched Mrs Richardson, a midwife who lived in Beauford Buildings, to the Countess at the private house, and there the Countess discovered to Mrs Richardson what condition she was in, and consulted with her how long it would be before her delivery, and Mrs Richardson being of the opinion the Countess would go a month longest, the Countess and [I] returned to Woodcott again ... During all the time the Countess was with Mrs Richardson, the Countess did not make herself known to Mrs Richardson, but talked with her all the time with her mask on ... On the 10th of July [I] and Countess Anne went from Woodcott to London to the house in Queen Street and Anne fell in labour in the house on the very same night, and one Mrs Pheasant, a nurse, went for Mrs Richardson, and about two of the clock in the morning ... she delivered of a female child in a fore room up one pair of stairs ... The Countess some part of the time of her labour kept her mask on, but in the height of the Countess's pains the mask fell off ... Before [I] left the Countess's service, [I] told the Countess that [I] had heard the business was discovered, and the Earl of Macklesfield did know of her being delivered of a child and that some man had discovered the same and the name of the father of the child, and the Countess replied, that is impossible ... During all the time [I] lived with the Countess [I] never saw the Earl of Macklesfield with the Countess Anne either in public or private ... About six days after the Countess was delivered of the child, [I] went with the Countess to Beaufort House, where the Countess afterwards lodged, and soon after the Countess had a swelling in her thigh and leg, which [I]

believe the Countess got by a cold received by her hasty retreat
from her lodging so soon after her delivery ... some short time
afterwards [I] went with the Countess to Bath ... Nurse Pheasant,
about three days after the child was born, told [me] that the child
was carried to nurse to some town near Epping Forest ... she
afterwards put the child to nurse at Chelsea, and the nurse at
Chelsea's name was Mountaine, and that she had agreed to pay her
six shillings a week for the nursing of the child ... after [I] had
returned from Bath with the Countess [I went] to Chelsea to see
the Countess's child, and the Countess did each time give nurse
Mountaine 5 shillings and charged her to be careful with the child
and seemed very fond of the child ... the last time the Countess
went to see the child at Chelsea, the child was very sick ... and
about three or four days afterward died, and the Countess sent
[me] for a lock of the child's hair ... In the month of June 1696
last past, [I] being then with the Countess at Woodcott in Surrey,
and having perceived that the Countess was again with child, [I]
did tell the Countess that [I] was well assured the Countess was
again with child and [I] desired leave to quit her service, for it
would ruin [me] to live with her any longer, and [I] would not get
another service, upon which the Countess was angry with [me],
and denied she was with child, but [I] told her [I] was sure the
Countess was with child, and [I] thought [I] ought in conscience
to acquaint the Countess's mother ... of it, and then the Countess
earnestly desired [me] not to tell her mother or any of her family
she was with child, and if [I] would go away she would give [me]
20 guineas and five pounds a year to go and live with [my] sister
in the country and accordingly [I] did go and live with [my sister]
... and the Countess gave [me] 20 guineas and sent one guinea
and three shillings to [me] in the country for the first quarter of
the five pounds per annum.

SIGNATURE

◆

NOVEMBER 1682

Deposition of Grace Lowndes, wife of Johnathan Lowndes; St. James Westminster, Middlesex; aged 37 years

[I] well remember Elizabeth Brook came to be [my] servant on the 29th or 30th day of August last in the year 1689 and continued in [my] service about seven months, and when [Brook] first came to be [my] servant, she went under the notion of a widow, and told [me] that her husband while living was postmaster at Thetford in Norfolk, and her husband's mother kept her children which were (as Elizabeth Brook told [me] three or four) ... about the latter part [Brook] lived with [me I] observed [Brook] to be sick and out of order and thereupon [I] told [her] that [I] wished she was not breeding or with child, and at such times [Brook] had made answer that she was big with fat and nothing else, and [I] having heard that [Brook] was brought to bed some few months after she left [my] service, [I] believe that [she] was with child when she lived with [me], but whether [she] was delivered of a bastard child [I] know not, nor knew Elizabeth Brook to be guilty of thieving, but [I] did always look upon her to be a bold, confident servant.

SIGNATURE

◆

JANUARY 1715

Deposition of Anna Giles, spinster; Bromley, Kent; aged 27 years

[I] was a servant to Edmund Thomas for about 6 months ending St. James's Day in the year 1714, within which time he prevailed upon [me] to lie with him, and several times had the carnal knowledge of [me] and [I] was with child by him and [I] never had the carnal knowledge of any other person whatsoever and [I] ... was then and now [am] a single woman and he [Thomas] then had a wife and child ... On or about the 27th day of Oct. 1714, [I] made an affidavit before Justice Emmit in the parish of Bromley, Kent (in which parish [I] then lived), that [Thomas] was the father of the child ... In or about the month of January in the year aforesaid, [I] was

delivered of a girl [who] was baptized by the name of Elizabeth and
in the extremity of [my] pain and labour [I] declared to [my] midwife ... that Edmund Thomas and no other person was the father
of the child.

MARK

Deposition of Thomas Giles, Bromley, Kent; labourer; aged 50 years

[I] well know Edmund Thomas ... [my] daughter Anne Giles lived
as a servant with [Thomas] about 8 or 9 months ending about St.
James's Day in the year 1714, at which time [my daughter] was with
child and then informed [me] that Edmund Thomas was the father,
and about four days afterwards [I] went to him and he then confessed that he had lain with [my] daughter (meaning that he had
carnally known her) and promised to come to [me] and make [me]
satisfaction for the same and then desired [me] not to make any
words of it, and about two or three months afterwards, there being a
discourse that he was to be apprehended by a warrant from a justice
of the peace, he came to [me] and endeavoured to persuade [me] to
send [my daughter Anna] out of the way and then promised to
maintain her ... [I] then insisting to have a bond or a note of his
hand to oblige him to perform his promise, he refused to give the
same, saying that his word was as good as his bond ... on or about
the 27th day of October 1714 Anna Giles made an affidavit before
justice Emmit that Edmund Thomas was the father of the child.

SIGNATURE

IV

APRIL 1735

*Deposition of Mary Stevens; Devonshire Street near Queens Square,
Middlesex; aged 25 years*

[I] came to know the Lady Susannah Clavering by going to live as a servant to her and continued to live with her for about half a year ... Elizabeth Hawsot [another servant] waited upon [Clavering] when [I] first went to live there and [she] was turned away ... about a month afterwards ... Elizabeth Hawsot being then out of place and [when I asked her] if she had not got a place she made answer ... No, that old bitch won't give me a character but God damn her I'll seek an opportunity at some time or other to be revenged of her for it ... [I] know that she behaved in a very impudent manner to [Clavering] and encouraged the rest of the servants to behave in the like manner ... [Elizabeth Hawsot told me] about the time of her first going to live there that if [I] did not use [Clavering] ill [I] would not stay there long and several times declared that she would get [Clavering] turned out of doors, and that a fortune-teller had informed [Hawsot] that she would live to be Lady Clavering or to that effect ... [I] was the housemaid and was kept by [Clavering] at the yearly wages of £6.

SIGNATURE

◆

APRIL 1735

Deposition of Mary Tilly wife of James Tilly; St. Andrew Holborn, Middlesex; servant to Mr Willie, Bury of St. Edmund in the County of Suffolk; aged 40 years

[I have] well known Dame Susannah Clavering for about seven years last past and lived with her and her husband ... as their cook for about six weeks ending almost four years since, and have ever since ... lived in the same neighbourhood with them ... During the time of [my] living with them ... Elizabeth Hawsot was the chambermaid [and] Mary [Stevens] was the housemaid, Thomas Smith butler, Robert Bainbridge coachman and William Knight was their footman ... Elizabeth Hawsot was [of] very poor [reputation] and a great liar and frequented a house which was reputed to be a bawdy house ... It was commonly reported that she had one or two bastards and that she had been turned away two or three times for misbehaviour ... [I] several times saw [Hawsot] intoxicated with strong liquor and know that she took all opportunities of drinking it when she could get it ... [I] once saw her and a charwoman ... and the housemaid all very much fuddled and at the same time saw three bottles of wine among the coats ... [and I have] seen her set her foot upon or against the kitchen grates and show her legs in the presence of the men servants ... [I] was married about eleven years since to [my] husband James Tilly in the presence of [my] brother John Preddon ... [My] husband lives as a servant with Squire Willie of St. Edmund's Bury, and [I] believe that he is to be found there ... [My] maiden name was Stone and [I] have lived with Daniell Burr of Great James Street Esq. as his cook almost four years and [am] worth more than what will pay [my] debts.

SIGNATURE

◆

APRIL 1735

Deposition of Mary Nugent formerly Parry, wife of Henry Nugent, mariner; St. George Hanover Square, Middlesex; aged 40 years and upwards

About or almost two years since [I] came to know [the Clavering family] ... by living with them as their cook and [I] continued to live with them as such for almost half a year ... [I] often heard [fellow servants] abuse [Clavering] ... behind her back ... by railing against her and have heard them often curse her by saying damn her and ... also several times give her saucy language to her face ... About nine weeks since [I] was married to [my] husband Henry Nugent at the Sign of the Hand and Pen, in the Liberties of the Fleet, in the presence of the maidservant at the house and a man who officiated as clerk ... [My] husband is the cook of a merchant ship at sea ... [My] maiden name was Perry, and [I have] lodged at Thomas Palmer's, a pastry cook, over against Carnaby Market about a year, and before that [I] was cook to Arthur

Onslow Esqr. near Leicester Fields almost a year ... and before
that [I] lived with [Clavering] ... before that [I] was cook to Mr
Whitworth in Burlington Gardens about 7 or 8 months ... [I am]
worth more than what will pay [my] debts.

MARK

♦

APRIL 1735

*Deposition of Elizabeth Pyne, wife of Richard Pyne; St. George/Hanover
Square; Middlesex; servant of the Spanish Ambassador; aged 30 years or
thereabouts*

[I] came to know [the Claverings] by their lodging in the same
house at Bath wherein [I] then lodged and they continued at Bath
for about 6 or 7 weeks and [I] was there all the time ... Elizabeth
Hawsot is guilty of drinking strong liquor to excess ... until she is
fuddled and [I] about 4 or 5 months since saw her ... drinking in a
public house at the Sign of the Coach and Horses in Ormond Yard
... About 4 years since [I] was married in the Abbey Church in
Bath to [my] husband Richard Pyne ... [My] husband is the groom
of the Spanish Ambassador and lodges with [me] in Ormond Yard
and is generally to be found there ... [My] maiden name was
Elizabeth Bradford and [I have] lodged in the Yard above a year, and
before that [I] lived as a servant with the Lord Kingsale almost half a
year, and before that with Mr Basnot in Picadilly almost four
months, and before that [myself and my] husband kept a public
house ... in Bristol from the time of [our] marriage ... [I] believe
that if [we] owe a penny [we] have two pence to pay it.

MARK

♦

JULY 1735

Deposition of Sir Francis Clavering, Baronet

[I] show no favours to any of [my] servants other than what they

merit by their good behaviour in their service and what is fit for
[me] as a master to do ... While [my wife] lived with [me, I] never
concerned [myself] with hiring or turning away any of [the house-
hold] maid servants, but left it entirely to her to act as she thought
fit, and believe [she] turned [Elizabeth Hawsot] out of her service
twice but for what reasons was beneath [me] to inquire ... [My
wife] did at her own instance take Elizabeth Hawsot into [my] service a third time without consulting [me; I am] an entire stranger to
the facts charged on Elizabeth Hawsot.

SIGNATURE

◆

DECEMBER 1693
Deposition of Margaret Keene alias Atkins, widow; St. James in the
Fields, Middlesex; aged 23 years

[I] was acquainted with one Christiana Lovegrove, who was servant
maid to Elizabeth Bound about two or three years since, when she
lived with her husband Samspon Bound in Old Southhampton
Buildings, upon which occasion [I] often went to see Christiana,
and so became acquainted with the family of Elizabeth Bound, and
with Hannah Hardcastle who was then waiting maid to Elizabeth
Bound ... Since the time Sampson and Elizabeth Bound parted
and broke up housekeeping, Hannah Hardcastle was entertained by
[me at my] house or lodgings ... For about a week or ten days,
Hannah lay with [me] in [my] own bed ... the first two or three
days Hannah Hardcastle lodged with [me, we were] talking of the
difference between Elizabeth and Sampson Bound [and Hardcastle]
did then swear God damn her, her master was a cocky dog, and
that her mistress was an honest woman, and she farther then swore
that her mistress would pay her twelve pounds which she said was
due to her, she would swear for Mrs Bound anything against
Sampson Bound, and Hannah Hardcastle then swore God damn
her, if she would not have the money of Elizabeth Bound she
would swear against her for Sampson, or on any side that would

give her the money, upon which [I] reproved [Hardcastle] saying she ought not be believed if she would swear for them that paid her the money ... After [Hardcastle] had been at [my] house for about five or six days, [she] came in between ten and eleven at night and brought a man with her in a red coat whom [she] called her husband, and [I] being angry thereat told [Hardcastle] that she would not keep such hours if she lodged with [me], and that she would have no men in her lodging ... thereupon [Hardcastle] fell cursing and swearing in such a violent manner, and swore damn her and sink her, she could not get any money off Mrs Bound, but that she had been with her master Sampson Bound who had given her a pistol which [Hardcastle] then showed [me], and that Sampson Bound had promised her the twelve pounds, with which money she said she would fetch her clothes out of pawn and then swore, by god she would swear for her master ... that Elizabeth Bound was a whore, and [I] then told Hannah that it was a hard matter to swear her mistress to be a whore, to which Hannah replied, why would not she give her the money then, and if swearing would do it [Hardcastle] swore she would be revenged of Elizabeth Bound ... While Hannah Hardcastle did lodge with [me, she] did behave herself very scandalously both by her behaviour and speech, and in discourse eventually swore and cursed violently and swore she would go into Flanders and strip the people before they were dead for money, and because [Hardcastle's] father and mother refused to give her something which she required of them (as she told [me]) Hannah Hardcastle did in [my] hearing swear she did not care what became of them, and that she would cut their throats rather than be so served by them and [I], perceiving [her] vicious practices ... in about a week or twelve days time, locked [Hardcastle] out of doors and would not nor have since that time kept any acquaintance or correspondence with her ... [I] have been nurse to several noble families, and take home persons belonging to such families when they are sick of the small pox ... [I] have been nurse to the Earl of Thanet's family for ten years together and have served Sir John Chicheley's family and the Lady

Cye's family, in whose several houses and several other eminent
families [I] have been a nurse, and [I] live now in Duke Street at
Mr Petty's where [I] have lived a year and a half before which time
[I] lived in Mr Field's rents in Duke Street for about fifteen years
and have lived thereabouts in the parish of St. Giles about 23 years
... [I] do not owe ten shillings in the world, and [I] have good
household goods about [me], and money enough to keep [me] in
[my] old age.

SIGNATURE

◆

JANUARY 1693
*Deposition of Christiana Lovegrove, spinster; St. Butolph Aldersgate,
Middlesex; aged 19 years*

[I] was cook maid to Elizabeth Bound for about 12 months and
upwards soon after the marriage of Elizabeth and Sampson Bound
when they lived at Mr Catridge's in Southton Buildings, and while
they kept house near Middle Row in Holbourn ... When Sampson
and Elizabeth Bound first went into their new house in Middle
Row, there was several valuable household goods, [such] as beds,
pewter, diaper and damask table linen and other necessary and
handsome furniture sent in from Mr Rouse, father of [Elizabeth] ...
Elizabeth Bound had then very rich and good wearing clothes and
linen and a pearl necklace of fifty pounds value ... Mr Rouse had
given Sampson with his daughter about two or three hundred
pounds in goods ... [I] well knew Richard Hooton when he was a
drawer at the Feather Tavern in Red Lyon Square, and at the Sun
Tavern in Holbourn ... by Richard's often coming to [my] master's
house to bring wine and the like, [I] had opportunity to hear his
talk, which [was] very lewd and debauched discourse, commonly
swearing and talking of his whoring, and a fellow servant ... Mary
called Richard a nasty pocky dog, to which Richard replied pox
was the fashion and he did not care, and she had been told by
Richard's fellow servants that they had seen his shirts, that they were

stained as is usual in the distemper called the clap or pox, and that
Richard kept a whore ... [I] well remember Margaret Smith, then
called Gibbons, when Sampson Bound had lodgings at Mr
Partridge's house, at which time [I] came to have some knowledge
of Margaret Smith by [her] coming to see Hannah Hardcastle, the
waiting maid of Elizabeth Bound, and when Smith first came to see
[Hardcastle, Smith] was with child and very big, which occasioned
[me] to inquire of [Hardcastle about Smith], and [Hardcastle] then
and at several other times told [me] that [Smith] was sometimes
kept or maintained by gentlemen, and that she was a common
whore and had nothing to kept her withall, but what she picked up
or got of men about the town ... Margaret Smith oftentimes confessed that she had lain with or been debauched by several gentlemen whose names [she] then mentioned ... that she was poxed by a
Lord ... Margaret Smith was Hannah Hardcastle's particular
acquaintance and they were often together ... and [I] have often
seen [Hardcastle dress Smith] in Elizabeth [Bound's] wearing head-
clothes and petticoats and gowns without the knowledge of
[Bound], and in the Christmas that [I] lived with Elizabeth Bound,
Margaret Smith was dressed by Hannah Hardcastle in [Bound's]
wearing clothes for about a week together during which time
Elizabeth Bound kept her Christmas at her father's house in
Southwark and at the week's end [Smith] returned the clothes to
[Hardcastle] at [Bound's] lodgings at Mr Partridge's, and then
Margaret Smith came with a young fellow who went with her and
Hannah Hardcastle into a room together, but at other times that
[Smith] was dressed in Elizabeth Bound's clothes she usually came
in the same back again at night ... [I get my] livelihood by going to
service ... [I] have lived at my Lord Walgreve's, at Mr Bound's and
at the George Inn in Aldersgate Street for about four or five years
and before that in the country ... [I am] not in debt.

MARK

◆

JANUARY 1693

Deposition of Mary Squib, wife of Arthur Squib, linen draper; Covent Garden, Middlesex; aged 31 years

About three years since Sampson Bound and Elizabeth his wife lodged at [my] house at the Queen's Head in Henrietta Street in Covent Garden and for about half a year of the time they so lodged there, Hannah Hardcastle was waiting maid to Elizabeth Bound, and [I] in some short time after Elizabeth had been at [my] house observed [Bound and Hardcastle] her maid to be very familiar and intimate together not becoming the decency of a mistress to her servant, and more particularly [I] had taken notice that at such times as Sampson Bound had been gone abroad, Hannah Hardcastle had fetch'd a coach and frequently gone out with her mistress and then [Bound and Hardcastle] usually returned late at night, when [I] had been abed, and [I] had been told by [my] servants that [Bound and Hardcastle] frequently came home drunk, and to [my] certain knowledge Hannah Hardcastle was a very impudent profligate wretch, and not fit to be entertained in a civil family, and Sampson Bound being well informed thereof had in my hearing often told his wife that Hardcastle was not a fit servant to live with her, and that it was scandalous to entertain her and that he would put her away, unto which Elizabeth Bound would never agree or consent, and Hannah Hardcastle continuing constantly in her loose carriage, Sampson Bound in [my] presence and [that] of his wife did give the order to Hardcastle to quit his service upon which Elizabeth Bound fell into a great passion and having a knife in her hand ... declared that if she was sure Sampson Bound would turn away [Hardcastle] she would stick the knife into his heart and wherever Hannah went she would go too ... [He] did not turn away and discharge Hannah from his service and Elizabeth Bound did thereupon persist in her leaving her husband, and did declare to him that she was resolved and would go with [Hardcastle], and on the day [Hardcastle] went away, Elizabeth Bound kissed her husband at parting, and Sampson Bound being gone out, [Bound and Hardcastle] went away in a coach together from [my] house and did not return at all again, and [I] have heard Elizabeth Bound never lived with her husband since ... [I] have been told by [my] servants that [Bound and Hardcastle] went often revelling together in men's apparel, and while Elizabeth Bound lodged at [my] house, [I] saw Elizabeth Bound dressing herself in men's clothes to go abroad, and she then had on men's shoes, stockings and breeches.

SIGNATURE

Deposition of Samuel Stanton, vintner; St. Andrews Holbourn, Middlesex; aged 40 years

About last Bartholomew Fair was three years that Benjamin Kellow (who was a constant customer to [my public] house) came to [my] house at the Sun Tavern in Holbourn with two other persons, and borrowed a cloak for the use of one of his company, and desired leave of [me] for [my] servant Dick Horton to go along with him and [his] company to go to Bartholomew Fair ... [which I] did give Horton leave to do, and [I] was afterwards informed by [my] servant that the two persons with Kellow were Elizabeth Bound and her maidservant Hannah dressed in men's clothes ... [I] very well know Elizabeth frequently came to [my] house and was in company with Sir Thomas Neysman ... Richard Horton was [my] apprentice and drawer, and while [Horton] was in [my] service, [he] was somewhat purblind or shortsighted, and would not read anything without drawing it pretty near to his eyes or sight.

SIGNATURE

'The great danger she had reason to believe she was in'

WIFE-BEATING IN THE EIGHTEENTH CENTURY

♦

BY MARGARET R. HUNT

Some time in the year 1711, Mrs Elizabeth Spinkes petitioned the Consistory Court of the diocese of London for a 'separation of bed and board' (in modern parlance, a legal separation) from her husband John, a physician. She alleged that her husband's abuse and cruelty had caused her permanent physical impairment, endangered her life and seriously limited her freedom of movement. The records generated by the ensuing case, referred to by the court simply as *Spinkes v. Spinkes*, comprise the next selection. They include Elizabeth Spinkes's original complaint (called, a little confusingly, the 'libel'); depositions by a number of witnesses, including Elizabeth's brother-in-law, her maidservant, and various neighbours; and a set of leading questions put forward by John Spinkes and his counsel that sought to air his side of the story and to cast doubt on his wife's veracity.

'Moderate physical correction' of a wife by her husband was legal in the eighteenth century, indeed expected if she disobeyed him or flouted community norms. But serious and systematic abuse that threatened permanent injury or loss of life was viewed in a more negative light. The historical record remains somewhat ambiguous, but in this period there appears to have been a growing, if hardly universal, tendency on the part of justices of the peace to make very violent husbands post bonds for their good behaviour (it is difficult to say how effective this method was in stopping the violence,

Seventeenth-century court records, Greater London Record Office.

however). This timid effort to cope with the problem was offset by the fact that the eighteenth-century authorities were very loathe to interfere in 'family matters' and even less willing to do anything that, in that staunchly hierarchical society, might be construed as usurping a husband's rightful authority over his wife.

Since wife-beating was not in and of itself illegal or socially unacceptable, it was extremely difficult either to interpret or to intervene in the vast grey area that lay between 'moderate correction' and violence that was 'excessive' or 'life threatening'. The situation was even more murky for other kinds of cruelty. What was one to do with a husband who locked his wife up, as many abusive husbands (including John Spinkes) did, or threw excrement in her face, or forced her to engage in 'forbidden' sexual acts? (Complaints of all these practices turn up in cases from this period.)

There were several possible routes out of an abusive marriage, and the Consistory Court was a less frequently travelled one. The Consistory Court was one of the courts administered by the Anglican church, and it was only in the seventeenth century that *some* church courts began permitting significant numbers (meaning perhaps a dozen per decade within a particular diocese) of legal separations on account of marital cruelty, as opposed to, say, adultery or nonconsummation. And though the church courts were relatively cheap to use, the expense of bringing a case could still prove an insurmountable obstacle to poorer women, indeed any woman, whatever her ascribed status, who lacked money of her own. Finally, the relatively public nature of court proceedings meant that women who were protective of their reputations were likely to look to quieter solutions: mediation by relatives, informal separation agreements, or, most common of all, simply suffering in silence. The church courts are no index, then, to how much marital abuse was actually taking place in eighteenth-century England: the cases that ended up there were only the tip of a presumably quite large iceberg.

Nor are the Consistory Court cases a representative sample of family violence cases more generally. Then, as now, those cases that got to court tended to cite quite severe abuse, and it seems likely that there were both formal and informal mechanisms in place to ensure that less serious cases (which, however, might still appear life-threatening from the victim's vantage point) never got far enough in the process to receive a hearing.

Why did men beat their wives in the eighteenth century? The answer is not a simple one, even if we forego the search for 'ultimate causes' and focus on immediate motives. Men beat their wives to coerce them into sexual relations, to stop them from being extravagant, or because they suspected them of flirting (or sleeping) with other men. Wives who did not dress in a manner that their husbands deemed appropriate—who burned the dinner, who talked when their husbands wished them to be silent, who balked at handing over their earnings, who kept company with people their husbands disliked, or who got pregnant (or as the case might be, failed to get pregnant)—all might find themselves the object of violent attacks.

A good many cases of wife-beating in the early eighteenth century, including the case of Elizabeth and John Spinkes, seem to have revolved, at least in part, around dowries, trusts or loans. The wife's family might not have paid her dowry, or the wife owned property in trust that she or her trustees were refusing to sign over to the husband, or the in-laws had rejected the husband's request that they lend him money. In cases like these, the husband might make a special point of beating up his wife in front of her family (as did John Spinkes) in order to coerce them to pay her dowry, to loosen the reins on a trust or to come up with a loan. In such a marriage the wife became, in effect, a hostage to her husband's financial ambitions.

The *Spinkes* case becomes somewhat more comprehensible if one has some basic knowledge about what marriage meant to eighteenth-century people. First, marriage tended to be much more embedded in family and neighbourhood than it is today. People generally lived near their relatives and visited them often; families and neighbours often intervened in marital disputes. It is striking how many of Elizabeth Spinkes's women neighbours were willing to testify on her behalf; presumably some of them were the same people who, at earlier points, sought to stop John Spinkes from beating her. This does not mean that these women were necessarily opposed to wife-beating (though this is not something one can ultimately know). But what is clear is that they thought that John Spinkes had stepped over the line of what was acceptable, and they did not hesitate to say so within their neighbourhood and in court. In this community, at any rate, the notion that a man's home was his castle did not mean an unrestricted license for husbands.

Marriage was also more overtly a financial partnership than most people are used to today. Though arranged marriages were a good deal less common in this period than they had been, many people married, at least in the first instance, for money, though generally with the expectation that love would follow. Within the upward-striving urban middle classes, from which the Spinkeses hailed, dowries were one of the main ways that men financed their entry into business or the professions. One result of this was that it was not considered at all tasteless, or even unusually mercenary, for a man to remark on the fortune of a prospective mate ('a woman worth £200 a year') or for a women to pride herself on how large her dowry had been ('I brought with me £1,000 when I married my husband'). John Spinkes clearly was more mercenary than some, but contemporaries would have had no trouble understanding why a man might feel cheated if his wife turned out to be less well off than she or her family had led him to believe during the period of courtship.

Married women laboured under many disadvantages in the eighteenth century. Apart from separate trusts (if any), all the money and other assets they had passed into their husband's possession on marriage. And anything women subsequently earned belonged to their husbands as well. This last was a perennial problem for women who left unhappy marriages and sought to support themselves on their own labour: they were liable to find their estranged husbands coming around to lay legal claim to their hard-won earnings. The principle that property belonged to the husband also meant that it was always wives who got thrown out of their houses by their husbands, and never the reverse: the house was, literally, his domain. And it also meant that fathers had automatic custody of all children. Finally, a woman did not technically have the right to leave her husband without his permission, even if he beat her or threatened her life. Of course, women did run away or flee to their relatives, but it could prove a delicate business, harbouring a fugitive wife if her husband insisted on having her back.

A wife did have at least one real 'right': the right to be supported by her husband at a level roughly commensurate with his income. This ancient entitlement owed less to any residual sense of fair play than to the desire of taxpayers not to have to support other men's wives on the poor rolls. But whatever its origins, women took this right very seriously, and they could and did haul husbands before the courts or parish officials for failing to provide them minimal support. In fact, one of the main motives women had for seeking a legal separation was the court's ability to award alimony, which was the same right in more coercive dress. (The term 'alimony' actually comes from the Latin, *alimonia*, or nutriment).

Eighteenth-century English society was profoundly hierarchical, explicitly committed to male supremacy and accustomed to the belief that the use of violence was essential for the maintenance of order among subordinate groups. There is no doubt that this regime had tragic implications and dehumanizing effects for countless numbers of women (and also for children, servants, slaves and poor people). But it is also important to distinguish between the ways hierarchical systems work in theory, and the more equivocal ways

they function in practice. The case of *Spinkes v. Spinkes* is a window
into a world that was undeniably patriarchal and, generally, hostile
to the idea of women wielding significant amounts of power. But it
also shows some of the ways women negotiated within and challenged that reality, using neighbourhood (and female) solidarity, ties
to relatives, principled stands against undue abuse of authority and
even magic.

People routinely lie in court, and they lie even more when the
financial and emotional stakes are high. In her statement to the
court, Elizabeth Spinkes probably exaggerated her husband's income
(she claimed he made £500 a year) because she knew the court
would use the information to set the alimony payments (by contrast
her brother-in-law puts John Spinkes's income at only £200 to
£300 a year). John Spinkes's luxuriant allegations about Elizabeth
Spinkes's sex life are likewise somewhat implausible, though we
should not assume too readily that eighteenth-century women (or
Elizabeth Spinkes herself) were as chaste as the culture told them to
be. But the job of the historian is less to catch witnesses in lies and
distortions than to ask what general truths about a particular time
and place can be gleaned from their testimony, whether or not it is
'true' in every detail. John Spinkes made the claims he did because
he lived in a society in which chastity was, at least in theory, the single most important element of a woman's character and reputation,
and he knew very well that if he could get the court to believe him,
Elizabeth's credibility would be seriously harmed.

By the same token, Marie Nuby exaggerates the degree to which
Elizabeth 'provoked' her husband's violence, and she certainly puts a
different gloss on Elizabeth's efforts to involve the neighbourhood
in her marital problems than a modern observer (or, for that matter,
Elizabeth's friends) might. But her account of Elizabeth's interest in
magic has a ring of truth about it that goes beyond the question of
whether or not Elizabeth herself actually tried to call up the devil
or bewitch her husband. Magic has always been one of the weapons

of the weak, and even if it cannot be proved incontrovertibly that Elizabeth dabbled in it, we can be quite certain that other abused wives did. In a world in which many, perhaps most people still believed in magic, it could be a real source of power.

Fear, disrupted families, blasted hopes: marital violence in the eighteenth century, like its modern counterpart, devastated individual lives at the same time that it helped keep women in a subordinate position within the family and in the larger society. But even in highly inegalitarian societies the victimized can, and at times do, find ways successfully to challenge their superiors. Elizabeth Spinkes's story is the story of one such woman, and of the people who helped and hindered her along the way.

From *Spinkes v. Spinkes*
1711

The Wife's Case

*The 'libel' or original complaint drawn up either by
Elizabeth Spinkes herself, or on her behalf, and signed by
her, gives the rough outlines of her brief and unhappy marriage to John Spinkes. It details John Spinkes's use of violence to wrest from Elizabeth's control a trust or 'separate
estate'[1] bequeathed to her on his death by her former protector, and, presumably, lover, Sir John Williams. It cat-
alogues the abuse to which she was subjected at John
Spinkes's hands. And it shows how neighbours, and especially women neighbours, intervened to try to moderate the
violence and, in Elizabeth's case, to help her extricate herself from the marriage.*

John Spinkes, finding that the fortune of his wife was not so great as
he expected to have and receive with her in marriage, or that he
did not receive it so soon as expected, did by degrees withdraw his
pretended love and affection from her and treated her with indiffer-
ence and [a] disrespect which he had not formerly used towards
her, with a design and intent thereby to force her to ... consent ...
[to] the selling of an estate of about two hundred pound p[er]
annum in lands lying in Monmouthshire within the principality of
Wales which was given her by the last will and testament of Sir
John Williams, baronet, deceased, wherein she was named executrix,

---

which for the procuring of her peace and quiet she accordingly did, in hopes and expectation of receiving a better usage [from her husband] than he had before treated her with ...

The statement goes into detail about the barbarities inflicted upon Elizabeth by her husband, including punching her in the face, cutting her with knives, threatening to murder her, and 'tearing off her head-cloths and hair therewith and throwing them in the fire and burning them ...' *John Spinkes also locked her in an upstairs room for days at a time. During one of these periods of enforced confinement, Elizabeth tried to escape by leaping out a window, unfortunately only succeeding in breaking a foot. But the commotion aroused the neighbours, and, as Elizabeth lay bleeding on the ground, there ensued an loud confrontation between* 'some of the women of the neighbourhood who came to her assistance' *and John Spinkes who* 'threatened ... to arrest their husbands if they offered to come near or meddle with her ...' *This time John Spinkes won the fight, but his victory was to be short-lived; once Elizabeth Spinkes recovered:*

[John Spinkes] did renew his cruelties in kicking, beating, striking and abusing her and with a case knife once in a threatening manner said 'Damn you you bitch I shall either be hanged for you or you for me' and at the same time cut her in and upon diverse parts of her hand which she held up to defend her face with ...

Some time after this, John Spinkes committed Elizabeth against her will to Dr Newton's madhouse in Newington, where she was to stay for some six weeks. Her statement suggests that she was sent to the madhouse in order to coerce her to appear in Chancery Court in connection with the dispute about the estate of her former protector, from which John Spinkes hoped to realize some money. On

being promised her freedom she finally agreed to appear in
court, but having done so, she was put in the madhouse
again for another three weeks. Dr Newton only gave her
her liberty when he was threatened with prosecution by her
relatives. On Elizabeth's release the statement relates that:

[Elizabeth] went back to her husband for her clothes and some
money for her subsistence but instead ... John Spinkes did not only
himself call her bitch and whore but suffered his maidservant to abuse
her with the same and worse language, by whose assistance forced her
downstairs into the cellar and threw a great brass candlestick after her
... The neighbours hearing the noise and knowing the occasion
brought a constable who threatened to break open the door if [John
Spinkes] would not let him in or deliver his wife out, upon which
[Spinkes] opened the door and did give liberty to his wife who went
out with the constable and neighbours and secured herself from the
great danger she had reason to believe she was in ...

Elizabeth Spinkes concluded her statement by confirming
that John was a physician and by estimating his income to
be some £500 per annum.

Deposition of Joseph Wilson, Elizabeth Spinkes's brother-in-law.
I have been acquainted with Elizabeth Spinkes, the producent in
this cause, for about eighteen or nineteen years, and first knew and
became acquainted with her by means of my courting and afterwards marrying her sister. I have also known and been acquainted
with John Spinkes, her husband, for about five or six years and ...
I became acquainted with him by means of his marrying
Elizabeth. Ever since [we met] John Spinkes has been frequently at
my house, as I have been at his house, whereby we became very
intimate with each other and [were] often in each other's company. And within a short time after John and Elizabeth own[ed] each
other to be man and wife, Elizabeth [began coming] often ... to

my house and complain[ing] to me and [to] my wife in my presence that John Spinkes had been very cruel and unkind to her and
frequently beat and misused her. And some of the said time[s] I
have observed her face to be discoloured and her eyes swollen
which she has told me were occasioned by blows she had received
from her husband John.

And about four years [ago], to my best remembrance of the
time, a message was sent to my house ... from John Spinkes that his
wife was very ill and that he desired to speak with my wife or her
mother who then lodged with us, and thereupon I advised my wife
to go to him, promising her I would come to her and bring her
home with me on the evening. Accordingly, on the evening of the
[same] day I went to the house of John Spinkes, then in Half Moon
Houses near Ludgate, London, and I was by him conducted
up[stairs] into a room ... in the house where Elizabeth Spinkes was.

I then and there found her sitting on a bedside and in tears, with
her eyes and face very much swollen, and my wife with her, and I
then asking [John Spinkes] the reason thereof, he told me that he
had sent for my wife for a witness and thereupon immediately with
his fists doubled and with all his force struck her [Elizabeth Spinkes]
over the face by which means her nose and eyes fell a-bleeding, and
at the same time cursed and swore at her and gave her very oppro-
brious language. And I thereupon endeavoured to make peace
between them and, as I apprehended [I had spent] some time with
them, thought that I had done so, and then left. By the force and
the violence of the blows Elizabeth's eyesight is very much impaired
as she has often since then told me and ... she frequently complained to me and [to] my wife ... that he continued his cruelty
towards her and [she] did at some times complain that he had
whipped her with a horse whip.

And within half a year after the [incident previously described]
John Spinkes told me that his wife had leapt out of a window from
one pair of stairs into the Court[yard] (which is paved with stones)
and had broken her instep and had so done it, because he had
locked her up and would not let her go out of doors. And I heard

and believe that a surgeon was employed in the care thereof and that [Elizabeth] was obliged by reason of the pain and misery she sustained thereby, and for the better cure thereof, to keep [to] her bed about six weeks and since then I have often heard her complaining of pain in that foot whereby I believe the [bone was] not … well set, the same since having very much inconvenienced her walking.

… Four years since, to my remembrance of the time, I was informed by my wife's mother that John Spinkes had sent Elizabeth his wife to the house of Dr Newton, being a house there kept for the care of lunatics, [under the] … pretense that she was mad, and I have heard and believe that she continued there as a lunatic for about the space of two months within which time I was five or six times to see her and she at such times appeared to me to be in her perfect senses, as I do verily believe she was for all the time of her so being there. And I heard Dr Newton say that he kept her there by order of John Spinkes, her husband, and that he did not find that she was any ways disturbed in her senses or understanding, and that he did at last give her liberty by reason that he had been threatened by some attorney to be sued for detaining her … And Elizabeth, as also John Spinkes, has since [that] time told me that within the time of such her confinement with Dr Newton, John Spinkes took her … [away] for one day in order to give an answer to a bill in Chancery [Court] and then returned her back again into the custody of Dr Newton.

And upon her being released by Dr Newton [Elizabeth Spinkes] came to my house in High Holborne and lodged there for some short time, but being destitute of clothes and other necessaries she … went home to her husband for the same … and upon her return complained to me that her husband would not let her have anything but had thrust or thrown her down into the cellar, and had thrown a candlestick after [her] and that he made so great a noise at her that the neighbours, overhearing the same, brought a constable to break open his door, whereby she escaped from him and went out of his house with such constable for her security.

Deposition of Elizabeth Thomas

> *Thomas lodged near the Spinkeses in Half Moon Court.*
> *She confirmed that:*

[Elizabeth Spinkes's] face was very much bruised and discoloured and her eyes very much swollen and which continued so to be for a considerable time ...

Deposition of Maria Graham

> *Graham's house apparently abutted on that of the*
> *Spinkeses. She reported that:*

... in the back room of my house I have often heard the voice of Elizabeth Spinkes (with which I am well acquainted) screaming and sometimes crying out 'Murder' as if she [was being] beaten by some person in the house of John Spinkes.

> *Two other neighbours, Elizabeth Farrand and Margaret*
> *Baynes, corroborated this account in separate depositions.*

THE HUSBAND'S CASE

> *Court procedure demanded that the party accused (in this*
> *case John Spinkes) submit a set of questions to be asked of*
> *witnesses and of the main complainant (that is, Elizabeth*
> *Spinkes herself). The Interrogatories, as they were called,*
> *were an opportunity to impugn the character and credibility*
> *of the complainant. Spinkes and his counsel used the inter-*
> *rogatories to paint Elizabeth Spinkes as a social-climbing,*

*quarrelsome, drunken whore, who lied to her husband, dis-
obeyed him and sought to ruin him financially.*

*Witnesses were asked to respond to such questions as
the following: was Elizabeth not at one time apprenticed
to a wire-drawer, and did she not go into service after that?
(This was intended to suggest that she was of lower-class
origins.) Didn't she co-habit with Sir John Williams, even
though she knew his wife to be living? Didn't she pretend
to have a child by Sir John, when it was really the child
of one Chambers, a poor tailor? And:*

[Wasn't Elizabeth] kept as a concubine by one Van, an outlandish
man, or by a trooper or life guardsman, during which time did he
not catch or take her in naked bed with another man and thereby
deserted and turned her off?

*These questions were designed to cast doubt upon her
chastity. A number of other questions concerned Elizabeth
Spinkes's allegedly quarrelsome, violent, disobedient and
unchristian character, both in relation to Sir John (didn't
she curse and swear at him, and throw things at him and
drink too much?) and in relation to John Spinkes:*

[Didn't she call John Spinkes] to his face and behind his back many
ill names, curse him, swear at him and treat him in a very provoking
and undutiful manner and threaten to stab him, murder him and
poison him? [And hadn't she] diverse times, endeavoured by
conversing with pretended witches and fortune tellers to perplex
and vex John Spinkes and put him to pain and anguish of mind
and body?

*One of John Spinkes's central grievances against
Elizabeth Spinkes had to do with the way she had
represented herself to him before they married. Witnesses
were to be asked if Elizabeth hadn't led her husband to*

believe before her marriage that:

... her father was own brother to Sir William Pritchard, our lord mayor of London, that her father left her £1,000 fortune, that she was married to Sir John Williams and had several children by him [and that he had left her £3-4,000 in his will] while in truth she was worth nothing.

> *And hadn't John Spinkes shown himself to be a devoted husband by redeeming some of Sir John's goods with his own money, paying his wife's debts and putting out hundreds of pounds in Chancery over the Williams case?*
>
> *Other questions apparently bore on the approximately three-year period that had elapsed between the time Elizabeth Spinkes exited her husband's house with help of the constable and the neighbours, and her filing for a separation. At some point during this period John Spinkes seems to have spent some time in debtor's prison, due, he claimed, to the difficulties brought on by the marriage. Witnesses were asked whether, during the time her husband was in the Fleet prison, Elizabeth didn't carry on a correspondence with one Brooker* 'in an incontinent and adulterous manner' *and lodge with him* 'in a suspicious manner' *and buy a gold ring for him using her husband's money?[2] John Spinkes and his counsel also used this opportunity to emphasize the financial hardship that paying alimony to Elizabeth would cause to her husband.*

[John Spinkes was] ... at great ... expenses in printing and dispersing printed bills in relation to certain cures he is skilled in and for drugs, medicines, chemical preparations, [also] house rent, housekeeping, parish taxes and servants' wages, and ... his disbursements since the time [of] his marriage have exceeded his income.

At the same time, the expense of litigation and the disputes with his wife had:

... much prejudiced his practice of physic and rendered the annual income there arising much less than in time past ...

John Spinkes's coup-de-grace was to impugn Elizabeth's relationship with her mother:

Have not you several times heard [Elizabeth Spinkes's] mother wish [Elizabeth] had never been born because of her having had an ill life and been an undutiful child to her?

And the interrogatories concluded:

[Elizabeth Spinkes] might have lived very happily with [John Spinkes] [if] she had behaved herself towards him as a wife ought to do towards her husband.

Deposition of Marie Nuby

None of the witnesses favourable to John Spinkes went so far as to argue that he did not beat his wife. Rather they took the position that Elizabeth Spinkes was disobedient, vengeful and prone to drunkenness; that she deliberately provoked her husband to violence; and that she had misled him as to how much she was worth in financial terms. In their view she deserved to be punished. The key witness for the husband's side was the couples' maidservant, Marie Nuby, the wife of a coachman of St. Laurence parish. According to her John Spinkes had to pay up to £200 of debts that Elizabeth had contracted before her marriage. Moreover, Elizabeth Spinkes was much given to drunkenness, and when drunk, had been known to verbally abuse her husband, calling him rogue and villain and 'little insignificant son of a bitch and such like names'. Elizabeth told neighbours her husband kept a whore, and she went about complaining that he physically abused her so as 'to scandalize his good name and reputation and expose him to the world.' In addition:

... she constantly gave him very ill language and endeavoured all she could to provoke him to be angry ...

Marie Nuby had overheard:

... [Elizabeth Spinkes] seriously declare[d] that she would lie with any porter she could meet with that her husband might be pointed at and said there goes a cuckold ...

Elizabeth also retaliated physically, once flinging a looking glass at her husband, and on another occasion, a stone mug.[3] Marie Nuby also testified that she had heard Elizabeth Spinkes threaten to poison John with opium. Moreover, the night before she was carried to the madhouse:

... [Elizabeth] several times ran up and down stairs with a case knife in her hand knocking at the door where [John Spinkes] lay and where he had locked himself up to secure himself from her fury, swearing and cursing and saying damn him and sink him she would that night either kill him, or be killed ...

Marie Nuby supplied the court with a vivid description of Elizabeth Spinkes's efforts to call up supernatural forces against her husband. She testified that Elizabeth used to pray that John wouldn't come home and:

... [she would] kneel on her knees ... and pray to God that he would send the Devil to her that she might make a contract with him to plague her husband ...

When Marie Nuby confronted Elizabeth about this, telling her that:

...she wondered she should have such thoughts and use such expressions as she did to her husband ...

Elizabeth is said to have replied that:

... she knew she should not be saved and she did not care what she did so she might be revenged of him ...

Elizabeth's attempts to enlist the power of magic went beyond the merely rhetorical. Marie Nuby describes her coming home and relating how:

... she had been with a fortune teller at Whitechapel to know when [John Spinkes] would die, in two months or two years but could not tell which and that [the fortune teller] had told her how she should plague her husband by taking her husband's urine, a Cat's heart and bull's blood, which she, Mrs Jones [the fortune teller], would mix for her and stick full of pins and that she was to give Mrs Jones 18 pence for the composition and when she had the heart she was to put it into a box and carry it about [with] her.

Marie Nuby goes on:

And she further told me that one Mrs Cunningham had such a thing from Mrs Jones and that her husband was so lamented thereby, that he was forced to fly the kingdom. And I afterwards heard Mrs Cunningham [herself] declare to the same effect and I twice went with Elizabeth Spinkes to the house of Mrs Jones, at which time

Mrs Jones and Elizabeth Spinkes [consulted together in] private.

... [And] some short time after Elizabeth had told me of the composition Mrs Jones was to make for her to plague her husband ... I saw Elizabeth pour some urine out of a chamberpot in her chambers in a glass vial and she told me that the same was her husband's and that she was carrying it to Mrs Jones to make the said composition for her, and I see her put the said vial in her pocket and go out of doors with it and upon her return home again she told me that she had left the vial of urine with Mrs Jones and a short time afterward, Elizabeth being in a madhouse, a kinswoman or daughter of the said Mrs Jones came to John Spinkes's house to enquire for Elizabeth and told me that she came from Mrs Jones and had brought something for Mrs Spinkes, which she would not leave nor declare what it was and I therefore believe that the same was the composition [previously described] ...

THE JUDGEMENT OF THE COURT

The court found Elizabeth Spinkes more convincing than it did her husband. The copious evidence that John Spinkes had used excessive violence proved more compelling than the evidence that Elizabeth Spinkes had been a less-than-dutiful wife. The court awarded her a legal separation and a modest alimony, thus bringing her troubles to an end, at least for the time being. The judgement is short and to the point:

That the cruelties libellate are proved and [the court] does decree that John Spinkes and his wife be separated *a thoro et mensa* [at bed and board] and does allow to Mrs Spinkes twenty-eight pounds per annum for alimony to be paid quarterly at seven pounds per quarter ... and such money as has already been received for alimony to be deducted. [*A further statement in Latin decreed that John Spinkes would be liable for Elizabeth's legal expenses*]

> Twenty-eight pounds a year would put Elizabeth Spinkes above bare subsistence, but it would be difficult for her to maintain an independent household. However, since it was considered morally suspect for women to live alone, the court probably assumed she would continue to lodge with relatives and adjusted the award accordingly. It is important to note that a legal separation, unlike today's divorce, did not permit either husband or wife to remarry during the lifetime of the other. This left both Elizabeth and John Spinkes with a rather narrow set of options, but would have been especially problematic for Elizabeth. On the other hand, the court could not easily prevent people from living together without the benefit of marriage.
>
> The overwhelming majority even of very serious cases of wife abuse only turned up in court when they resulted in the death of one or the other of the parties.[4] Spinkes v. Spinkes is, in this sense, somewhat unusual. But the complex and contested history of the Spinkeses' marriage, as narrated in the complaints and depositions from both sides, gives us a very rich sense of the way eighteenth-century English people responded to spousal violence, in their own families and in other people's. It is an especially rich source for finding out about both formal and informal separations, the response of relatives and neighbours, and even the role of magic. The case of Spinkes v. Spinkes illuminates a world that was both like our own and very different from it. It gives us a powerful sense of the disadvantages for women of social subordination, but it is also a good reminder that victimization is not always absolute, and that the abused can find ways to fight back.

NOTES

1. The separate estate (or separate settlement) was an amount of money set aside in trust for the benefit of a married woman and her children. In theory, husbands were not supposed to meddle with it, and a husband's creditors could not take it in payment of debts. The separate estate was the major exception to the rule that a woman's assets became the property of her husband upon marriage. But, as this and other cases show, husbands often sought to coerce their wives into signing over their rights to their separate estates. It used to be thought that separate estates were solely the prerogative of rich women. But evidence has been accumulating that, by the eighteenth century, the institution reached quite far down the social scale, so that a number of 'middling' or middle-class women had them.

2. Any and all of a wife's money (apart from her separate settlement, if any) still belonged legally to her husband, even if she was living apart from him and earning it through her own labour. Thus, in theory, Elizabeth Spinkles could not pay for anything except her basic upkeep without her husband's permission, nor could she buy gifts for anyone else.

3. This was a very serious charge, because a woman was not supposed to strike out at her husband, no matter how violent he became.

4. In that age, as in ours, battered women were known to kill their husbands, generally in a fashion that looks to us today like self-defence, but sometimes in a premeditated fashion. But killing a husband was petty treason, a more serious crime than ordinary murder because of the way it subverted the proper order of authority. Women who killed their husbands were therefore executed in a particularly painful and shameful way, by being burned at the stake. Wife-murderers were executed in the more usual way, by hanging, though a man who murdered his wife after discovering her in bed with another man often got off with justifiable homicide or manslaughter.

'Hard-pressed to make ends meet'

WOMEN AND CRIME IN AUGUSTAN LONDON

◆

BY JOHN BEATTIE

Studies from across several centuries have found that women have generally been responsible for a small proportion of serious crimes, including crimes against property. This was the case in eighteenth-century England. In the countryside, where the bulk of the English population continued to live, women accounted for only fifteen to twenty percent of cases involving theft, robbery, burglary and other offences in which someone's property was stolen. In London, on the other hand, women were much more prominent at the sessions of the Old Bailey, the main criminal court of the metropolis. Indeed, through much of the century they came close to rivalling the numbers of men charged with property crimes in London. That was the case in the period in which the following documents have been drawn from the Old Bailey records, for between 1690 and 1720, close to fifty percent of the defendants before the court were women.

Women differed from men in the kinds of offences they committed. They were more likely than men to be charged with offences that did not involve the threat of violence and the direct confrontation with a victim. But, while their forms of appropriation differed, the prosecution of men and women for crimes against property followed broadly similar tracks; their numbers before the courts rose and declined in similar ways over time. When times

William H. Pyne, 'Rabbit-woman,' 1805. Watercolour, from
British Costumes.

were good—when food prices were low and work plentiful—
women's offences decreased in the same way as did men's; and they
both rose when circumstances changed for the worse for the
working population.

It is possible that women were prosecuted at an unusually high
level in the late seventeenth and early eighteenth centuries because
of heightened anxiety about their behaviour in this period and a
greater willingness of victims and the authorities to bring women
to court. There is a suggestion of such an anxiety in the campaigns
to reform the manners of the poor that began soon after 1689, for
while these groups of reformers wanted to eradicate all evidence of
immorality, their principal targets in fact were 'lewd and disorderly'
women, primarily prostitutes. Perhaps more directly, the shoplifting
statute of 1699 and the act that made servants' theft a capital offense
in 1713 reveal a particular anxiety about women. The former was
certainly aimed directly at women, who were always more frequently charged with shoplifting than men; and a large proportion
of the domestic servants of the capital, against whom the 1713
statute was aimed, were women. That Parliament brought the heavy
weapon of the gallows to bear on these essentially minor offences
suggests that men of the propertied classes were becoming particularly alarmed about women's crime and were anxious to bring
women under control.

The pattern of prosecution of women seems to me to have arisen
very largely from the reality of their behaviour, from changes in the
number of offences they were actually committing. That was in turn
the result of the difficulties that many women found themselves in
as they attempted to support themselves in London. Perceptions of
women's behaviour were important, but they were almost certainly
formed because women were unusually hard-pressed to make ends
meet in London and because theft was one of a number of
options—the poor law, charity, the support of friends and relatives,
begging and prostitution were others—when starvation threatened.

A large proportion of the women in London had come to the capital—typically in their early twenties—in search of work. The problems that such women faced arose from their position of fundamental inequality: they were very largely confined to a limited range of occupations and their wages were significantly lower than men's. Most of the work they could seek was unskilled or semi-skilled, badly paid and sensitive to seasonal variations. That was particularly true of work in the textile and clothing trades, but it was also true of large numbers of other jobs in a variety of trades in London and in street-selling and work in the market gardens, in taverns and shops, and so on. Domestic service, which attracted large numbers of young women, carried no guarantee of continuous work.

The justification for low wages arose from the notion of the woman as dependent, the notion that women were expected merely to supplement the earnings of a male. The reality was that such wages (and the irregularity of work) left many women destitute, or at least close to the edge and easily tipped into serious circumstances. The wives of the large number of poor unskilled men, who themselves could only patch together a living, had to work to supply simple necessities to their families, and commonly had to work hardest during their child-raising years because extra mouths could not be fed without their labour. But single women, or widows with children, or wives who had been deserted by their husbands (a situation that was all too common among the very poor), were likely to feel the threat of starvation the soonest from loss of work or a sudden increase in prices.

The pattern of prosecutions thus suggests that women stole for the same reason that men stole in this period—largely as a means of survival, as a way of supplementing inadequate wages or of supplying the most basic wants. And the frequency with which women were brought before the courts suggests, too, that women found themselves in difficulties in the city much more often than in small towns and rural parishes. For single women especially, the capital offered a greater degree of independence and privacy—a certain freedom from the surveillance and controls of patriarchal and paternalistic social relationships. At the same time, however, and as an inevitable consequence, the urban world forced on them a greater need for self-reliance. That must have been true of single women and widows in particular, and it is hardly surprising that not only were larger numbers of women drawn into theft in London, but that fully eighty percent of the women before the Old Bailey on property charges in this period were unmarried. For many of these women crime may well have been a matter quite simply of survival.

FROM THE COURT RECORDS

THEFT BY SERVANTS

OCTOBER 1693

Examination of Darkest Needham ... this 18th day of September 1693

[She says] that, as [for] the watch ... which she is accused [of having] stolen, she knows nothing of it. Being asked whether she did acknowledge to Mr William Bright that she had taken the watch, she answers no, but says that she remembers she told him that she believed the [watch would be restored] and the reason [for] her belief was [that] some of the family had been [to see] a cunning man about it, [and he] had told them they should have it again. And being further asked why she made her escape out of her master's house, and run away, she answers and says, because they confin'd her in her master's house and threatened to carry her from thence to Newgate, and further says not.

DARKEST NEEDHAM HER MARK

OCTOBER 1700

Examination of Emblem Gold, servant to William Battersby of Holborn, stationer ... who confesses that at divers times she has taken out of her master's house aforesaid several goods without her said master's knowing thereof of which goods these named hereafter are part, viz:

[She] says that at one time she took of her said master's house privately a large silver tankard which she pawned by the assistance of one Mary Stratford at one Mr Dunn's, a broker in Show Lane, for seven pounds and spent the money.

[She] says that she stole out of her said master's house at another time a black tabby petticoat with 3 fringes that she pawned at Mr Dunn's and a black-flowered petticoat that Mary Stratford pawned for her at Mr Dunn's the Broker, [and] another time a flowered petticoat that Mary Stratford pawned for her at Dunn's. Another time 3 yards of scarlet serge that Mary Stratford pawned for her at Mr Dunn's. And at several other times 2 silver spoons, 2 shell spoons adorned with silver, a silver needle and thimble case, 2 sad-coloured cloth coats, a black calamanco waistcoat and breeches, 4 pairs of gold buttons, a new beaver hat, a Camblett cloak lined with blue, a white halland petticoat ... a child's silver corrall, a silver fork. [These] goods [she] says she gave to Mary Stratford to pawn at Mr Dunn's aforementioned and they spent part of the money together that they pawned the goods for ... The residue [she] says that she spent herself. And [she] says that she stole divers other goods out of her ... master's house [that] Stratford pawned for her at other places ...

◆

MAY 1711

THE CASE OF ANN WARD
Examination of Madam Dorothy Waite

On her oath [she says] that on or about Monday the 17th day of April in the year 1710, one Ann Ward (now present) came to be hired [by her as] a servant by the name of Mary Rodes, [who was] pretending she had been a servant to the Lady mayor and Mr Cooper. [She was] impersonating one Mary Rodes, who had been a servant in those families ... Ann Ward, alias Mary Rodes, continued to be a servant [to her] until the Monday following, and then took and stole away a gold watch and chain, a pair of candlesticks and snuffers of silver, a silver coffeepot ... and divers other goods to the value of fifty pounds. And Ann Ward, alias Rodes, being left at home by [Mrs Waite when she] went out about eleven o'clock and returned again about twelve. [By] then, Ann Ward, alias Mary Rodes, was absented from the service of [Mrs Waite], and the goods abovementioned were gone. [She] does on her oath say that ... Ann Ward, now present, is the same person that was a servant to this deponent by the name of Mary Rodes and stole the goods above-mentioned.

SIGNATURE OF DOROTHY WAITE

Examination of Elizabeth Marriott

On her oath [she] says that one Ann Ward, now present ... who is charged with robbing ... Mr Waite, [her] master, is the same person that lived there about April was twelvemonth. [Mrs Marriot] being then and still is a servant in [that] family, and ... Ann Ward, who then went by the name of Mary Rodes, was [her] bedfellow. [And at the] time the goods abovementioned was stolen ... Ann Ward, alias Mary Rodes, absented.

SIGNATURE OF ELIZABETH MARRIOTT

Examination of Mary Waver

... who on her oath says that Anne Ward, now present, did fre-quently come to one Mrs Richardson, where [she] lodged, a little after Christmas was twelvemonth.

THEFT BY A LODGER

JULY 1708
Information of Sarah Ware

[Mrs Ware] says that on Witsunday last about two of the clock in the afternoon, ... being a lodger with Mrs Mary Brown, wife of

William Brown of the parish of St Leonard Shoreditch in the County of Middlesex, Barber, she ... entered the chamber of Mrs Brown by virtue of the key thereof left upon the kitchen table, wherewith she unlocked the same and therein broke open a wainscot box of Mrs Brown and feloniously took thereout two silver porringers, two silver cups, three silver spoons, one silver salt and eighteen pence in money, which goods except one of the silver cups this informant sold to Dorothy Deale for four pounds and five shillings and gave her the silver cup gratis and at the same time told her that she had stolen the same.

MARK OF SARAH WARE

SHOPLIFTING

JULY 1695

[Examination] and Confession of Alice Stephens, wife of Walter Stephens of the parish of St Andrews Holbom

[Mrs Stephens] says that between two and three of the clock in the afternoon on this present day, she was at the shop of Susannah Sale in the parish of St Botolph (without Bishopsgate) in the City of London, and she being there did cheapen and ask the price of several pieces of ribbon, but did not buy any. [And] at the same time she ... did steal and carry away one piece of blue ribbon, called Spanish blue, which was showice [sic] unto her as aforesaid. Which said piece of ribbon she, this examinant, presently after she got out of the shop, gave to a woman of her acquaintance but does not know her name, which she accidentally met in the street.

The above said Alice Stephens did make the aforesaid confession but refused to set her name or mark.

TRAFFICKING IN STOLEN GOODS

OCTOBER–DECEMBER 1699

Mary Parker has this day made oath ... that the persons within named did ... steal the goods herein mentioned and that [those who] bought the [goods] knew them to be stolen.

The latter end of Aug. last, Mary Pynes and Rachell Lewes, for a piece of muslin taken out of a shop in Fanchurch Street, sold to Mrs Jane Lewes;

The beginning of Sept., Mary Pynes and Rachell Lewes, for a piece of flowered damask, sold to Old Mrs Jane Whittell;

The middle of Sept., Mary Pynes for 8 yards 1/2 of silver lace from Middle Row (val £6), sold to Jane Willson for [blank];

Beginning of Sept,. Mary Pynes for a silver cup from the Old Jury, sold to Nurse Waide for 45s;

Beginning of Sept., Mary Pynes and Rachell Lewes for 13 yards of stuff from Bartholomew Close, sold to Mrs Jane Whittall;

Beginning of August, Benjamin Harding, Mary Pynes, Rachell Lewes for a pair of britches from Long Lane.

Nineteen further shoplifting offences are alleged by the accomplice, Mary Parker, most of them involving Mary Pynes and Rachell Lewes, and invariably naming the receiver.

TWO PETITIONS FOR PARDON

1701

Petition of Ann Hartley

To the Rt Hon. Sir Tomas Abney Kt Lord Mayor and the rest of the Court, now sitting in the Old Bayley: The Humble Petition of Anne Hartley, al[ia]s Jinings, who [has] been above 4 months a prisoner in Kent and Newgate.

Most humbly sheweth:

That your petitioner being a poor, ignorant woman and not knowing the dangerous consequences of making a false oath, was seduced by Rebecca Harrison [into giving] the present evidence against her.

That [she is] a poor, indigent woman and having two small children to provide for, and no subsistence but what she was, and is, forc'd to work hard for, was by Harrison's persevations and her own necessities prevailed on to counterfeit herself [as] the widow of Henry Hudson, lately deceased on board His Majesty's Ship *Oxford* ...

That [she] immediately deliver'd the [proceeds] to ... Rebecca Harrison by virtue of which Harrison sold Hudson's wages, [she has] not gain[ed] any advantage thereby.

That [she] is extremely poor, and [has] had nothing to live on during her confinement but the allowance of the gaol, which is only bread and water, [and] which great hardship [has] thrown her into a sickness under which she now languishes, and must inevitably perish if your Lordships be'n't pleas'd to commiserate her ... condition.

Your petitioner therefore most humbly begs that your Lordships will be pleas'd, according to your usual goodness and clemency, to commiserate her offence and moderate the punishment due to her crime, so as she may obtain her liberty to provide for her poor children.

1696

The humble petition of several women that have pleaded to a pardon of transportation now in Newgate

To the Rt Hon. Sir John Houblon Knt Lord Mayor of the City of London and justices now sitting at Justice Hall in the Old Bailey.

That your petitioners pleaded [for] a pardon of transportation last December, and the ships being gone, there is no hopes of being sent away [for] a great while. [Your] petitioners must inevitably perish in the gaol, many of them being sick and in a languishing condition. Neither indeed have [they] any hopes of being sent away at all, [since] the merchants [are] refusing to take them without the men.

Humbly pray that they may be admitted to bail to transport themselves in some convenient time, whereby their lives might be preserved and the gaol eased.

CRIMES OF VIOLENCE

2 MAY 1707

From The Ordinary of Newgate his Account

Alice Gray [was] condemned for assisting one Thomas, alias John Smith, in committing a rape upon the body of Katherine Masters, on the 28th of February last. She denied the fact, and said she never was guilty of anything like it, though she had otherwise much offended God, and particularly in her having of late kept company with a man, whom she was to have marry'd, but was not actually marry'd to him. She said very little else; only, that she was about 32 years of age, born at Andover in Hampshire; that she had all along worked very hard for her livelihood; that she had liv'd several years (both as a wife and a widow) in the parish of St.Clement Dane; and had since her husband's death (as in his life's time) maintain'd herself by her honest and constant labour; she making up clothes for soldiers, and sometimes ... washing and scouring, and at other times watching with sick folks, and being a nurse to them ... [In denying her part in the offence, she said] that there was a man in the room that night when the fact was said to have been committed; that he lay across the feet of the bed, but never offer'd to force or lie with the young woman; and, that that man was a stranger to her, and that she did not know what became of him afterwards.

11 JANUARY 1709

Examination and Confession of Elizabeth Cole, wife of John Cole, mariner of the parish of St. Buttolph without Aldgate London ... this 11th day of January ... 1709

[Mrs Cole] confesses that on Sunday last, being the ninth ... about seven of the clock in the evening, she did murder her own female child, called Elizabeth Cole, about three years of age, by pushing it wilfully off a wall near London Bridge into the River Thames, where she saw it go under the ice after which she never saw her said child any more.

SIGNATURE

MARCH 1713

From The Ordinary of Newgate his Account

Susan Perry, alias Dewy, [was] condemn'd for stripping naked, robbing and murdering ... John Peirce, an infant of 4 years of age, on the 27th day of January last. She said, she was not above 22 years old; that she was born at Greenwich, and had liv'd a considerable time in or about London; that she at first learned to make manteaus; but when she was out of her apprenticeship, not being able to find work in that calling for her maintenance, she then went to live with a seamstress, with whom she stayed but a little while ... [she] then betook herself to cry [i.e. sell] sometimes newspapers, and other times fruit, etc. about the streets. She confess'd, she was before now (viz. in October last) tried at the Old Bailey, for a felony, which she was found guilty of, and whipped for; and, that after her discharge out of Newgate she liv'd a poor, miserable, wretched life; which as she had no thought to render better by honest means, so she was easily tempted to make it worse, as she did by committing the fact she is now to die for.

The Real
and the Ideal

'Though it be the part of every good wife'

MARGARET CAVENDISH, DUCHESS OF NEWCASTLE

◆

BY HILDA L. SMITH

Margaret Cavendish, Duchess of Newcastle, was a fascinating individual, a woman of great character possessing varied and unpredictable intellectual interests. Once one has begun to study her, she occupies a place permanently in one's consciousness. A creature of mid-seventeenth century England—a period that has attracted the most historical and literary interest (especially for women) for its political and religious left—she was an uncomplicated royalist and mostly uninterested in the major social and political debates of the day. Her political efforts were generally directed towards aiding her husband, a military leader under Charles I who lost his fortune in supporting the king and who, in the opinion of himself and his wife, was not sufficiently recognized and recompensed by the restored Charles II. With few clear religious convictions, her interests were situated in social and educational structures, the sciences and an overriding concern about women's status and abilities.[1]

Margaret Cavendish was born a Lucas, according to her account, a respected and prosperous Essex gentry family. Even so, her father had been exiled for killing a relative of Lord Cobham in a duel in 1597, and he languished in France for five years after his betrothed gave birth to their eldest son; Margaret was ultimately the last of eight children. In all likelihood, we would not have heard of her (except as a passing eccentric in some local account of her family)

Here on this Figure Cast a Glance,
But so as if it were by Chance,
Your eyes not fixt, they must not stay,
Since this like Shadowes to the Day
It only represent's; for Still
Her Beuty's found beyond the Skill
Of the best Paynter, to Imbrace,
These lovely Lines within her face,
View her Soul's Picture, Judgment, witt,
Then read those Lines which Shee hath writt,
By Fancy's Pencill drawne alone
Which Peece but Shee, Can justly owne.

Peter van Schuppen, 'Margaret Cavendish, Duchess of Newcastle 1604–
1674.' Engraving, National Portrait Gallery, London.

had she not married William Cavendish, first Marquis and ultimately Duke, of Newcastle. The duke's encouragement was surely the most important reason that her works were published, and her social prominence made her eccentricities of interest to people such as Samuel Pepys and Dorothy Osborne. Born in 1623, she was the youngest daughter of a large family, and, according to her autobiography, the subject of much love and adulation from her older sisters and brothers. She wrote lengthy stories and gained much praise and attention from her family because of her precocity. In the account of her life, appended to the more prominent biography of her husband, she noted that such attention made her shy outside the family circle.

As a young woman she sought her mother's permission (and then had second thoughts) to join Queen Henrietta Maria's court in exile, and thus she travelled to France in 1644. Here she mostly avoided court society but still managed to attract the eye of the Marquis of Newcastle (about thirty years her senior), who was deemed the most eligible bachelor at the court. The duke demonstrated a not unusual affection for a younger woman endowed with a range of charms, not the least an ample bosom. She, although barely twenty, kept her distance and accused him of acting in ways that would undercut her reputation. She admitted her affection, but held out for marriage. He wooed her with typically bad verse in the Cavalier mode, but he did work some surprising assurances into his claims as a suitor. One of the more interesting was his guarantee that an older man was less apt to dominate women than a young one, who he accused of being a 'self lover' who 'bridles no Passion but is loose to Sinne, Takes lust for love, runnes over Woman kinde'.

she made her husband work for her established power [handwritten marginal note]

In reacting to the duke's discussion of the twin motives of passion and respect in his desire to wed her, she demonstrated a kind of common sense and sceptical vision that underlay her later feminist sentiments. While acknowledging the great admiration he showed

financial, political, social, intellectual freedom!

women & finance freedom

her while courting, she still explained his reasons for selecting her thus: 'having but two sons' he so wanted to marry to 'increase his issue, that I have heard him say, he cared not, (so God would be pleased to give him many sons) although they came to be persons of the meanest fortunes; but God frustrated his designs, by making me barren.' The Duchess of Newcastle was not far wrong, for in the inscription he wrote for her tomb (intended for both), he began 'Here leyes the Loyall Duke of Newcastle, and his Dutches, his second wife, by whom he had noe issue'; also, although in his eighties, he still was planning to remarry when he died not so long after her. Another example of her looking behind verbal expressions for a more realistic understanding of male and female behaviour was her scepticism over her mother's wish that Margaret's brother, rather than herself, should take over the estate's management following her husband's death. 'She was very skilful in leases, and setting of lands, and court keeping, ordering of stewards, and the like affairs. And though she would often complain that her family was too great for her weak management ... yet I observe she took a pleasure and some little pride, in the governing thereof.' While others took women's words at face value, and those of men when discussing their interactions with the opposite sex, the duchess was not inclined to do so. She was more apt to say what made sense to her as an individual than to conform to social customs or to interpretations that raised few hackles.

For those who seek early seeds of feminism, she is especially unsettling. She at once wrote the most radical critique of women's nature and women's status penned in the seventeenth century, yet expressed some of the strongest doubts about women's intellectual and personal competence. Through her one can find the unexpected viewpoint, the uncontrollable and unpredictable mind, an individual willing to take on any subject, even while apologizing for taking pen to paper at every turn.

In many ways, she was a blazing star among early modern authors

122

questioning women's place in society. In her writings she created an imaginative world where she could be at the intellectual and political centre, and in real life she offered opinions not spoken by others. And, she emerged from a background that provides little explanation for her ideas. What does one make of an author who writes the following seemingly contradictory statements:

> It cannot be expected I should write so wisely or
> wittily as men, being of the effeminate sex, whose
> brains nature has mix'd with the coldest and softest
> elements.

And, on the need for men to extract and process precious metals, for it could not be accomplished:

> If none but women were to melt and hammer them
> out whose weak spirits would suffocate and so faint
> with the heat, and their small arms would sooner
> break than lift up such a weight.

But on the other side she claimed:

> Men from their first Creation usurped a supremacy to
> themselves, although we were made equal by Nature.
> [This] tyrannical government they have kept ever
> since, using us either like children, fools, or subjects,
> that is, to flatter us to obey, and ... not let us divide
> the world equally with them.

In the intellectual arena, it

echoes of mary wollstonecraft

> has so dejected our spirits, as we are become stupid ...
> whereas in Nature we have as clear an understanding
> as men, if we were bred in schools to mature our

brains, and to manure our understandings, that we
might bring forth the fruits of knowledge.

intellect

If one concentrated on the thoughts excerpted above, Margaret
would seem an interesting, and perhaps even extreme, advocate for
women's equal mental abilities and equal access to a serious education, but not the most fundamentally radical of seventeenth-century
feminists. A range of writers agreed with these sentiments going
back at least to Christine de Pizan, and including Bathsua Makin,
Hannah Woolley, Anna van Schurman, Poullain de la Barre, and
most prominently, Mary Astell in her own day.[2] Rather, it is the areas
where she disagreed with or went further than her contemporaries—and in many ways, beyond later feminist movements—that
establish her uniqueness. It is through her 'Female Orations' and
portions of her introductions that she takes on a broader spectrum
of female experience than did her contemporaries. Here, perhaps
rhetorically, but in a rhetoric that fits with her other views and in
many ways with her own life, she questioned the value of marriage
altogether, the need for women to bear children and any gain to be
had from them; she questioned women's relationship or loyalty to
the state. Her topics and her language in many ways make her sound
similar to the views of radical feminists of the late 1960s expressed
perhaps most clearly in 'The Redstockings Manifesto' published in
Sisterhood Is Powerful in 1970.

marriage
children
state

Thus to study Margaret Cavendish has never been comfortable
for those desiring intellectual or feminist consistency, but it has
been richly rewarding for those seeking someone who tests the
boundaries of acceptable views. She represented no movement or
group and was an individual who spoke against or outside the
values held by her class, her sex and her age. About gender primarily, but also on issues of class, the pomp and circumstance of
academics and academic life, and the social customs of the age, she
was singularly original. At least for me, this has always made her

the most intriguing of women writers during the seventeenth century. She was, of course, not a member of the radical sects who often spoke more for the religious and political values of the group, normally articulated by male leaders. Nor was she an ideological tool for either royalist or revolutionary cause during the Civil War or later. And she was not a member of an intellectual circle pushing women's higher education. She selected her causes and her positions in ways that seem idiosyncratic, remaining loyal only to husband (and indirectly to monarch), but never becoming a mouthpiece for others, either human or godly. And, although we might have some clues, for the most part no one has adequately explained the radical and often unseemly things she uttered. Her intellectual interests were as broad as her views were daring; her works encompassed the physical and biological sciences, drama, poetry, essays, moral philosophy and model letters.

In sampling such views in this introduction, I want to establish the breadth and radical critique at the heart of her writings. Margaret Cavendish often wrote in an evolutionary manner, and she edited her works minimally, so that the beginning of a sentence or paragraph often does not seem to conform to or agree with the ending. But long-term reading makes clear that her thought process continued as she wrote, and she came to the point only as she completed the argument she was making. Such a style of writing and argumentation dominated many of her works (especially the non-scientific) and is evident in her analyses of women's relationships with marriage, children and the state.

Marriage was a questionable bargain for women. In two orations she constructed, 'A Young New-Married Wife's Funeral Oration' and 'A Child-Bed Woman's Funeral Oration' she questioned the value of marriage and the pain and suffering attached to childbirth. In the first, she noted that marriage may be happy at the beginning, 'Yet, after a time, it is displeasing; like meat which is sweet in the mouth, but proves bitter in the stomach'. Its displeasing qualities

marriage

came from the typical culprits: 'neglects, disrespects, absence, dissembling, adultery'. In the oration, given future prospects, she notes the woman might have been better off experiencing an early death. In the oration on childbirth, she contrasted men's easier lives with those of women, and questioned their courage. 'Although all women are tender creatures, yet they endure more than men.' But men harbour opposing views:

childbirth

> Men think all women mere cowards, although they do
> not only venture and endanger their lives more than
> they do but endure greater pains, with greater
> patience, than men usually do.

Men's valour on the battlefield was contrasted with women's courage and pain and suffering in childbirth and found wanting. Yet, though women risked their lives having children, they came to belong to men.

And, in a letter addressed to a woman, who, like herself, did not bear children, she noted:

> I know no reason why she should be troubled for
> having no children, for though it be the part of every
> good wife to desire children to keep alive the memory of
> her husband's name and family by posterity, yet a woman
> has no such reason to desire children for her own sake.

The woman's lack of attachment to children emerges from the fact that males take the father's name and inherit his property while

> Daughters are but branches which by marriage are
> broken off from ... whence they sprang, and grafted
> into the stock of another family, so that daughters are
> to be accounted but as moveable goods or furnitures
> that wear out.

126

Whether or not one agrees with the duchess's interpretation of marriage and motherhood, she took the greater power of men within the family closer to its logical conclusion than did any of her contemporaries, male or female.

In 1938, Virginia Woolf in *Three Guineas* questioned whether women had reason for a national loyalty and rather saw them as citizens of the world. Margaret Cavendish was a rare individual of the sixteen-hundreds to question such loyalties three centuries earlier. In her discussion of women's relationship to the state, she began:

> And as for the matter of governments, we women
> understand them not; yet, if we did, we are excluded
> from intermeddling therewith, and almost from being
> subject thereto;

She continued the logical progression she began with the phrase, 'almost from being subject thereto'.

> We are not tied, nor bound to state or Crown; we are
> free, not sworn to allegiance, nor do we take the oath
> of supremacy!

This has led women to 'hold no offices, [nor] bear any authority, [and be] accounted neither useful in peace nor serviceable in war'. And thus she has reached her startling conclusion:

> If we be no citizens in the Commonwealth, I know *state*
> no reason we should be subjects to the
> Commonwealth.[3]

It has been difficult for her contemporaries or for later scholars to accept the radical nature of her works. They are often dismissed as fanciful, or as cries for acceptance or as indications of her unique social and intellectual background. She was of the wrong social rank, on the wrong side of the English Civil War, tied (if only slightly) to the wrong religious establishment, to have reason to question gender or other relationships. Yet, even if offered in a rhetorical manner, grounded in an inconsistent vision of male-female relationships, and coming from a woman who was both admired and ridiculed as an eccentric, her writings posed a more broadbased, fundamental critique of women's legal, political, educational and social status than did those of her contemporaries. In many ways her life exemplified the desire expressed by a heroine in one of her plays, to be 'a meteor singly alone' rather than a 'star in a crowd'.

NOTES

1. Since I discussed Margaret Cavendish's feminist writings in *Reason's Disciples: Seventeenth-Century Feminists* (Urbana: University of Illinois Press, 1982), there has been a significant growth in the scholarship about her, especially concerning her scientific writings and works of fantasy. The standard biography remains, however, Douglas Grant's *Margaret the First* (London: Rupert-Hart Davies, 1957) with a more recent substantial account in Sara Heller Mendelson's *The Mental World of Stuart Women: Three Studies* (Amherst: University of Massachusetts Press, 1987), and a new lengthy introduction by Kate Lilley to *The Blazing World and Other Writings* (London: Penguin Classics, 1994), the first book-length edition of any of her works in paperback. Important articles include: Lisa T. Sarasohn, 'A Science Turned Upside Down: Feminism and the Natural Philosophy of Margaret Cavendish,' *Huntington Library Quarterly* 1984 47(4): 289-307; Sylvia Bowerbank, 'The Spider's Delight: Margaret Cavendish and the "Female" Imagination,' *English Literary Renaissance* 1984 14(3): 392-408; and Rachel Trubowitz, 'The Reenchantment of Utopia and the Female Monarchical Self: Margaret Cavendish's *Blazing World*,' *Tulsa Studies in Women's Literature* 1992 11(2): 229-245. Finally, Lilley's edition of *The Blazing World* has complete and up-to-date references.

2. Christine de Pizan (c.1365-c.1431), a late medieval French author who questioned the treatment of intellectual women; Bathsua Makin (c.1610-c.1682), a late seventeenth-century educator who favoured women's advanced learning; Hannah Woolley (fl. 1670), a late-seventeenth century author of cookbooks who was critical of women's inferior education; Anna van Schurman (1607-1678), a Dutch scholar who favoured women's higher education and recognition of their writings; Poullain de la Barre (1647-1723), a late-seventeenth century French Cartesian who criticized the assumptions of male superiority and revealed their lack of rational basis; and Mary Astell (1666-1731), a prominent late seventeenth and early eighteenth-century feminist who supported institutions of higher education for women.

3. Margaret Cavendish, Marchioness [later Duchess] of Newcastle, *CCXI Sociable Letters*, Number Sixteen (London: Printed by W. Wilson, 1664), 27

FROM *POEMS AND FANCIES*
1653

To All Noble, and Worthy Ladies

Noble, Worthy Ladies,

Condemn me not as a dishonour of your sex, for setting forth this work; for it is harmless and free from all dishonesty; I will not say from vanity: for that is so natural to our sex, [that it would be] unnatural, not to be so. Besides, poetry, which is built upon fancy, women may claim, as a work belonging most properly to themselves: for I have observ'd, that their brains work usually in a fantastical motion; as in their several, and various dresses, in their many and singular choices of clothes, and ribbons, and the like; in their curious shadowing, and mixing of colours, in their wrought works, and divers sorts of stitches they employ their needle, and many curious things they make, as flowers, boxes, baskets with beads, shells, silk, straw, or anything else; besides all manner of meats to eat: and thus their thoughts are employed perpetually with fancies. For fancy goes not so much by rule, and method, as by choice: and if I have chosen my silk with fresh colours, and matched them in good shadows, although the stitches be not very true, yet it will please the eye; so if my writing please the readers, though not the learned, it will satisfy me; for I had rather be praised in this, by the most, although not the best. For all I desire is fame, and fame is nothing but a great noise, and noise lives most in a multitude; wherefore I wish my book may set [to] work every tongue. But I imagine I shall be censur'd by my own sex; and men will cast a smile of scorn upon my book, because they think thereby,

---

women encroach too much upon their prerogatives; for they hold books as their crown, and the sword as their sceptre, by which they rule, and govern. And very like they will say to me, as to the lady that wrote the Romancy,

> Work Lady, work, let writing Books alone,
> For surely wiser Women nere wrote one.

But those that say so, shall give me leave to wish, that those of nearest relation, as wives, sisters and daughters, may employ their time no worse then in honest, innocent, and harmless fancies; which if they do, men shall have no cause to fear, that when they go abroad in their absence, they shall receive an injury by their loose carriages. Neither will women be desirous to gossip abroad, when their thoughts are well employed at home. But if they do throw scorn, I shall entreat you, (as the woman did in the play of the wife, for a month, which caused many of the effeminate sex) to help her, to keep their right, and privileges, making it their own case. Therefore pray strengthen my side, in defending my book; for I know women's tongues are as sharp, as two-edged swords, and wound as much, when they are anger'd. And in this battle may your wit be quick, and your speech ready, and your arguments so strong, as to beat them out of the field of dispute. So shall I get honour, and reputation by your favours; otherwise I may chance to be cast into the fire. But if I burn, I desire to die your martyr; if I live, to be

YOUR HUMBLE SERVANT,

M. N.

An Epistle to Mistress Toppe

Some may think an imperfection of wit may be a blemish to the family from whence I sprung: But Solomon says, A wise man may get a fool. Yet there are as few mere fools, as wise men: for understanding runs in a level course, that is, to know in general, as of the effects: but to know the cause of any one thing of Nature's works, Nature never gave us a capacity thereto. She has given us thoughts which run wildly about, and if by chance they light on truth, they do not know it for a truth. But among many errors, there are huge mountains of follies; and though I add to the bulk of one of them, yet I make not a mountain alone, and am the more excusable, because I have an opinion, which troubles me like a conscience, that 'tis a part of honour to aspire towards a fame. For it cannot be an effeminacy to seek, or run after glory, to love perfection, to desire praise; and though I want merit to make me worthy of it, yet I make some satisfaction in desiring it. But had I broken the chains of modesty, or behav'd myself in dishonourable and loose carriage, or had run the ways of vice, as to perjure myself, or betray my friends, or denied a truth, or had lov'd deceit: then I might have prov'd a grief to the family I came from, and a dishonour to the family I am link't to, raised blushes in their cheeks being mentioned, or to turn pale when I were published. But I hope, I shall neither grieve, nor shame them, or give them cause to wish I were not a branch thereof. For though my ambition's great, my designs are harmless, and my ways are plain honesty: and if I stumble at folly, yet will I never fall on vice. 'Tis true, the world may wonder at my confidence, how I dare put out a book, especially in these censorious times; but why should I be ashamed, or afraid, where no evil is, and not please myself in the satisfaction of innocent desires? For a smile of neglect cannot dishearten me, no more can a frown of dislike affright me; not but I should be well pleased, and delight to have my book commended. But the world's dispraises cannot make me a mourning garment: my mind's too big, and I had rather venture an indiscretion, then lose the hopes of a fame. Neither am I ashamed of my simplicity, for Nature tempers not every brain alike; but 'tis a shame to deny the principles of their religion, to break the laws of a well-governed kingdom, to disturb peace, to be unnatural, to break the union and amity of honest friends, for a man to be a coward, for a woman to be a whore; and by these actions, they are not only to be cast out of all civil society, but to be blotted out of the roll of mankind. And the reason why I summon up these vices is to let my friends know, or rather to [remind] them, that my book is none of them: yet in this action of setting out of a book, I am not clear without fault, because I have not asked leave of any friend thereto; for the fear of being denied, made me silent: and there is an old saying; That it is easier to ask pardon, [than] leave: for a fault will sooner be forgiven, [than] a suit granted: and as I have taken the one, so I am very confident they will give me the other. For their affection is such, as it does as easily obscure all infirmity and blemishes, as it is fearful and quick-sighted in spying the vices of those they love; and they do with as much kindness pardon the one, as with grief reprove the other. But I thought it an honour to aim at excellencies, and though I cannot attain thereto, yet an endeavour shows a good will, and a good will ought not to be turned out of noble minds, nor be whipped with dispraises, but to be cherished with commendations. Besides, I print this book, to give an account to my friends, how I spend the idle time of my life, and how I busy my thoughts, when I think upon the objects of the world. For the truth is, our sex has so much waste time, having but little employments, which makes our thoughts run wildly about, having nothing to fix them upon, which wild thoughts do not only produce unprofitable, but indiscreet actions; winding up the thread of our lives in snarls on unsound bottoms. And since all times must be spent either ill, or well, or indifferent; I thought this was the harmelessest pastime: for sure this work is better [than] to sit still, and censure my neighbours' actions, which nothing concerns me; or to condemn their humours, because they do not sympathize with mine, or their lawful recreations, because they are not agreeable to my delight; or ridiculously to laugh at my neighbours' clothes, if they are not of the mode, colour, or cut, or the ribbon tied with a mode knot, or to busy myself out of the sphere of our sex, as in politics of state, or to preach false doctrine in a tub, or to entertain myself in hearkening to vain flatteries, or to the incitements of evil persuasions where all these follies, and many more, may be cut off by such innocent work as this. I write not this only to satisfy you, which my love makes me desire so to do; but to defend my book from spiteful invaders, knowing truth and innocence are two good champions against malice and falsehood; and which is my defence, I am very confident is a great satisfaction to you. For being bred with me, your love is twisted to my good, which shall never be undone by any unkind action of mine, but will always remain

YOUR LOVING FRIEND,
M.N.

FROM *DIVERS ORATIONS*
1662

A Young New-Married Wife's Funeral Oration

Beloved Brethren,

We are met together at this time, to see a new-married wife, which is here dead, to be buried. She has made an unequal change from a lively hot husband, to a deadly cold lover, yet will she be more happy with her dull, dumb, deaf, blind, numb lover, than with her lively, talking, listening, eyeing, active husband, were he the best husband that could be; for death is far the happier condition than marriage; and although marriage at first is pleasing, yet after a time it is displeasing, like meat which is sweet in the mouth, but proves bitter in the stomach. Indeed, the stomach of marriage is full of evil humours, as choler, and melancholy; and of very evil digestion, for it cannot digest neglects, disrespects, absence, dissembling, adultery, jealousy, vain expenses, waste, spoil, idle time, laziness, examinations, cross answers, peevishness, forwardness, frowns, and many the like meats, that marriage feeds on. As for pains, sickness, cares, fears, and other troubles in marriage, they are accounted as wholesome physic, which the gods give them; for the gods are the best physicians, and death is a very good surgeon, curing his patients without pain, for what part soever he touches, is insensible. Death is only cruel in parting friends from each other, for though they are happy, whom he takes away, yet those that are left behind, are unhappy, living in sorrow for their loss. So ... this young new-married wife, that is dead, is happy, but her husband is a sorrowful widower. But leaving her to her happiness, and him to be comforted, let us put her into the grave, there to remain until the day of judgement, which day will embody her soul with everlasting glory.

A Child-Bed Woman's Funeral Oration

Beloved Brethren,

We are met together to see a young dead woman, who died in child-bed, to be laid into the bed of earth, a cold bed, but yet she will not take any harm there ... we shall not fear she will catch her death, for death has catch'd her; the truth is, that although all women are tender creatures, yet they endure more than men, and do oftener venture and endanger their lives than men, and their lives are more profitable than men's lives are, for they increase life, when men for the most part destroy life, as witness wars, wherein thousands of lives are destroyed, men fighting and killing each other, and yet men think all women mere cowards, although they do not only venture and endanger their lives more than they do, but endure greater pains with greater patience than men usually do. Nay, women do not only endure the extremity of pain in childbirth, but in breeding, the child being for the most part sick, and seldom at ease. Indeed, Nature seems both unjust and cruel to her female creatures, especially women, making them to endure all the pain and sickness in breeding and bringing forth of their young children, and the males to bear no part of their pain or danger. The truth is, Nature has made her male creatures, especially mankind, only for pleasure, and her female creatures for misery. Men are made for liberty, and women for slavery, and not only slaves to sickness, pains, and troubles, in breeding, bearing, and bringing up their children, but they are slaves to men's humours, nay, to their vices and wickedness, so that they are more enslaved than any other female creatures, for other female creatures are not so enslaved as they; wherefore, those women are most happy that never marry, or die while they be young, so that this young woman that died in childbed is happy, in that she lives not to endure more pain or slavery, in which happiness let us leave her, after we have laid her corpse to rest in the grave.

FROM *DIVERS ORATIONS*
1662

Female Orations
I

Ladies, Gentlewomen, and other Inferiors, but not less worthy, I have been industrious to assemble you together, and wish I were so fortunate, as to persuade you to make a frequentation, association, and combination among our sex, that we may unite in prudent counsels, to make ourselves as free, happy, and famous as men, whereas now we live and die, as if we were produced from beast rather than from men; for men are happy, and we women are miserable, they possess all the ease, rest, pleasure, wealth, power, and fame, whereas women are restless with labour, easeless with pain, melancholy for want of pleasures, helpless for want of power, and die in oblivion for want of fame. Nevertheless, men are so unconscionable and cruel against us, as they endeavour to bar us of all sorts or kinds of liberty, as not to suffer us freely to associate among our own sex, but would fain bury us in their houses or beds, as in a grave; the truth is, we live like bats or owls, labour like beasts, and die like worms.

II

Ladies, Gentlewomen, and other Inferior Women, the lady that spoke to you, has spoken wisely and eloquently in expressing our unhappiness, but she has not declared a remedy, or show'd us a way to come out of our miseries; but if she could or would be our guide, to lead us out of the labyrinth men have put us into, we should not only praise and admire her, but adore and worship her as our goddess. But, alas, men, that are not only our tyrants, but our devils, keep us in the hell of subjection, from whence I cannot perceive any redemption or getting out. We may complain, and bewail our condition, yet that will not free us; we may murmur and rail against men, yet they regard not what we say. In short, our words to men are as empty sounds, our sighs as puffs of wind, and our tears as fruitless showers, and our power is so inconsiderable, as men laugh at our weakness.

III

Ladies, Gentlewomen and other more Inferiors, the former orations were exclamations against men, repining at their condition, and mourning for our own; but we have no reason to speak against men, who are our admirers, and lovers; they are our protectors, defenders, and maintainers; they admire our beauties, and love our persons; they protect us from injuries, defend us from dangers, are industrious for our subsistence, and provide for our children. They swim great voyages by sea, travel long journeys by land, to get us rarities and curiosities; they dig to the centre of the earth for gold for us; they dive to the bottom of the sea for jewels for us; they build to the skies houses for us. They hunt, fowl, fish, plant, and reap food for us; all which we could not do ourselves, and yet we complain of men, as if they were our enemies, when we could not possibly live without them. Which shows, we are as ungrateful, as inconstant. But we have more reason to murmur against Nature than against men, who has made men more ingenious, witty, and wise than women; more strong, industrious, and laborious than women, for women are witless, and strengthless, and unprofitable creatures, did they not bear children. Wherefore, let us love men, praise men, and pray for men, for without men we should be the most miserable creatures that Nature has, or could make.

IV

Noble Ladies, Gentlewomen, and other Inferior Women, the former oratoress says, we are witless, and strengthless; if so, it is that we neglect the one, and make no use of the other, for strength is increased by exercise, and wit is lost for want of conversation; but to show men we are not so weak and foolish, as the former oratoress does express us to be, let us hawk, hunt, race, and do the like exercises as men have, and let us converse in camps, courts, and cities, in schools, colleges, and courts of judicature, in taverns, brothels, and gaming houses, all which will make our strength and wit known, both to men and to our own selves, for we are as ignorant of ourselves, as men are of us. And how should we know ourselves, when as we never made a trial of ourselves? Or how should men know us, when ... they never put us to the proof? Wherefore, my advice is, we should imitate men, so will our bodies and minds appear more masculine, and our power will increase by our actions.

V

Noble, Honourable, and Virtuous Women, the former oration was to persuade us to change the custom of our sex, which is a strange and unwise persuasion, since we cannot change the nature of our sex, for we cannot make ourselves men; and to have female bodies, and yet to act masculine parts, will be very preposterous and unnatural. In truth, we shall make ourselves like as the defects of nature, as to be hermaphroditical, as neither to be perfect women nor perfect men, but corrupt and imperfect creatures. Wherefore, let me persuade you, since we cannot alter the nature of our persons, not to alter the course

of our lives, but to rule our lives and behaviours, as to be acceptable
and pleasing to God and men, which is to be modest, chaste, temperate, humble, patient, and pious; also to be housewifely, cleanly, and of
few words, all which will gain us praise from men, and blessing from
heaven, and love in this world, and glory in the next.

VI

Worthy women, the former oratoress's oration endeavours to persuade us, that it would not only be a reproach and disgrace, but unnatural for women in their actions and behaviour to imitate men. We
may as well say, it will be a reproach, disgrace, and unnatural to imitate the gods, which imitation we are commanded both by the gods
and their ministers. And shall we neglect the imitation of men, which
is more easy and natural than the imitation of the gods? For how can
terrestrial creatures imitate celestial deities? Yet one terrestrial may
imitate another, although in different sorts of creatures. Wherefore,
since all terrestrial imitations ought to ascend to the better, and not to
descend to the worse, women ought to imitate men, as being a degree
in nature more perfect, than they themselves, and all masculine
women ought to be as much praised as effeminate men to be dis-
praised, for the one advances to perfection, the other sinks to imperfection, that so by our industry we may come at last to equal men
both in perfection and power.

VII

Noble Ladies, Honourable Gentlewomen, and Worthy Female
Commoners, the former oratoress's oration or speech was to persuade
us out of ourselves, as to be that which nature never intended us to
be, to wit masculine; but why should we desire to be masculine, since
our own sex and condition is far the better? For if men have more
courage, they have more danger; and if men have more strength, they
have more labour than women have. If men are more eloquent in

speech, women are more harmonious in voice; if men be more active, women are more graceful; if men have more liberty, women have more safety; for we never fight duels, nor battles, nor do we go [on] long travels or dangerous voyages. We labour not in building, nor digging in mines, quarries, or pits, for metal, stone, or coals. Neither do we waste or shorten our lives with university or scholastic studies, questions, and disputes. We burn not our faces with smiths' forges, or chemist furnaces, and hundreds of other actions, which men are employed in; for they would not only fade the fresh beauty, spoil the lovely features, and decay the youth of women, causing them to appear old, while they are young, but would break their small limbs, and destroy their tender lives. Wherefore, women have no reason to complain against Nature, or the God of Nature, for though the gifts are not the same they have given to men, yet those gifts they have given to women, are much better; for we women are much more favour'd by Nature than men, in giving us such beauties, features, shapes, graceful demeanour, and such insinuating and enticing attractives, as men are forc'd to admire us, love us, and be desirous of us, in so much as rather than not have and enjoy us, they will deliver to our disposals, their power, persons, and lives, enslaving themselves to our will and pleasures; also we are their saints, whom they adore and worship, and what can we desire more, than to be men's tyrants, destinies, and goddesses?

FROM *SOCIABLE LETTERS*
1664

XCIII

Madam,
You were pleased in your last letter to express to me the reason of the Lady D.S.'s and the Lady E.K.'s melancholy, which was for want

of children. I cannot blame the Lady D.S. [since] her husband is the last of his family unless he have children, but the Lady E.K.'s husband being a widower when he married her, and having sons to inherit his estate, and to keep up his family, I know no reason why she should be troubled for having no children, for though it be the part of every good wife to desire children to keep alive the memory of their husband's name and family by posterity, yet a woman has no such reason to desire children for her own sake, for first her name is lost as to her ... in her marrying, for she quits her own, and is named as her husband. [She also loses] her family, for neither name nor estate goes to her family according to the laws and customs of this country. Also she hazards her life by bringing [children] into the world, and has the greatest share of trouble in bringing them up. Neither can women assure themselves of comfort or happiness by them, when they are grown to be men, for their name only lives in sons, who continue the line of succession, whereas daughters are but branches which by marriage are broken off from the root from whence they sprang, and grafted into the stock of another family, so that daughters are to be accounted but as moveable goods or furnitures that wear out; and though sometimes they carry the lands with them, for want of heir-males, yet the name is not kept nor the line continued with them, for these are buried in the grave of the males, for the line, name and life of a family ends with the male issue; but many times married women desire children, as maids do husbands, more for honour than for comfort or happiness, thinking it a disgrace to live old maids, and so likewise to be barren, for in the Jews' time it was some disgrace to be barren, so that for the most part maids and wives desire husbands and children upon any condition, rather than to live maids or barren. But I am not of their minds, for I think a bad husband is far worse than no husband, and to have unnatural children is more unhappy than to have no children, and where one husband proves good, as loving and prudent, a thousand prove bad, as cross and spendthrifts; and where one child proves good, as dutiful and wise, a thousand prove disobedient and fools, as to do actions both to the dishonour and ruin of their families.

Besides, I have observed, that breeding women, especially those that have been married some time, and have had no children, are in their behaviour like new-married wives, whose actions of behaviour and speech are so formal and constrain'd, and so different from their natural way, as it is ridiculous; for new-married wives will so bridle their behaviour with constraint, or hang down their heads so simply, not so much out of true modesty, as a forced shamefulness. And to their husbands they are so coyly amorous, or so amorously fond and so troublesome kind, as it would make the spectators sick, like fulsome meat to the stomach; and if new-married men were wise men, it might make them ill husbands, at least to dislike a married life, because they cannot leave their fond or amorous wives so readily or easily as a mistress. But in truth that humour does not last long, for after a month or two they are like surfeited bodies, that like any meat better than what they were so fond of, so that in time they think their husbands worse company than any other men. Also women at the breeding of their first children make so many sick faces, although oftentimes the sickness is only in their faces, not but that some are really sick, but not every breeding women. Likewise they have such feigned coughs, and fetch their breath short, with such feigning laziness, and so many unnecessary complaints, as it would weary the most patient husband to hear or see them. Besides, they are so expensive in their longings and perpetual eating of several costly meats, as it would undo a man that has but an indifferent estate. [And] to add to their charge, if they have not what they please for child-bed linen, mantles, and a lying-in bed, with suitable furniture for their lying-chamber, they will be so fretful and discontented, as it will endanger their miscarrying. Again to redouble the charge, there must be gossiping, not only with costly banquets at the christening and churching, but they have gossiping all the time of their lying-in, for then there is a more set or formal gossiping than at other ordinary times. But I fear, that if this letter come to the view of our sex besides yourself, they will throw more spiteful or angry words out of their mouths against me, than the unbelieving Jews did hard stones out of their hands at Saint Stephen. But the best is, they cannot kill me with

their reproaches, I speak but the truth of what I have observed among many of our sex. Wherefore, pray Madam, help to defend me, as being my friend, and I yours, for I shall continue as long as I live,
Madam,

YOUR LADYSHIP'S MOST FAITHFUL
AND HUMBLE SERVANT.

CLII

Madam,
The messenger you sent is returning to you again, and with him I have sent some babies, and other toys this city affords, as a token to your daughter, I do not send them for bribes, to corrupt her from edifying learning, and wise instructions, for I would not have her bred to delight in toys, and childish pleasures, but I send them as gifts, to allure her to that which is most profitable, and happiest for her life, for children are sooner persuaded by the means of tinsel-toys, and flattering words, to listen to wise instruction, to study profitable arts or sciences, to practise good, graceful behaviours, and civil demeanours, than they can be forced thereto, by terrifying threats, and cruel blows. 'Tis true, they may be forced to the outward forms, or actions of learning, but not to the understanding, profit, grace, or becoming, for force breaks the understanding, destroys all ingenuity, for the fear of punishment confuses the brain, and disquiets the mind so much, as it makes them incapable of right impressions, whereas the hope of rewards delights the mind, and regulates the motions in the brain, and makes them so smooth, as the least impression of learning prints fairly therein, and so plainly, as to be remembered in their elder years. Also it makes their thoughts and actions industrious, to merit those rewards, and their endeavours will be the more active, through a covetous desire to increase those rewards, so that those toys which are given to children in their childish years, may be a means to teach them, when grown to elder years, to know, and acknowledge, that all toys are vanities, and

that nothing is to be prized, or esteemed, but what is useful, and best, either for their present, or future life, as the life of their memory, or renown. Thus, Madam, the toyish present is to a good design, and may prove to a good end, which is the wish of,

Madam,

YOUR *FAITHFUL FRIEND*
AND SERVANT.

'The pleasing objects
of our present researches'

WOMEN IN BOTANY

◆

BY ANN B. SHTEIR

During the eighteenth century, before science was formalized in terms of professions and institutions, the activities of science took place not only in learned academies, but also in polite drawing rooms, in public lecture halls, in fields and in gardens. Interest in natural knowledge was an important part of the European Enlightenment, and knowledge gleaned from one's own observations was particularly prized. Astronomy and natural philosophy were early eighteenth-century sciences of choice, and natural history was on the ascendancy by the century's end. Botany became particularly popular. Perhaps because it stood at the junction of gardening, art and science, the study of plants had wide acceptability and even social cachet. Books, magazines, essays, poetry and handbooks about the Vegetable Kingdom proliferated. Botany was recommended to men, women and children in the middle and upper ranks of society as a worthy activity, good for health and for mental and moral well-being. Women, benefitting from the favourable climate within science culture, participated in botanical work as audience and as agents, reading, studying, researching and writing about plants.

Priscilla Wakefield's *An Introduction to Botany* (1796) illuminates the role of women in eighteenth-century botanical culture. A work of informal science education, Wakefield's book situates the study of

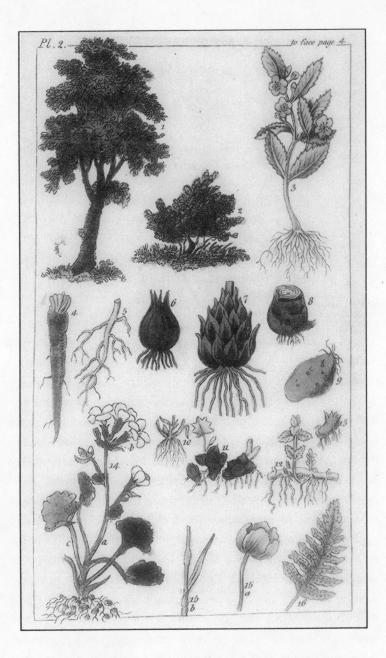

Engraving from *Introduction to Botany*, Priscilla Wakefield, 1796.

botany as part of general education, inside everyday family life and within a world of women. The book teaches its readers the parts of plants and the system of plant classification developed by the influential Swedish botanist Carl Linnaeus. It also describes indigenous English plants that belong to the twenty-four Classes of the Linnaean system. Wakefield places her exposition inside a narrative framework that is part of the book's larger teaching: a governess, under instruction from a mother, gives botanical lessons to one of her teenaged pupils who in turn reports on what she is learning in letters to her sister. There is no suggestion that science teaching is inappropriate to the sex or station of the girls. On the contrary, the governess has already taught the girls about other sciences, and now she is adding botany to the curriculum.

The narrative framework of letters from one sister to another was a genre familiar to eighteenth-century readers, for this was the century that shaped the epistolary novel. Letters were frequently used as a narrative form for didactic teachings. In France, Jean-Jacques Rousseau, for example, wrote letters to a young mother about botany in the 1770s so that she could teach her children about plants. The letter form offered a pedagogical protocol that matched assumptions about women's lives, while it inserted intellectuality into conventional social forms. Priscilla Wakefield herself used the epistolary form in other books too, notably in *An Introduction to the Natural History and Classification of Insects* (1816) and in a series of didactic, family-based travel books.

The appearance of *An Introduction to Botany* in 1796 shows us a writer with a finger on a cultural pulse in promoting science for girls and women. Priscilla Wakefield (1751-1832) became a professional writer in mid-life when family money troubles called upon her resources. This forty-five-year-old Quaker mother and grandmother took up her pen in the mid-1790s and wrote seventeen books during the next two decades. Her writing included travel books, natural history miscellancies and an adult book on female education and employment.[1] She issued her books with well-known publishers of the day, including Elizabeth Newbery, Longman, the radical Joseph Johnson and the Quaker firm of Darton and Harvey.

Priscilla Wakefield wrote principally for what she labelled 'the rising generation', and her books for young people display keen attention to audience. Like many other writers of the Enlightenment, she worked under an aesthetic that combined instruction and amusement. She shaped her books as letters and as conversations, and when she taught science or other subjects, she created characters and family settings. Her authorial tone was always adult and teacherly but not stern; 'an air of kindness and sympathy', she once wrote, 'is an essential ingredient to render admonition palatable'.[2]

Priscilla Wakefield drank from both the intellectual well-spring of the Enlightenment and the moral and teacherly well-spring of the Society of Friends. Not a close Quaker, she declared her independence from the stringent observances in dress, behaviour and relationship to the secular world practised by some in the Society of Friends. But she shared Quaker philanthropic commitments deeply, and she performed many community services. These included establishing a lying-in charity and a 'frugality society' (the origin of the Savings Bank) and supporting educational ventures for girls and for the labouring poor. Like other Quakers, she promoted spiritual, moral and intellectual self-improvement and valued natural history as a worthy activity of leisure. Priscilla Wakefield was celebrated in her day in reviews and in magazines that featured biographical sketches of exemplary women. *The Ladies' Monthly Museum*, for example, described her as 'author of many well-known publications for young people; in which she has industriously embraced all the leading objects of early instruction, whether of Travels, Foreign or Domestic; or of History, Natural, or Moral; or of Science and Philosophy; with appropriate Reflections, moral and religious, that may influence and direct in the dangerous and difficult passage through life.'[3]

The Preface to *An Introduction to Botany* illustrates the extent to which Priscilla Wakefield viewed science instruction in terms of larger socio-cultural objectives. Wakefield presents science for girls as part of a curriculum of intellectual and moral development. Botany, she maintains, sharpens the powers of observation, provides topics of conversation, teaches method and order and leads the student towards religious reflection. It also prevents boredom and depression of spirits. A body of knowledge worthy in itself, its greater value is as a stopgap against more harmful occupations for girls and women. The book holds out the promise that Wakefield's ideal female reader will be saved from the dangers that cluster under the headings of 'accomplishments' and 'fashion'.

In the eighteenth century, botany was understood for the most part to be a 'safe science', one that inculcated method, regularity and order. One feature of this science was problematic, however. The Linnaean system of plant classification was based on ideas about plant sexuality and reproduction. Linnaeus counted the 'male' and 'female' reproductive parts of flowers and thereby classified plants according to Classes and Orders. Writings by Linnaeus, and by English Linnaeans such as Erasmus Darwin, paraded anthropomorphized and eroticized accounts of the sexual politics of plants, with the result that botany became a problematic female activity in the eyes of some writers and commentators. One would not know from Priscilla Wakefield's account, however, that the Linnaean system in botany was a sexual system; her text sidesteps the issue of sexuality in its choices of vocabulary and in her approach to Linnaean explanatory categories. This was partly the strategic decision of a fledgling professional writer. Working with a publisher, and alert to the marketplace, Priscilla Wakefield shaped an accessible introductory botany book for her target audience, one that would be neither too expensive nor too technical and that would not affront the sensibilities of readers and the book-buying public.

Starting in the eighteenth century, women wrote about science for women, children and general readers in genres such as fiction, periodical essays, expository poetry, letters and dialogues, and they helped shape the early textbook tradition in science. Women's popular science writing was one prominent, though now unfamiliar, area of the history of science and the history of women's writing more generally. Popular science books like Priscilla Wakefield's *Introduction to Botany* are cultural narratives through which to interpret the experiences of girls and women in the science culture of their day. They show that science was a resource for women in ways we have not explored sufficiently and that women science writers challenged, negotiated and accommodated the ideologies of science and gender with impressive dexterity.

NOTES

1. e.g., *The Juvenile Travellers: Containing the Remarks of a Family during a Tour through the Principal States and Kingdoms of Europe* (1801); *Domestic Recreation; or Dialogues Illustrative of Natural and Scientific Subjects* (1805); and *Reflections on the Present Condition of the Female Sex, with Suggestions for its Improvement* (1798).

2. This statement comes from an unpublished letter housed in the British Library. (BL Add. Mss. 9828, f.209) Transcriptions of journals kept by Priscilla Wakefield are available in xeroxed form in the Library of the Society of Friends, London, England.

3. (1818, 8:63). The sub-title of the journal is *Polite Repository of Amusement and Instruction; Being an Assemblage of Whatever can Tend to Please the Fancy, Interest the Mind, or Exalt the Character of the British Fair.*

From Priscilla Wakefield's
An Introduction to Botany
1796

Preface

The design of the following introduction to botany is to cultivate a
taste in young persons for the study of nature, which is the most
familiar means of introducing suitable ideas of the attributes of the
Divine Being, by exemplifying them in the order and harmony of the
visible creation. Children are endowed with curiosity and activity, for
the purpose of acquiring knowledge. Let us avail ourselves of these
natural propensities, and direct them to the pursuit of the most judi-
cious objects: none can be better adapted to instruct, and at the same
time amuse, than the beauties of nature, by which they are continually surrounded. The structure of a feather or a flower is more likely
to impress their minds with a just notion of Infinite Power and
Wisdom, than the most profound discourses on such abstract subjects
as are beyond the limits of their capacity to comprehend. In the
important business of forming the human mind, the inclination and
pleasure of the pupil should be consulted: in order to render lessons
effectual, they should please, and be sought rather as indulgences, than
avoided as laborious toils. Botany is a branch of natural history that
possesses many advantages: it contributes to health of body and
cheerfulness of disposition, by presenting an inducement to take air
and exercise; it is adapted to the simplest capacity, and the objects of
its investigation offer themselves without expense or difficulty, which
renders them attainable to every rank in life. But with all these allure-
ments, 'til of late years, it has been confined to the circle of the

learned, which may be attributed to those books that treated of it, being principally written in Latin: a difficulty that deterred many, particularly the female sex, from attempting to obtain the knowledge of a science, thus defended, as it were, from their approach. Much is due to those of our own countrymen, who first introduced this delightful volume of nature to popular notice, by presenting it in our native language: their labours have been a means of rendering it very generally studied, and it [is] now considered as a necessary addition to an accomplished education. May it become a substitute for some of the trifling, not to say pernicious objects, that too frequently occupy the leisure of young ladies of fashionable manners, and, by employing their faculties rationally, act as an antidote to levity and idleness. As there are many admirable English books now extant upon the subject, it may require some apology for obtruding the present work upon the public. It appeared that everything hitherto published was too expensive, as well as too diffuse and scientific, for the purpose of teaching the elementary parts to children or young persons; and it was therefore thought that a book of a moderate price, and divested as much as possible of technical terms, introduced in an easy, familiar form, might be acceptable.

Letter I
Felicia to Constance

SHRUBBERY, FEB. 1

My Dear Sister,
As it is an unusual thing for us to be separated, I do not doubt that we equally feel the pain of being at a distance from each other. When I consider that you are really gone to pass the whole summer with my aunt, and that I have parted with the beloved companion of my walks and amusements, I think I shall but half enjoy either during the fine season that is approaching. With you, indeed, the case will be different:

new scenes will present themselves, which will entertain by their novelty and variety; and the kind attentions of my aunt and cousins will compensate, in some degree, for the absence of those friends you have left at home. Every place here looks solitary, especially our own apartment, and our favourite haunts in the garden. Even the approach of spring, which is already marked by the appearance of snowdrops and crocuses, affords me but little pleasure. My kind mother, ever attentive to my happiness, concurs with my governess in checking this depression of spirits, and insists upon my having recourse to some interesting employment that shall amuse me and pass away the time while you are absent. My fondness for flowers has induced my mother to propose the study of botany to me, as she thinks it will be beneficial to my health, as well as agreeable to my inclination, by exciting me to use more air and exercise than I should do without such a motive. Because books ought not to be depended upon alone, recourse must be had to the natural specimens growing in fields and gardens. How I should enjoy this pursuit in your company, my dear Constance! But as that is impossible at present, I will adopt the nearest substitute I can devise, by communicating to you the result of every lesson. You may compare my descriptions with the flowers themselves, and by thus mutually pursuing the same object, we may reciprocally improve each other. I am impatient to make a beginning, but am full of apprehension of the number of hard words which must occur. However, I am resolved not to be deterred by this difficulty: perseverance and patience will overcome it; and, as I know the easy method of instruction adopted by my dear governess in other sciences, I confide in her skill to render this easy and pleasant. Farewell.

FELICIA

Letter II

The morning being fine, tempted us abroad: botany supplied us with subjects for conversation. Mrs. Woodbine took the opportunity of remarking that a PERFECT PLANT consists of a *root*, a *trunk* or *stem, leaves, supports, flower,* and *fruit;* for (botanically speaking) by fruit in herbs, as well as in trees, is understood the whole formation of the seed. And as each part needs a particular explanation to a novice, she began her lecture by pointing out the uses of the root. The first and most obvious, is that of enabling the plant to stand firmly in the ground, by serving as a balance to the head. By what means could the enormous oaks in the park be kept upright and fixed but by their extensive turgid roots? These serve as a counterpoise against the weight of the trunk and branches. The chief nourishment of the plant is received by the fibrous part of the roots, which, like so many mouths, absorb the nutritious juices from the earth. The root also performs the part of a parent, by preserving the embryo plants in its bosom, during the severity of winter, in the form of bulbs or buds: bulbs are properly but large buds, eyes, or gems, including the future plants. Nature is an economist, and is sparing of this curious provision against the cold, where it is unnecessary. In warm countries, few plants are furnished with winter buds. Roots are distinguished by different names, according to their forms: as, fibrous, bulbous, and tuberous; with many lesser distinctions, expressive of their form and manner of growth. (*f.* 4—13.)*

The next part of a plant that claims our notice is the TRUNK or stem, which rises out of the root, and supports the flower, leaves, &c. (*f.* 14—16.) The trunk of a tree or shrub (and it is supposed that the stem of a more diminutive plant in the same manner) consists of several distinct parts; as, the bark; the wood; the sap-vessels, corresponding to the blood-vessels in animals; the pith; the tracheae,

---

* For figures 1-16, see p.146 of this book. The other plates referred to in Wakefield's text have not been included here.—ED.

or air vesicles; and the web or tissue. Each of these parts has its peculiar use, and its construction is admirably adapted to its purpose. The bark of plants seems to perform the same offices to them that the skin does to animals; it clothes and defends them from injury, inhales the moisture of the air, and extracts, or conveys from the plant, the superfluity of moist particles. The cause of evergreens retaining their foliage during the winter is supposed to arise from an abundant quantity of oil in their barks, which preserves them from the effects of cold. The bark (as well as the wood) is supplied with innumerable vessels, which convey the fluid to and from every part of the plant; the wood is also furnished with others, which contain air, and are distributed throughout its substance. The stability of trees and shrubs consists in the wood, which corresponds with the bones of animals. The seat of life seems to reside in the pith or medullary substance, which is a fine tissue of vessels, originating in the centre. The fluids of plants are the sap, analagous to the blood of animals; and the proper juice, which is of various colours and consistencies in different individuals; as, white or milky in the dandelion, resinous in the fir, and producing gum in cherry or plum trees, &c. Hoping that I have given you such a clear description of the root and stem, as will enable you to form a general idea of their parts and uses, I shall proceed to the LEAVES, which contribute at the same time, to the benefit and ornament of the plant. I need not tell you, that the variety of their forms and manners of growth is great; your own observation has long since informed you of this particular, and prepared you to understand the terms by which botanists arrange them, according to their forms and shapes; as, simple, compound, rough, smooth, round, oval, heart-shaped, &c. these minutiae must be learned by referring to plates (3 and 4.) Leaves are supposed to answer the purpose of lungs, and, by their inclination to be moved by the wind, in some degree serve also that of muscles. They are very porous on both their surfaces, and inhale and exhale freely. The annual sun-flower is an extraordinary instance of this fact; it is said to perspire nineteen times as much as a man, in twenty-four hours. Fine weather encourages the perspiration of vegetables; but in heavy, moist, and wet weather, the inhalation exceeds. The effluvium of plants is thought unwholesome to persons of delicate constitutions, more particularly so at night, and in a dull state of the atmosphere; but it is worth observing, that the air emitted from the leaves is never prejudicial; that which is noxious proceeds from the corollas only.

The next parts to be considered are the SUPPORTS or props; by these are meant certain external parts of plants, which are useful to support and defend them from enemies and injuries, or for the secretion of some fluid, that is either baneful or disagreeable to those insects that would otherwise injure them. They are divided into seven kinds: 1st. *Stipulas;* small leafy appendages, situated on either side of the leaf or a little below it, in order to protect it when first emerging from the bud, (*f.* 92.) 2ndly. *Floral-leaves* (*f.* 93.), are small leaves placed near the flower, smaller, and mostly of a different form from those of a plant. 3rdly. *Spines* (*f.* 94.); these are sharp-pointed projections, growing from the woody substance of a plant. 4thly. *Prickles* (*f.* 95.), or sharp-pointed projections formed from the bark. 5thly. *Tendrils* (*f.* 92): small spiral strings, by which some plants, that are not strong enough to stand alone, sustain themselves by embracing trees, shrubs, or other supports. 6thly. *Glands,* or little tumours, which discharge a viscous or resinous kind of fluid. 7thly. *Hairs,* or down, (Pl. I. *f.* 2.) In order to enliven a dry detail of names, and a mere description of parts, Mrs. Woodbine favoured me with an account of some curious contrivances of nature, observed in some particular plants, for their defence against insects, or larger animals, that would, without this precaution, greatly annoy them; and as I know the pleasure you take in such recitals, I shall repeat them to you before I close this long letter. The viscous or clammy matter which surrounds the stalks, under the flowers of the catchfly, prevents various insects from plundering the honey, or devouring the pollen which fertilizes the seed. In the *dionaea muscipula,* or Venus's fly-trap, there is a still more wonderful means of preventing the depredations of insects. The leaves are armed with long teeth, like the antennae of insects, and lie spread upon the ground round the stem; they are so irritable, that when an insect creeps upon them, they fold up, and crush or pierce it to death. The sundew, a plant very common in our marshes, is likewise furnished with the same means of defence against its enemies. The flower of the *arum crinitum* has the smell of carrion, which invites the flies to lay their eggs in the chamber of the flower; but the worms which are hatched from these eggs, are unable to make their escape from their prison, being prevented by the hairs pointing inwards, which has also given the epithet of fly-eater, or *muscivorum,* to this flower. The same purpose is effected in the *dipsacus,* vulgarly called teasel, by a basin or receptacle of water, placed round each joint of the stem.

The nauseous and pungent juices of some vegetables, and the fragrance of others, are bestowed upon them, in common with thorns and prickles, for their defence against the depredations of animals. Many trees and shrubs supply grateful food to a variety of creatures, and would be quickly devoured, were they not armed with thorns and stings, which protect them not only against some kinds of insects, but also against the naked mouths of quadrupeds. It is worth remarking, as a further analogy between plants and animals, that the former frequently lose their thorns, &c. by cultivation; as wild animals are deprived of their ferocity, by living in a domestic state, under the government and protection of man. My letter is already spun out to a tedious length; I must, therefore, reserve the description of the fructification 'til a future opportunity. Adieu: your

FELICIA

Letter V

SHRUBBERY, MARCH 1

It is with renewed pleasure I devote the present half hour to your service, since you assure me that my letters contribute to your amusement, and that you pursue the same object that occupies me daily, from the hints I have given you. I wish you had a better guide, who could satisfy your enquiries, and animate your industry by superior skill. Affection and a desire to please will stimulate me to repeat Mrs.

Woodbine's lectures accurately. I wish I may be able to give you a clear idea of what I describe: but, as I find it difficult to express forms and shapes by writing, I believe I shall be obliged to have frequent recourse to my pencil, which will represent, in a more lively manner, the pleasing objects of our present researches. In order to assist you in the examination of the minute parts of small flowers, it will be necessary to provide a magnifying glass, a needle, a lancet, and a pair of small scissors, to render the dissecting them easier; as many of their parts are too delicate to be handled, a pair of small nippers will be a useful addition to the instruments that I have already named. Although I have wandered far from the subject, I have not forgotten my promise of describing the curious mechanism exhibited in the structure of the pea-flower.

On examining this elegant and wonderful blossom (f. 109,) you will observe that the calyx is of one piece, divided at the edge into five segments, or distinct parts, two of which are wider than the other three, and are situated on the upper side of the calyx, while the three narrower ones occupy the lower part. The corolla is composed of four petals; the first is broad and large, covering the others, and standing, as it were, on the upper part of the corolla, to defend and shelter it from the injuries of the weather, in the manner of a shield; by way of pre-eminence it is called the Standard, or Banner. In taking off the standard, remark how deeply it is inserted on each side, that it may not easily be driven out of its place by the wind. The side petals, distinguished by the name of wings, are exposed to view by taking off the banner. They are as useful in protecting the sides of the flower, as the banner is in covering the whole. Take off the wings, and you will perceive the keel, called so on account of its fancied resemblance in shape to the bottom of a boat: this encloses and preserves the centre of the flower from harm, which its delicate texture might receive from air and water. If you are curious to examine the contents of this little casket, slip the keel gently down, and you will discover a membrane terminated by ten distinct threads, which surround the germ, or embryo, of the legume or pod. The uppermost of these threads, or filaments (f. 157,) is not united to the rest, but each is tipped with a yellow anther, the farina of which covers the bearded stigma, that terminates the style, or grows along the side of it. The filaments form an additional defence to the germ, from external injuries. As the other parts decay and fall off, the germ gradually becomes a legume, or pod. This legume is distinguished from the silique of the cruciform tribe, by the seeds being fastened to one side only of the case, or shell, though alternately to each valve of it. Compare the pod of a pea and that of a stock together, and you will immediately perceive the difference. The foot-stalk which supports this flower is slender, and easily moved by the wind. In wet and stormy weather the pea turns its back to the storm, while the banner enfolds the wings, by closing about them, and partly covers them; they perform the same office to the keel, containing the essential parts of the fructification. Thus is this flower curiously sheltered and defended from its natural enemies, rain and wind; and, when the storm is over, and fair weather returns, it changes its position, as if sensible of the alteration, expands its wings, and erects its standard as before. Wonderful are the means of preservation, used by the all-wise Creator, to defend the tender and important parts of the fructification of plants from injury; but he seems to have provided, in an especial manner, for the security of those which serve as nourishment to men and animals, as does the greater part of the leguminous or pulse kind. I imagine, by this time, that you are pretty well acquainted with the several parts that compose a flower, and would recognize them, though in an individual that was an utter stranger to you. Confirm your knowledge by practice, and do not suffer a day to pass without amusing yourself in dissecting some flower or other. When you are perfectly acquainted with this entrance to the science, Mrs. Woodbine says that I may proceed to give you a sketch of the arrangement and classification of plants; for it is by method only that it is possible to obtain a knowledge of so many particulars. Botany would be indeed a most fatiguing and almost unattainable science were we obliged to learn the peculiarities of every plant, one by one; but the difficulty ceases, or at least is greatly diminished, by classing those together, in which there is a similarity in some one point. Eminent naturalists have, at different times, exerted their talents to perform this task. Tournefort is a name that was highly distinguished on this list, before the time of Linnaeus, whose superior genius has raised him above all his predecessors, and whose system is now universally adopted ...

Letter VI

SHRUBBERY, MARCH 6

Dear Sister,

I am fearful, lest by this time you are wearied with my minute descriptions of the separate parts of flowers and plants, and that you wish for something more amusing. Botany, like all other sciences, has its elements, which must be patiently learned by the pupil, before sufficient knowledge can be obtained, to enjoy the most pleasing parts of it. I have already hinted the necessity of forming some system, that may reduce the innumerable species of the vegetable kingdom to the compass of human memory and comprehension. All the known vegetable productions upon the surface of the globe have been reduced by naturalists to Classes, Orders, Genera, Species, and Varieties. The CLASSES are composed of Orders; the Orders are composed of Genera; the Genera of Species; and the Species of Varieties. Let us endeavour to obtain a clearer idea of Classes, Orders, &c. by comparing them with the general divisions of the inhabitants of the earth.

Vegetables resemble mankind in general;

Classes—Nations of men;

Orders—Tribes, or divisions of nations;

Genera—The families that compose the tribes;

Species—Individuals of which the families consist;

Varieties—Individuals under different appearances.

Do not think, dear sister, that I am capable of methodizing so accurately, without the kind assistance of one who superintends my letters, and points out what I should write: it is not necessary to say, that Mrs. Woodbine is that attentive, affectionate friend, who will not allow me to do anything without some degree of regularity. Many great men, as I told you in my last, have formed systems after different plans. Those of Tournefort and Linnaeus are most esteemed. Both are ingenious; but as that of Linnaeus has superseded all others, it will not be necessary to confuse your memory with any other; his being the universally adopted, it is that in which it is proper to be completely instructed.

Linnaeus, dissatisfied with every system invented before his time, undertook to form a new one, upon a plan approaching nearer to perfection, and depending on parts less liable to variation. The stamens and pistils are the basis of his classification. He has divided all vegetables into twenty-four classes. These classes are subdivided into nearly one hundred orders; these orders include about two thousand families, or genera; and these families about twenty thousand species, besides the innumerable varieties produced by the accidental changes of cultivation, soil, and climate. As you have acquired accurate notions of stamens and pistils, you will find but little difficulty in making yourself mistress of the classes and orders: the former depending principally upon the number, the length, the connexion, or the situation of the stamens; the latter are founded, in the thirteen first classes, on the number of pistils; in the others, on circumstances to be hereafter explained. The characters of the genera are marked from some particulars in the flower, unnoticed in the definitions of the classes or orders. The specific description includes *all* the most obvious appearances in the flower. In a science depending so much on observation and minute definitions, it is advisable for you to proceed step by step, and make yourself perfectly acquainted with the classes, before you advance to the orders. Should you gather a flower, in order to know to what class it belongs, observe, first, whether it be a perfect flower, containing both stamens and pistils; if that be the case, examine whether the stamens are entirely separate from the pistil and each other, from top to bottom. If you find that they are perfectly distinct, and not so many as twenty, the number of them alone will be sufficient to determine the class ...

Letter VIII

SHRUBBERY, APRIL 2

Whenever you set out on a botanical excursion, remember to put your magnifying glass and dissecting instruments into your pocket, that you may not be obliged to neglect those flowers that are small, for want of this precaution. Always gather several flowers of the same kind, if possible; some just opening, and others with the seed-vessels almost ripe: and as I intend to select our examples from plants of British growth, you must seek for them growing wild in their native fields, and not confine your walks within the limits of a garden wall. Thus, I hope, you will obtain health and a knowledge of vegetables at the same time. That nothing might be left undone by Linnaeus, the great master of method and arrangement, to render the acquisition of his favourite science easy, he has divided the orders, when numerous, into several divisions, each including one genus or more, which is a means of diminishing the pupil's labour. Let us suppose that you have a plant under observation, belonging to an order that contains a great number of genera: you are confused, and know not to which to refer it. But on remarking these divisions, you are enabled to place it among a few of its brethren: there remains but little difficulty to discover its peculiar marks, and to assure yourself of the identical plant. The first class, MONANDRIA, contains but two orders, both depending upon the number of the pistils. Most of these plants are natives of India. Our ditches and muddy ponds, however, produce one example, that you may easily procure. It is called *Marestail,* (Hippùris,) and has neither calyx nor corolla. Its single stamen grows upon the receptacle, terminated by an anther slightly cloven, behind which you will find the pistil, with its awl-shaped stigma, tapering to a point. The stem is straight and jointed; and the leaves grow in whorls, round the joints;

at the base of each leaf is a flower, so that the number of flowers and leaves is equal. Its season of flowering is the month of May. As there are but few objects of native growth to arrest our attention in this class, we will proceed to the next, the class DIANDRIA.

The *Privet* (Ligustrum) is a shrub common enough in the hedges in many parts of England, and, when mixed with other shrubs, makes a pleasing variety in our gardens. It bears a white blossom, and generally flowers in June. It has a very small tubular calyx of one leaf, and its rim is divided into four parts. The blossom is also monopetalous and funnel-shaped, with an expanded border, cut into four egg-shaped segments. Its stamens are two, which determine it to belong to this class, placed opposite to each other, and nearly as long as the blossom. The seed-bud is roundish, the style short, and terminated by a thick, blunt, cloven stigma. The seed-vessel is a black berry, containing but one cell, which encloses four seeds. The leaves grow in pairs, and are sometimes variegated with white or yellow stripes. The berries are useful to the dyers, as they give a durable green colour to silk or wool, with the addition of alum.

In the second division of this order is a genus, the Latin name of which is *Veronica,* but commonly known by that of Speedwell. There are a great many species of it, which has induced Linnaeus to treat it in the same manner as the orders, and to divide it into three principal divisions. First, Flowers growing in spikes. Secondly, Flowers in broad bunches. Thirdly, Fruit-stalks with one flower. The monopetalous wheel-shaped corolla, divided into four segments, the lowest of which is narrower than the rest, and that opposite to it the broadest, easily distinguish this genus, as well as the heart-shaped, flatted capsule with two cells. Several of the species are cultivated, and increase the beauty of the flowerbeds in the early part of the summer. You will soon be tired of these descriptions, if you do not unite them to the living objects. Search for some others in the same class, and oblige me with your account of them. In this manner we may contribute to each other's amusement, though we cannot enjoy each other's company. Yours, with warm affection,

FELICIA

'The passion for public speaking'

WOMEN'S DEBATING SOCIETIES

◆

BY DONNA T. ANDREW

Writing of the intellectual and historical background of Mary Wollstonecraft's *Vindication*, her biographer has noted:

> The overwhelming majority of Englishwomen of the time had known little freedom ... The majority of women of the eighteenth century accepted their inferior status without complaint ... They had their little liberties and their little triumphs, but always they were obliged to confine themselves to such liberties and triumphs as were approved by the code in which they lived. They were bound, as [Wollstonecraft] said in 'silken fetters'.

Accounts like this one portray Wollstonecraft as a shooting star, miraculously escaping the iron gravity that bound most of her contemporaries, briefly illuminating the sky and then tragically sinking out of sight. But historians have grown sceptical of these sorts of explanations and have begun to contextualize the life and writings of this remarkable woman. This new historical activity is not designed to denigrate Wollstonecraft; rather it strives to re-create the social milieu that nourished her and made her writings popular. To date, this contextualizing effort has been most successful in embedding Wollstonecraft's thoughts in a framework of the radical political

Rowlandson & Pugin, 'Debating Society' (detail). Engraving, from *The Microcosm of London*, 1904.

ideas and practice that characterized London's extraordinary community of rational dissenters. What I wish to do is to suggest another context—an earlier, larger and more public context—in which Wollstonecraft's project would seem neither radical nor surprising. To do this, an introduction to a wildly successful form of contemporary entertainment, the debating society, is necessary. Costing only 6 pence for the evening (half the price of the cheapest theatre ticket) these clubs advertised a question for discussion, allowed comments and views from the audience, then voted at the end of the evening on the outcome of the debate.

Though some version of male debating societies had been around for several decades, by the late 1770s many of the societies moved from pubs to places more accessible to virtuous females, and with this move, liquor (and rowdiness) tended to decrease. The total number of such societies in the metropolis grew enormously. By the end of 1780, thirty-three separate venues were operating all over the city; meetings often drew between 400 and 1,200 people a night. Finally, in 1780, four all-female debating societies were founded— La Belle Assemblee, the Female Parliament, the Female Congress and the Carlisle House Debates for Women—where men could attend, but only women could speak. This proliferation of both separate and mixed-gender societies made it possible, and profitable, to discuss topics of particular interest to women: love, marriage and sexuality as well as the education and social role of women.

The following items are derived from the advertisements these societies placed in London papers and from subsequent reports of those debates. They display both the range of topics discussed, and the mixed reactions of Londoners to this novel form of public entertainment. I have chosen to concentrate on the year 1780 and to give merely a sample of the sorts of debates and newspaper comments that such discussions aroused when unnamed women and men expressed in debate, not in print, their views on those 'silken fetters'.

Announcements of the Meetings and Reports on the Debates
1780

They all have to do about appearance, or how to attract man or relationships.

JANUARY 4

The Oratorical Academy, Old Theatre, Portugal Street

Ought the bold or the timid lover to succeed best with the ladies?

Mr Dodd, President

London Courant

JANUARY 5

Coachmakers Hall

Would it not be a just and equitable law, that every man who had seduced a woman should be obliged to marry her?

Gazetteer, January 4

JANUARY 18

Oratorical Academy

Is female beauty more often of advantage or detriment to the possessor?

London Courant, January 17

JANUARY 27

Coachmakers Hall

Whether the virtues and qualifications of men, or those of women, are most conducive to the good and happiness of society?

Gazetteer, January 25

FEBRUARY 8

The Oratorical Academy is removed to the Mitre Tavern, Fleet Street
Is the prude or the coquette, the most odious character?
LONDON COURANT, FEBRUARY 5

FEBRUARY 22

LONDON COURANT:

The passion for public speaking is become epidemical, not content with Forums, Apollo's, Lyceum, and Schools of Eloquence, we have now on the tapis La Belle Assemblee, which is to be opened this week at the Haymarket. This plan, we are informed, is set on foot by several ladies of distinguished abilities in the literary world, where public and free debate will be agitated by ladies only.

FEBRUARY 26

La Belle Assemblee
Whether oratory is, or should be, confined to any sex?
The chair will be taken by Rev. Mr Phillips ... Admittance two shillings each.
LONDON COURANT, FEBRUARY 24

FEBRUARY 28

MORNING CHRONICLE:

There were 700 persons at Mr Greenwood's Room on Saturday evening to pay their compliments to La Belle Assemblee; some of the ladies spoke well, but the moderator appeared to be but very moderately qualified for his office. After quitting a post he gave no proof of his being fit to hold, a sprightly female seized it, and entertained the audience highly by an excellent recital of a well-known poetical tale. Various are the opinions formed by the public, of the entertainments to be presented on Wednesday evening at the Haymarket; some think the fabricators are suborned by the Majority, to ridicule the associations, others, that the protests are their subject of satire, and others, that the Lord-Mayor of London, and Court of Alderman, are to be virulently abused.

A correspondent informs us that a most exact representation of the House of Commons, is to be exhibited at the Haymarket next Wednesday evening, and a mock budget to be opened in the manner, and in imitation of the peculiarities of the noble Lord, to whose share this important part of the national business generally falls.

MARCH 4

La Belle Assemblee

Would it be sound policy to make the Salique Law general?*

The debate to be wholly maintained by ladies, but, for the sake of preventing tumult, a gentleman will be in the Chair.

LONDON COURANT

MARCH 6

LONDON COURANT:

The meeting at La Belle Assemblee on Saturday night was exceedingly crowded, many gentlemen being obliged to go away for want of room. Among the female part of the Assembly were many ladies, who, while they *struck the sight* with the elegance of their persons, displayed in the debate such superior accomplishments and refined understandings, as may truly be said *to win the soul.* The subject for that evening's discussion was *Whether it would be sound policy to make the Salique Law general?*

There were several speakers who took different sides of the question, which, nevertheless, was disputed with the utmost candour and moderation, and with real ability. Those ladies, who were for abolishing a law so tyrannical to the softer sex, instanced the glorious reigns of our Elizabeth, of Margaret of Denmark, and Christina of Sweden, while others, who, with humble modesty, were for declining all female pretensions to imperial sway, urged that from the natural softness and sensibility of their minds, women were too liable to be seduced from their attention to the public weal by the smooth and

* The Salic Law, as it is commonly spelled today, was the rule that certain aristocratic and dynastic families followed to bar women (as well as descendants in the female line) from succeeding to titles and offices.—ED.

silken parasites who constantly infest a court, and who leave no arti-fice unemployed to captivate and ensnare the weaker sex. One of the fair orators asserted in a charming tone, that 'there was one ingredi-ent in the cup of sovereignty, which ought peculiarly to discourage females from tasting its flattering contents'. It is, said she, when the rigid voice of inexorable justice demands the execution of the guilty delinquent; how shall woman, with all the trembling tenderness and sympathetic pity of her sex, sign the dreadful warrant denouncing death! This sentiment, delivered in a most graceful and expressive manner, was received with universal, and repeated tokens of deserved applause. A most elegant, and beautiful figure in one of the galleries, with a black mask on the upper part of her face, spoke with uncom-mon propriety, elegance and dignity. At ten o'clock the lady who opened the debate, rose up to speak some lines in conclusion, which however could not be heard, some persons among the audience, being shamefully noisy and tumultuous, but who on her sitting down called to her to proceed; the lady seemed confused, but replied, with great politeness to the gentlemen, that she should be very happy *to entertain them all night,* but that she had already finished what she had to say. The unguarded innocence of this expression produced a gen-eral laugh, which increasing her confusion, a very general acclamation of applause from the company made amends for the temporary dis-tress which they occasioned.

MARCH 11

La Belle Assemblee
Whether is connubial felicity more likely to arise from similarity or contrast of temper?
LONDON COURANT

MARCH 16

Coachmakers Hall Society
Does the present mode of educating the fair sex in boarding schools, con-tribute more to corrupt or to reform the manners of the rising generation?
LONDON COURANT

MARCH 17

MORNING CHRONICLE:

A correspondent informs us, that the next question of debate at the Ladies Assembly is, 'Whether such public publications as the pamphlet called the *Picture Gallery*, tend to improve or injure the morals of the sex'. As there are near two hundred of the most distinguished women in this kingdom taken notice of it in the above pamphlet, and very few of them pleased in an advantageous point of view, it is expected there will be a crowded room and warm debates; it is also said the author of the pamphlet intends to open the business, disguised in women's clothes, which he has borrowed of Lady L——, who is to accompany him.

MARCH 18

La Belle Assemblee
Whether variety is more predominant in the male or female breast?
LONDON COURANT

MARCH 22

Free Masons Hall, The Palladium, or Liberal Academy of Eloquence
What reason can be assigned for precluding the fair from the privilege of civil society, or from a liberal participation in their discussions?
Admittance two shillings and six-pence.
GAZETTEER

MARCH 25

La Belle Assemblee, Greenwood's Rooms in the Haymarket
Whether do the innocent gaieties of youth, or the mature wisdom of age, afford the greatest happiness?
N.B. It has been thought necessary to make some arrangements: For the future the galleries will be appropriated to ladies only; and in the other part of the house the ladies and gentlemen may sit together. Tea and coffee. Masks and dominos provided.
Admittance two shillings.

Such is the great propensity, as well as the propensity of the great, to frequent La Belle Assemblee, that on Saturday last soon after seven, Mr Greenwood's room was crowded with persons of the first distinction, and the street rendered impassable by the great number of coaches of nobility, gentry, &c. who had left their homes to hear the ladies argue.

GAZETTEER, MARCH 22

MARCH 27

MORNING CHRONICLE:

An admirer of every institution which has ever a probability of enlightening the understanding and polishing manners, was much pleased to see the first meeting at the Palladium at Free Mason's Hall, attended by so brilliant and respectable an audience. This institution most undoubtedly completes a system of oratory, upon a pleasing and rational plan; at the Belle Assemblee, ladies will accustom themselves to lay aside all mauvaise honte, and gentlemen become familiarized to their pleasing style: ladies by attending Carlisle House, will learn to adopt the eligible part of gentlemen's style of reasoning: and at Free Masons Hall both will have it in their power to display their talents, and give their unconstrained opinions.

APRIL 1

La Belle Assemblee

Is the spirit of duelling esteemed by the ladies, to proceed from a true or a false sense of honour?

The new arrangements that were made in the mode of sitting last evening, produced some inconveniences that will be provided against in future. Several applications to this purpose have been made by ladies who came with an intention to deliver their sentiments on the question, but who were intimidated by the company's sitting promiscuously. For the future, therefore, the lower part of the house and the galleries will be appropriated to the ladies only—the ladies and gentlemen may sit promiscuously in the other part of the room.

GAZETTEER

APRIL 2
Free Masons Hall, The Palladium or Liberal Academy of Eloquence
Whether is fortitude superior in the male or female breast?
Thirteen speakers; decided that 'fortitude was more superior in the female than in the male breast'.

Admittance two shillings and six-pence.
MORNING CHRONICLE, APRIL 3

APRIL 6
Coachmakers Hall
Is the practice of public oratory a fit accomplishment for the ladies?
On the decision of the question ... respecting the propriety of the ladies speaking in public, a numerous company were almost unanimously against it; so that, as our correspondent remarks, that species of female departure from a reserved and modest character is not chargeable on the ladies in general, nor on the public but only on some particular characters.
GAZETTEER, APRIL 4

APRIL 11
Oratorical Society, Old Theatre
Have not the ladies as good a right to a classical education as the men?
The lady who opened the question on Tuesday last being greatly confused by the repeated testimonies of applause given her by the society, it is earnestly requested in future of the ladies and gentlemen present to reserve their plaudits to the conclusion of the speech, when they will be more competent judges of the merits of the speakers; which will at the same time prevent the confusion that must obviously occur from the natural timidity of those who have but lately assumed their rights and privileges, by bursting those chains, with which through custom and illiberality, they have hitherto been fettered.

APRIL 12

MORNING POST:

Mr Adam, the famous combatant of Charles Fox, in a speech last Thursday night, at the Oratorical Academy, held at Coachmakers Hall, took an occasion to animadvert, with great severity, upon the Quakers. He was attacked, in reply, with very considerable acrimony, as well as great strength of argument, for the absurdity of pronouncing such vague unproved imputations against general characters and large bodies of men. A little struck with the impropriety of what he had said, Mr Adam rose again to apologize for his rashness, when a neat, genteel, well dressed, female Quaker, got up and said, 'Thou mayst hold thy peace; thou hast already spoken to very little purpose, and thou wilt hardly improve by saying more.' This brief rebuke, coming from so engaging a character, was received with the loudest applause, and Mr Adam was stunned into silence.

APRIL 21

Female Parliament, University for Rational Amusements

Is that assertion of Mr Pope's founded in justice which says, 'Every woman is at heart a rake'?

It was decided this was unjust.

LONDON COURANT

APRIL 21

The Palladium or Liberal Academy of Eloquence

Is there not cruelty in the law, that punishes a woman with burning, for the same crime which a man is only hanged for?

GAZETTEER, APRIL 19

APRIL 22

La Belle Assemblee

Whether is jealousy the result of extreme love, or the effect of mental depravity?

The rooms are altered for the better accommodation of the ladies. Determined that jealousy was the result of extreme love. An Italian lady, who was supposed to have given the question, spoke to it herself.

GAZETTEER

APRIL 25

Oratorical Academy, Mitre Tavern

Is that maxim of the poet true, which affects, that
Women born to be controll'd
Stoop to the forward and the bold

This question was sent by some ladies who promised to join in the debate.

LONDON COURANT, APRIL 20

APRIL 28

Free Masons Hall, The Palladium, or Liberal Academy of Eloquence

Which is most in danger from flattery, a woman of singular beauty, or ample fortune?

GAZETTEER, APRIL 27

APRIL 28

University for Rational Amusements, Female Parliament

Are not male encroachments on female occupations, an hardship on the sex, which ought to be remedied by a restrictive law?

LONDON COURANT, APRIL 26

APRIL 29

La Belle Assemblee

Which is the most amiable accomplishment in woman, fine natural sense or extensive learning?

The debate was spirited, and the language pointed and chaste. The question was carried in favour of fine natural sense.

LONDON COURANT

MAY 1

School for Oratory, China-Hall, Rotherhithe

In most instances, where the affections of the female sex are improperly attached, who is most blameable, the man or the woman?

GAZETTEER

MAY 2

GAZETTEER AND NEW DAILY ADVERTISER:

A *male* correspondent, who was on Saturday evening last at La Belle Assemblee at the Haymarket, was filled with chagrin and admiration; admiration at the very able manner the question then discussed [was] treated; and chagrin to perceive, that with all the disadvantages of education which the fair sex labour under, how infinitely superior those who are formed by nature *to excite* the *tender* passions, are to excite *every other.* In short, not only to lead captive by all the graces of colloquial harmony, of pure diction, of varied and expressive emphasis, of language clothed in the diversity of the several passions which were felt or wished to be personified, but likewise by sterling sentiments, founded in truth, forcibly directed to ultimate persuasion, and presenting in the whole to the attentive auditor, the *unmixed result* of well supported facts, or well-presumed premises, sufficient to bring home indubitable conviction to every mind capable of determining upon the only test of all human knowledge, logical conclusion, deduced from facts not denied, or premises not controverted.

MAY 2

Carlisle House, Ladies Only

Is the study of politics and the affairs of state compatible with the station and character of the fair sex?

LONDON COURANT, APRIL 29

MAY 2

Oratorical Society, Portugal Street

Which is more to be desired by a female, beauty or good sense?

MORNING CHRONICLE

MAY 2

ST. JAMES CHRONICLE:

Carlisle House

Tuesday evening a room was opened for debate by *Ladies only*, at this House. The inconsistency of this measure with the academical plan delivered to the public, and the advertisement of the moderator, that neither he nor the principal of the Academy had any concern in the business, gave the public a disadvantageous impression of it, as a desperate expedient of the tenants to get money.

The Chair was not taken 'til half after eight; and we were sorry to see that a gentleman of character should be the person engaged in such unworthy and dishonourable business. He proposed the question, to which some women spoke; or rather read speeches out of papers; but the chief dependence of the evening was on a Mr McNally in woman's clothes. He squeaked several speeches to eke out the time, but the offence taken at such an indecent artifice, and the impatience of the audience from want of entertainment, induced them to precipitate poor Marriott from the Chair, and to place an old discarded actress in his stead. She acquitted herself to the satisfaction of those who surrounded the Chair, and who seemed to wish, like the Praetorian Band, to be occupied in placing and displacing presidents. Whether the freedom of her behaviour, and the luxuriance of her language, aided by the appearance of men in women's clothes, may have any effect in rendering this Assembly popular, and profitable to the tenants, we leave to the determination of the public.

MAY 6

La Belle Assemblee, Mr Greenwood's Rooms in the Haymarket
Do the manners of the ladies, in the present day, tend more to invite the gentlemen to, or to deter them from matrimony?
LONDON COURANT, MAY 6

MAY 7

University for Rational Amusements, Female Parliament
Was Adam or Eve more culpable in Paradise?
LONDON COURANT

MAY 9

Carlisle House, Ladies Only

Is the diffident or resolute, the most persuasive lover?

LONDON COURANT, MAY 8

MAY 9

Oratorical Academy, Mitre Tavern

Can friendship subsist between the two sexes, without the passion of love?

LONDON COURANT, MAY 8

MAY 11

ST. JAMES CHRONICLE:

SIR,

At present I shall confine myself to that one head of the Hydra, called La Belle Assemblee. I am really, Sir, ashamed. I blush at seeing the lovely, tender, timid sex, appear in a light so very disadvantageous; and I am sorry for the countenance given to their eccentricity by the men, who, by insidious applauses, encourage the folly they laugh at.

Were it really a fact that these female orators were anything more than the *hired* reciters of a studied lesson, it would be very little to their honour: for what women of the slightest pretensions to modesty, or common decency could stand up in an assembly of a thousand persons, and hazard their thoughts and language on subjects which they are supposed never to have studied 'til the moment they begin to hold forth? Would not such assurance and effrontery render them absolutely disgustful? Is there a man on earth who from such a set of women would choose a wife? or a husband, father, or brother, who would not be shocked to find his sister, daughter or wife in this garrulous society?

But the truth is (and it is a fact in favour of the women who speak) their lessons are all composed for them; so that they have no more to do with the arguments they utter, than my pen has with the characters I force it to trace. But this though in favour of the *speakers*, is no sort of recommendation of the *society*, for our newspapers and magazines present us infinitely better essays on the same subjects, and these we may enjoy in our parlours, without the disadvantages of hearing them from mouths where they seem unnatural (for not the least trace of *feminine thinking* is to be found in these female orations), or having them clipped and murdered by a vulgar pronunciation.

INDIGNUS

MAY 13
La Belle Assemblee
Do the exhibitions of the stage tend more to the promotion of vice or virtue?
The arguments adduced by the fair orators were genteel and sprightly, free from that censure and invective which so ample a field might have afforded, and the question was unanimously carried, that stage exhibitions, well regulated, tend more to the promotion of *virtue*.

Tea-rooms open at six. Ice creams, &c.

GAZETTEER AND NEW DAILY ADVERTISER

MAY 16
Carlisle House, Ladies Only
Is not a liberal acquiescence with the prevalence of fashion, in the improvements of the person, as necessary as an attention to the cultivation of the understanding?

GAZETTEER

MAY 19
University for Rational Amusement, Female Parliament
Is an old woman marrying a young man, or a young woman marrying an old man, the more blameable?
As the decorations of the rooms gave such universal satisfaction on the night of the Carnival Masquerade, they will be illuminated this evening in the same style of elegance.

Admittance 2s6d. Refreshments of tea, coffee, capillaire, orgeat &c. included.

GAZETTEER

MAY 22

MORNING POST:

Lines on hearing the debates of the Female Parliament at the Casino
May 19, 1980

Lo! Now the mandate of despotic fate
Is fled—and women mingle in debate!
Op'd are those lips which bashful prudence clos'd,
And bar'd that breast where modesty repos'd.
Anxious in every course to win the bays,
They start, undaunted, candidates for praise!
But this ambition asks not for redress,
If human acts are measured by success!
Not *Fletcher* fills the Senatorial Chair
With more applause, than when a B——'s there.
Even in this infancy of female fame,
A Fox already lisps, and Burkes declaim!
An embryo minister the sex shall yield,
And young Minorities dispute the shield.
Ah! long victorious in the realms of Wit,
In all to thee must humbled man submit?
Content not *Phoebus'* envied heights to reach,
Ye claim the dormant privilege of *speech!*—
Learned-like, the lucky moment seize,
Gain what ye ask, and ask what'er ye please!
Thus the immortal Amazons of yore,
In *Mar's* red field, the palm of conquest bore;
Even he, whose labours filled earth's circuit wide,
Here first in arms a foe superior try'd.
To pining youths, who left the myrtle bough,
And plucked the laurel from the warrior's brow!

MAY 26
MORNING CHRONICLE:
The encouragement shown by the public to the Female Parliament, makes it almost as difficult to obtain a seat at the Casino, Marlborough Street, as at the Great House of Parliament in Westminster.

MAY 27
Coachmakers Hall
Is the man who never marries, or he who marries merely for pecuniary advantage, the greater enemy to the fair sex?
GAZETTEER, MAY 25

SEPTEMBER 21
Debating Society, King's Arms Tavern, Cornhill
Would it not be conducive to the happiness of the marriage state, that no woman should have a marriage portion?
GAZETTEER, SEPTEMBER 20

SEPTEMBER 27
MORNING CHRONICLE:
On a late decision, by the King's Arms Society, 'That the
Abolition of portions would be conducive to matrimonial happiness.'
As 'twas lately determin'd, that no one from hence,
When taking a wife, should accept of few pence;
'Tis presum'd, that the ladies in gratitude ought
To prefer the poor lover, who's not worth a groat:
That thus destitute both, they both may be sure,
Themselves are alone, not their purses the lure.
Then contemplate ye lads, and ye lasses, the blisses!
When sans bread and cheese, you exist but on kisses!
And if love, in nine months, a fine boy should complete,
They who live but on love, sure its produce may eat!
So cherish your wives, all as much as you're able,
As you value the sight of a joint at your table.

M. R.

OCTOBER 5
Coachmakers Hall
Would it not tend to the happiness of mankind, if women were allowed a scientific education?
GAZETTEER, OCTOBER 3

OCTOBER 5
King's Arms Society
Is the general charge of depravity of manners more applicable to the male or female character?
The room is conveniently adapted for the accommodation of the ladies.
GAZETTEER, OCTOBER 3

OCTOBER 14
La Belle Assemblee
Ought not the women of Great Britain to have a voice in the election of Representatives, and be eligible to sit in Parliament as well as the men?
LONDON COURANT

OCTOBER 18
MORNING POST:
On Saturday evening La Belle Assemblee opened for the winter season, and were honoured with a very brilliant and respectable audience. The debate was admirably supported, and many pointed good things said which would be no discredit to a much higher assembly. Several ladies who evidently came as auditors with no intent to speak, could not refrain from favouring the audience with their sentiments, in a language remarkably chaste, elegant and convincing. A well wisher to this *nouvelle* and rational amusement, recommends to the proprietors to make three prices instead of one, and have boxes, pit, and gallery, for which the place is well calculated. Thus would the pockets and persons of each class be more agreeably accommodated.

OCTOBER 21

La Belle Assemblee

Would it not be for the benefit of society, if the plan of female education was extended to the arts and sciences?

Places may be taken for the boxes 3s. Pit 2s. Gallery 1s.

LONDON COURANT, OCTOBER 19

OCTOBER 27

MORNING POST:

A correspondent observes with pleasure, that the wise resolution of the Common Council to exclude their wives from the Lord Mayor's feast, is to become the subject of debate and ridicule of the ladies of La Belle Assemblee. He should not be surprised, if it should turn out that the question originated with one of the offended ladies, that they might have an opportunity of making reprisals. There is no doubt but that it will afford ample scope for laughter and ridicule, and should Mrs——, who has been a constant patroness of La Belle Assemblee, take it into her head to communicate her sentiments on the subject, she will undoubtedly be able to give the most highly finished picture of the Aldermanic body, as she is certainly more acquainted with the *constitution* and *abilities* of the Court than all the poets or poetesses of England.

OCTOBER 28

La Belle Assemblee

Was it consistent with justice or politeness to think of excluding the ladies of the Common Council from the Lord-Mayor's feast?

LONDON COURANT, OCTOBER 26

NOVEMBER 2

Coachmakers Hall

Which is to be preferred in the choice of a wife, beauty without fortune, or fortune without beauty?

GAZETTEER, OCTOBER 31

NOVEMBER 11
La Belle Assemblee
*Can the Rev. Mr Madan's doctrine of a plurality of wives be justified
either by the laws of policy or religion?*
LONDON COURANT, NOVEMBER 9

NOVEMBER 16
King's Arms Society
*Can the doctrine of a celebrated Divine, in his treatise in behalf of a plu-
rality of wives, be justified upon the principles of religion, reason, or
sound policy?*
GAZETTEER AND NEW DAILY ADVERTISER, NOVEMBER 14

NOVEMBER 16
Coachmakers Hall
*Is it the love of the mental or personal charms of the fair sex, that is more
likely to induce men to enter into the married state?*
GAZETTEER, NOVEMBER 14

NOVEMBER 19
Christian Society
Genesis iv. vers. 19 *'And Lamech took unto him two wives'.*
MORNING CHRONICLE, NOVEMBER 18

NOVEMBER 30
Coachmakers Hall
*Is not the deliberate seduction of the fair, with an intention to desert, under
all circumstances worse than murder?*
GAZETTEER, NOVEMBER 28

DECEMBER 2
La Belle Assemblee
Whether the sports of the field are proper amusements for the ladies?
LONDON COURANT, NOVEMBER 30

DECEMBER 10

School of Theology, Coxe's Museum, Spring Garden

'Wherefore they are no more twain, but one flesh'. St. Matthew ch. xix, vers. 6. This text is selected as a critique upon Mr Madan's defense of polygamy.

Admission 1 shilling.

DAILY ADVERTISER, DECEMBER 9

DECEMBER 11

Robin Hood, Butcher Row, Temple Bar

Whether any increase of population on the Rev. Mr Madan's plan would compensate for the confusion polygamy would create in society?
Admittance (men only) six-pence, liquor included.

This undertaking is at the instance of many gentlemen desirous of renovating the old constitution of debating societies.

Adjourned.

MORNING CHRONICLE

DECEMBER 12

The Female Congress, Great Room, at the late King's Arm Tavern, Cornhill, for Ladies Only

Was Adam or Eve the more culpable in Paradise?

Admittance one shilling.

LONDON COURANT, DECEMBER 5

DECEMBER 14

Coachmakers Hall

Whether, if the idea of indelicacy, which custom has affixed to any advances of the fair sex, to enter into the married state, was abolished, it would not tend to the happiness of both sexes?

GAZETTEER, DECEMBER 12

DECEMBER 14

MORNING POST:

Last Tuesday evening a society for debate by *Ladies only* was opened at the late King's Arms Tavern, Cornhill, under the name of the Female Congress. The company was splendid and respectable, and so very numerous, that there was a considerable overflow. The chair was taken by a lady, who made an elegant exordium, which lasted near twenty minutes. She traced the practice of eloquence through the medium of the debating societies, 'til at length ladies were admitted to speak. She paid a delicate compliment to the Belle Assemblee, as the first institution in which women were restored to their natural rights, and declared the Female Congress was not opened from any spirit of rivalry or opposition, but solely to accommodate the ladies of the east and south ends of the town, whom the distance of the Haymarket deprives of hearing ladies debate so frequently as they might wish. She then mentioned the common objections, or rather cavils, against women speaking in public, and very ably defended the propriety of it, as well as the character of such who spoke. During the whole evening she maintained the dignity of the chair, and filled it with astonishing ability, so as to convince all present, that where a woman can be found equal to the task, a *woman alone* ought to preside over a *female society.* The debate that ensued was carried on with great spirit and vivacity. Some of the ladies were capital in wit, humour, and eloquence, and all were agreeable, though it was apparent that *three* of them spoke under the disadvantages consequent on a first attempt: in short, the company were entertained with twelve pleasing speeches, and departed after giving every mark of general approbation.

DECEMBER 19

Female Congress, King's Arms Tavern, Cornhill

Does jealousy in women more frequently arise from love or pride?
Admission one shilling.

GAZETTEER, DECEMBER 16

...iety
...e of advantage to the fair sex, that every man who had
...oman, should be obliged to marry her?
...TTEER, DECEMBER 19

DECEMBER 28
King's Arms Society
Does not the present mode of educating females in boarding schools greatly prejudice their rising morals?
GAZETTEER, DECEMBER 26

'The vortex of dissipation'

GEORGIANA, DUCHESS OF DEVONSHIRE

◆

BY PHYLLIS DEUTSCH

Born to John Spencer (the first Earl Spencer) and Georgiana Margaret Poyntz on 7 June 1757, Georgiana Spencer was raised in the comfortable and cosmopolitan world of the Whig élite. As a child, she travelled extensively with her parents on the Continent, where she acquired fluency in French and Italian, along with a more general appreciation of European art and culture. When she was sixteen, the Spencers arranged her spectacular marriage to William Cavendish, fifth Duke of Devonshire and one of the richest men in England. Georgiana was married in Wimbledon on 5 June 1774. She was not yet seventeen. The duke, nine years her senior, brought to the marriage a mistress, an illegitimate child and the manners of a man of the *ton*. Georgiana brought a native intelligence, a warm heart and a penchant for gambling that virtually ruled her life.

Like most late Georgian noblewomen, Georgiana wrote voluminous letters, mostly to her mother, but also to her sister, Harriet; to her banker, Thomas Coutts; and to assorted celebrities of the British and French élites. She also wrote to Lady Elizabeth Foster, a dear friend and the duke's mistress from 1782 until his death in 1811. Indeed, the Devonshires supported Lady Foster and the two children she and the duke conceived; the success of this long-term *menage á trois* suggests the flexibility of aristocratic sexual mores as late as 1800.

Thomas Gainsborough, 'Georgiana, Duchess of Devonshire' 1783. Andrew
W. Mellon Collection, Board of Trustees, National Gallery of Art, Washington.

Georgiana wrote passionately about politics, society, her health, her husband and her children. There were four: Georgiana (b. 1783), Harriet (Harry-o, b. 1785), William Hartington (Hart, b. 1790) and Eliza Courtney, her child by Charles, second Earl Grey (b. 1792). Mostly, however, she wrote about her gambling debts and how to manage them. Indeed, an early autobiographical novel, *The Sylph* (1777), recounts the misadventures (and ultimate salvation) of a newlywed bride ensnared by her husband's self-serving gamester friends. The duchess also wrote poetry (in English and French) and plays.

Given the volume of written material she has left us, it is a challenge to select letters that convey the richness and difficulty of the duchess's life. To simplify matters, I've chosen correspondence focusing on two central issues: politics and debts. The first set of letters concern the hotly contested Westminster election (February-April 1784), in which Whig statesman Charles James Fox sought re-election to one of two seats in that borough. Fox, the duchess's candidate and, like her, a well-known gamester, opposed increasing the power of the king and the House of Lords at the expense of the Commons. Fox's chief opponent (although not running against him directly) was the Tory leader William Pitt, whose sober image in the popular press sharply opposed the public's view of Fox as an unregenerate gamester.

Fox's campaign was unusual (even notorious) for its demotic pretensions and for the public violence it engendered. In addition, Fox came under fire for his extensive use of noblewomen as canvassers. The duchess, who loved politics, canvassed on foot for Fox in the crowded city borough of Westminster; her sister Harriet and several other noblewomen joined her. Georgiana, young, beautiful and ardent, was most visible, however, and as her letters imply, she got most of the negative press. These letters suggest the paradoxes and limitations of noblewomen's political participation in the late eighteenth century.

The second set of letters is correspondence from January-May 1787—a particularly bad year for the Devonshire expenses. An incessant gambler, the duchess had accrued serious debts in the course of her marriage. In her extremity, she turned to Thomas Coutts, a well-respected Scots banker. From his office in the Strand, Coutts served a pantheon of élite English debtors, including the Prince of Wales and several of his royal brothers. As the tone of Georgiana's letters to him suggests, Coutts was as much mentor and friend to her as moneylender; he did not, in fact, fully recover all she owed him (over £20,000) until several years after her death.

Other letters in this sequence show how Georgiana's gambling—indeed, her indebtedness—fit into a larger cultural pattern of aristocratic spending. Indeed, deep play (gaming for high stakes) occurred in gentlemen's clubs and in aristocratic homes, as well as at Newmarket and other racetracks. Spending in excess of immediate capital was part of aristocratic show. Even after the duke called in the estates agent Heaton to recommend retrenchments at Chatsworth, their Derbyshire estate, the Devonshires barely altered their standard of living. Georgiana's gaming and indebtedness, then, must be contextualized within a wider critique of a spendthrift élite.

Nevertheless, Georgiana's response to her gaming and her debts was personal and profound. As a woman with extensive credit (because of her husband) but very little real income, she spent most of her life buying, co-ordinating and transferring bills, annuities and pledges. She worried constantly that her debts would destroy her. I've included Georgiana's letter to her son Hart, written three weeks before her death, and an epitaph she wrote for herself, to show that her life did not comprise merely, or only, familial, social and political interests. Her gambling remained, until her death, a critical component of daily existence. Her remorse over this was real; at the end, remorse was her prevailing emotion. Indeed, her final illness, painful, protracted and disfiguring, itself signalled just how much her life of chance had cost her.

FROM THE CORRESPONDENCE

ON POLITICS

The Duchess to her mother

[8 FEBRUARY 1784]

... It is a very odd thing and a great waywardness, I believe, in my nature, but often, especially when as now I feel nervous and shy, I had much rather converse with people I know but little of, than with those I know very much [better]. I feel a dread of going to London, tho' Lady Melbourne, whom I love, and Lady Jersey, whose society is so remarkably amusing, would certainly do the best to entertain and dissipate me ... I am really sorry politics goes to such a height. I am sorry Lord Fitz* was personal, tho' I believe it is diffi-cult to avoid it. I give you, I think, a little political lesson ev'ryday— here is one now. If Mr Pitt succeeds he will have brought about an event that he himself as well as ev'ry Englishman will repent ever after, for if the King and House of Lords conquer the House of Commons he will destroy the consequence of that house and make the government quite absolute, for a majority in the House of Lords is always in the King's power by creating new peers. Now there are people and (tho' we never hear them mentioned without horror) well meaning people perhaps, who are call'd King's friends, who from being shock'd at the personal violence that has been some-times us'd against the King, and from having a love of kings and an

* The second Earl Fitzwilliam

awe at the idea of them, that would not think this absolute power a bad thing; but the proof that it is, and that the constitution we have hitherto enjoy'd is a good one, is, that [in] spite of ev'ry public misfortune and of a ruinous war, England is still a flourishing and glorious country, and bore her losses better than any other country could do. You see then that those who are interested in the welfare of their country, for I declare I believe the D. of P.* and Lord Fitz to be as honest and independent disinterested men as ever breath'd, cannot without some degree of warmth and disdain see a young man take upon him, and rest it upon its being his *opinion,* the entirely changing the happy constitution of his country. This is an odious subject and yet considering all things, do what one will, it is a subject one must think and feel about.

◆

The Duchess to her mother

[? MARCH 1784]

... The Duke is, I fancy, going to York. I should wish to be with you during his absence, but the Duke thinks that my being in town without [him] will have a good effect, as in case of there having been any ill natur'd reasons given for our stay out of town it will show his confidence in me.

You cannot conceive how good he has been, and he knows everything, but when I shall see you I shall explain more to you.

◆

The Duchess to her mother

MARCH 17TH 1784

... I went to the opera with Lady Jersey and my sister, the *Reine de Golconde.* It was very pretty and the march I compos'd in it. The Prince has been blooded three times today, he has drunk himself into this illness.

* The third Duke of Portland

I have seen again a whole tribe. D'Adhémar* is all humble to me, but I hear he says nothing can equal *le despotisme de M. Fox que la bassesse de ses amis*. Lord William Gordon, you know, has been a rat and chang'd sides. They thought he would not, as he jok'd 'til the last, asking them if they saw his tail growing, it is to oblige his brother. All our uncles din'd here today. The dissolution is not credited in the city ...

The Dss of Rutland came from her Cabinet dinner, which is a fact. The D. of Richmond din'd with her and the D., Lord Sidney and Lady Sidney.

> *In Rutland's place his Dss see*
> *Not shd the change surprise*
> *A prettier counsellor is she*
> *And at the least as wise.*

The idea is not mine but Charles F's, tho' the rhyme is mine ...

Tir'd to death, I am dressing for the opera. I am going out dingdong, but it shall not last. I am oblig'd to yield to those who wish to see me at first ...

George Hanger† has sent me a black boy, 11 years old and very honest, but the Duke don't like my having a black, and yet I cannot bear the poor wretch being ill us'd. If you lik'd him instead of Michel I will send him to you. He will be a cheap servant and you will make a Christian of him and good boy (perhaps a Sancho) ... I am tir'd to death with what I have gone thro' today. I can't get my bills in 'til the Duke and Heaton come back from York, and Heaton

---

* Count d'Adhémar, the French Ambassador.

† Afterwards fourth Baron Coleraine, though he refused to assume the title, preferring to be known as Colonel Hanger. He was a well-known figure in society and for some years a close friend of the Prince of Wales. He died unmarried in 1824 aged 73.

accuses me from this delay of want of confidence. In short, I wonder, for except by the D. I have been cruelly vex'd all day. I have made D'Adhémar, *tous courtisan quil est,* give me an opposition supper, Charles Fox, Grenville, D. of Portland, and all my tribe.

◆

The Duchess to her mother

SATURDAY THE 20TH [MARCH 1784]

I was at the opera, it was very full and I had several good political fights. Lady Sefton* says this is a great *aria* in the history of England. The Duchess of Rutland said D—— Fox, upon which Colonel St Leger with great difficulty spirited up Lady Maria Waldegrave† to say D—— Pitt. We had quite an opposition supper at D'Adhémar's much against the grain with him. There was Mr Fox, Grenville, Lord Malden‡, Colonel St Leger, all our men in short. We play'd a little after supper, and I very moderately won a few guineas ...

WEDNESDAY

The Election confusion is so great I can only tell you, my Dst M., that I shall be with you Saturday. The great seals were stole this morning. The King declar'd he would dissolve Parliament and it will be tomorrow ... I am dressing, and the D. of Portland and C. Fox are waiting in my room ...

◆

* Isabella, second daughter of the second Earl of Harrington; married the first Earl of Sefton (1748-95). She died in 1819.

† Charlotte Maria, second daughter and co-heir of James, second Earl Waldegrave, by Maria, illegitimate daughter of Sir Edward Walpole, brother of the Prime Minister. She married on 16 November 1784 George Henry, Earl of Euston, son of the fourth Duke of Grafton. She died in 1808 aged 46.

‡ Afterwards fifth Earl of Essex. As M.P. for Lostwithiel, and a supporter of the North and Fox coalition, he was one of those who lost their seats in 1784 and were known as 'Fox's Martyrs'. He was a player of the violoncello.

The Duchess to her mother

[MARCH-APRIL 1784]

I would give the world to be with you, for I am unhappy beyond measure here and abus'd for nothing, yet as it is begun I must go on with it. They will not give it up and they insist upon our all continuing to canvass. In short, they say, having begun and not going on would do a deal of harm. I shall go to church today, but I am really so vex'd (tho' I don't say so) at the abuse in the newspapers that I have no heart left. It is very hard they should single me out when all the women of my side do as much ... Dear Mama, I repent, as I often do, the part I have taken, tho' I don't see how I could have done otherwise. My Sr and Ly [name illegible] were both kiss'd, so it's very hard I who was not should have the reputation of it.

◆

The Duchess to her mother

[END OF MARCH OR EARLY APRIL 1784]

... We are ahead again today and have hopes, but the few unpoll'd people seem so resolv'd to be neuter that I know not how to hope. Have you any guile or anger in your Dear heart—if you have, call it forth from its lurking hole against the Dss of Beaufort, who was brutal enough to dispute with Miss Fielding, insisting upon it you would play again—and why should you not—why should you not have any amusement to your mind, and how dares she, with a heart the texture and merit of old wood, dry, harsh and worm eaten with envy, dare to talk of the intention of such an angel as you ...

◆

The Duchess to her mother

[? EARLY APRIL 1784]

... I give the Election quite up and must lament all that has happen'd. However, the circumstances I was in will justify me to those it is most essential for me to please, and I must *pocket* the opinions of the rest ...

◆

The Duchess of Portland to the Duchess

[APRIL 1784]

I do verily believe Mr Fox will succeed, every body seems to be of that opinion, if people will continue to exert themselves. I am worn out almost and must beg of you to come tomorrow. There are a great many votes that you can command and no one else, and now if you only stop at people's doors it will be quite sufficient, and really your presence is quite expected, so tomorrow morning pray be here early.

◆

The Duchess to her mother

[APRIL 1784]

As I felt tir'd and heated I don't go out, but my sister is gone to the opera quite well to sport her cockade. D'Adhémar, before he got my letter, boasted last night that he had *des sures,* and I believe he said, *bonnes nouvelles* that we should be beat, and so did Lady Essex—that our triumph was complete as the news came there. Charles Fox is last on the poll, but we hope to get forward on Monday, at all events St. Albans is a great comfort …

ON DEBTS

The Duchess to Lady Elizabeth Foster

MARCH THE 8 1784

At length, my ever dearest Bess, I am going to reveal the long kept secret from you. I should have told it you sooner but I knew that the very mention of my having been distress'd about such a thing as money would have alarm'd you, and made you fancy that what I have had the more than happiness of expending for you could have hurt me, and there too you would be mistaken for indeed, indeed, indeed, all that has come to you flow'd from Canis*, and if you ever try to prevent our being conducive to your comfort you will be cruel and make those that love you best in the world wretched. Before I say a word more you must promise, my dearest, dearest, dst angelic love, never to let Canis know I have told this secret to you, and you must neither change any way of living or give the least hint to him, unless you will make me wretched. You must know then, from circumstances I will tell you, I had incurr'd a very, very large debt. I never had courage to own it, and try'd to win it at play, by which means it became immense and was grown (I have not the courage to write the sum, but will tell you when I see you) many, many, many thousands. I would not tell Canis, (tho' I have kept absolute ruin to myself scarcely off) while I was with child and suckling, because I thought it ungenerous to be protected by my situation. Now that I was neither of these two I resolv'd to tell him, and I did with fear. What had I to offer for the kind of ruin I brought on him (for ev'ry year of my life I have cost him immense sums) a mind he could not trust in, a person faded, and 26 years of folly and indiscretion. And how do you think he has received the avowal—with the utmost generosity, goodness and kindness. His whole care has been that I may not vex myself, and you would think he was the offender, not me ... Now my Dst Dst Dst Bess, the little expense you are at is like a drop of water in the sea, and were you to retrench it would be making Canis and me cruelly feel the consequences of my extravagance. My angel Bess, write to me, tell me you don't hate me for this confession, oh love, love, love me ever.

◆

---

* The Duke of Devonshire.

Lady Spencer to the Duchess

JANUARY 4 1787

... I hope you are steady in your purpose of coming to Newmarket, and above all not residing in London this year. Think of the difficulties you will have to encounter, and the thousand disagreeable things that will be said, let your behaviour be what it will. Besides, between Newmarket and Bath the winter may pass easily. I dread the Duke's being persuaded by well meaning ill judging people to alter the fundamental plan about London, where I am sure there can be neither peace nor security for you at present.

◆

The Duchess to her mother

BUXTON THE 8TH [JANUARY 1787]

You are between 40 and 50, and I will not allow you to make yourself a day older. You are between 40 and 50 'til the 8th of May which is an age off ...

I shall be but 4 days in town then Newmarket for a good space with you or where you will. But Dearest, Dst M., I must entreat you from the bottom of my heart not to oppose about a fortnight or 3 weeks town between N. and Bath. The Duke's kindness is so great, and his plans of reform so *stable* and sensible, that if he desires this let me, Dearest, Dearest M., have the happy pride of giving him a specimen of my good behaviour, and of not by any great *éclat* and severity disgusting him with his plans. Our situation is much better than we thought. We are distress'd, but prudence will set us right, and you shall see you shall have no reason to repent your trust in me for so short a time.

◆

The Duchess to her mother

[14 JANUARY 1787]

... I must tell you that I am vastly pleas'd with Heaton. His appearance at first is against him, tiresome on ordinary subjects, with

200

some degree of insolence, but he has a comprehensive, laborious, active mind, and a spirit of order and regularity in the arrangement of business, very pleasing. He has just now finish'd the extricating the Duke of Portland from distress, and even by useful speculations gives him the prospect of affluence. I hope and think he will be as successful with us, as our case is not so desperate as their's was ... I think the plan of reduction will be Gilbert, Mason, 2 footmen and some of the horses, and as much as *can*, without hurting the interest, be reduc'd in keeping Chatsworth &cc. Any reduction that would hurt the interest would occasion a future expense. The Duke wishes it to be a *permanent reform,* not a violent and painful one for a year or two, but one that may go on. This would of course prevent entirely residing in one place, especially as the Duke wishes to be at Bath, but I shall be very little in town ...

◆

The Duchess to her mother

THURSDAY THE 25 [JANUARY 1787]

... I have made a good beginning, having forbid all milliner &cc. Dst M., I shall be with you in the lottery time and will only have 2 tickets and no insurance of any kind ...

◆

Lady Spencer to the Duke

NEWMARKET FEBRUARY 28 1787

... I am very conscious that I am the last person who ought to mention the subject of expenses, but indeed I am uneasy that no reform of any consequence has yet taken place, and I likewise dread the Dss's staying long in town, for her health and peace of mind as well as her pocket, for I am sure the money demands upon her must be very vexatious and troublesome. I have observed with pleasure that the very few things she bought here she paid for immediately, and tho' she has lost considerably for the moderate play we have had, it has been from a most obstinate and unalterable run of ill luck and not from gambling. As proof of this, I who have been her partner can answer for having won in the whole time but one single rubber at whist of two guineas.

◆

The Duchess to Thomas Coutts

MONDAY NIGHT 12TH MARCH 1787

With very little acquaintance, and that acquaintance having only given you a knowledge of my extravagance, I feel myself perfectly unauthoriz'd to the address I am making to you, and yet I cannot help applying to you, and feeling whether I will or not, a kind of confidence that you will befriend me. I must begin by informing you that whatever you do it is of essential importance to my ease and future happiness that you do not inform Craufurd of the measure I am taking. You were inform'd, I know, of his former goodness and assistance to me. Since that the Duke has step'd forth to the arrangement of my affairs, but I find I am still above the sum the Duke has in his mind allotted to my debt. The horror and misery I am at this moment in, I cannot express to you. I am indebted 1,200 to Mr Hammersley*, 1,000 to a person the steward has given his acceptance to, and which will bring him into distress if not paid, 1,100 more in small debts and 1,100 to you.

$$1,000$$
$$1,200$$
$$1,100$$
$$1,100$$
$$\overline{4,400}$$

That I have been more extravagant than can be conceiv'd is very true, but as true, I hope, that my mind is cur'd of its errors. But the despair that the Duke or even Craufurd's knowing of my distress would put me to, would, I am afraid, drive me to ev'ry ruinous expedient. If I am assisted the Duke will settle my affairs now, and at

*Thomas Hammersley (?1747-1812), banker in Pall Mall.

the end of a year that I shall have liv'd in prudence, will with pleasure, I am sure, reward me by the settling this debt. In this situation I
entreat and conjure you to give me this chance, this trial of my conduct. For one year from this day lend me 3,300. Give me the
chance of retrieving myself. I do not send you a common *note* but a
letter to the Duke in case of any accident to me. I must observe to
you that I have 2,000 a year, part of which I can pay to lessen this
in the course of the year. May I expect to see you Wednesday
morning at 11—and if you can give me any comfort by a line, I
entreat you to do it.

I enclose the stock you was so good as to purchase for me. I had
appropriated it for the establishment of a child whose parents were
related to me, but it must be better days before I can renew this
purpose. I am, dear Sir, your ever oblig'd.

◆

The Duchess to Thomas Coutts

[13 MARCH 1787]

Having been very ill thro' anxiety I have but this moment
receiv'd your letter, but you, oh, God bless you, restore me to peace,
health, happiness and prudence. It does indeed take me out of ev'ry
hand but yours. I have been so ill, with a return of the violent
spasms I had in the summer that I receive nobody, therefore shall
expect you directly, as there can be no fear of interruption. You
restore me to health and happiness, and my prudence shall prove my
gratitude. Pray, dear Sir, come directly, your ever affectionate.

◆

The Duchess to her mother

[17 MARCH 1787]

It is very true that I have been worry'd and distress'd to death.
The reason has been that from Martindale being paid a report has
got about that I have lost a new sum, some say at Newmarket ...

◆

The Duchess to her mother

MONDAY [19 MARCH 1787]

I write to you with more pleasure tonight than I have done hitherto, because *mes affaires sont en meilleure train et que je vois clair dans nos projets.* The reports of my new losses have been as cruel as false. I lost 40,000 at Newmarket—that is one, now 40,000 to Lady Essex, whom I never saw 'til Saturday, but the ridicule of these have cur'd them. I go a little more out as the staying at home increas'd the reports. I have however gone out sparingly. Cumberland House on Thursday, on Friday the rehearsal at Lady Aylesbury of Mrs Damer's play, which was delightfully acted, and then to Mrs St John. Saturday the opera, Sunday I had Morteloni here for Lady Bristol, Lady Clermont and a few men, and afterwards to D'Adhémar's ...

◆

The Duchess to Thomas Coutts

CHELTENHAM THE 24 MAY 1787

Your kind letter is an addition to all your other favours. I have the pleasure to assure you that I have not *play'd* once the whole season of my being in London, and that I am under a sacred promise with regard to playing at faro and insurance in the lottery, which no temptation could make me break. This promise and my never having play'd prevents me from entering into my opinion of a woman's gaming, because it is henceforward useless to me, but I assure you my opinion has ever coincided with yours, tho' I have so much err'd against it. All the money I shall ever have I will place in your hands and the purpose of making me more exact will be fully answer'd, especially if I keep a book likewise; but I must mention a few previous things to you. The Duke has paid amazing sums for me, he has taken now all my debts upon him, and pays them by degrees. It was arrang'd that my income was to be lessen'd from 2,000 a year to 600, but he has generously, and not to alter Mr Denne's* books, regiven me the 2,000 yearly. Only, what you will

* The Duke's banker.

think very natural for some time to come, when I receive my quarter I am to give him what part of it he wants. He always pays me my quarters and the moment I receive them I will pay them to you. The last money you advanc'd, dear Sir, is a distinct matter, and I shall be repaid it, and repay you, the first money at the end of the year. I have now no money, unless about 30£ has been paid to you since my departure. I suppose I shall have 250 of my summer quarter to pay you next month. My chief burden is a number of allowances or annuities to some relations, they amount to above 500 a year, and keep me very poor, as you may imagine, yet I cannot bear to stop them. Pray let me hear from you again, my dear Sir, and believe me your very affectionate G.D.

◆

The Duchess to her mother

[CHELTENHAM, 28 MAY 1787]

... In a few days I shall be 30, a great period of my life over, and, God knows, over in folly. However I hope from henceforward to bid adieu to many, many follies, I may, I hope, say with certainty to take leave of the follies that reflection may teach me to surmount, such as too great love of dissipation, admiration, dress—of those I have had enough to be even sick of them ...

◆

The Duchess to her son Hartington

MARCH 9TH 1806

... I feel and fear that I give too much latitude to my pleasure in writing to you, but indeed, indeed no mother ever lov'd a son as I do you. I live in you again. I adore your sisters, but I see in you still more perhaps than even in them what my youth was. God grant that you may have all its fervours and cheerfulness without partaking of many of the follies which mark'd with giddiness my introduction into the world. I was but one year older than you when I launched into the vortex of dissipation—a Duchess and a beauty. I ev'ry hour, however, thank my protecting angel that all I have seen never weaken'd my principles of devotion to Almighty God or took from my love of virtue and my humble wishes to do what is right. But I was giddy and vain. You will have great temptations in the same way, but you have judgment and sense to protect you ...

I hope to live to see you not only happy but the cause of happiness to others, expending your princely fortune in doing good, and employing the talents and *powers of pleasing,* with which nature has gifted you, in exalting the name of Cavendish even beyond the honour it has yet ever attain'd. God bless you, Dst Dst Hart. If it will not bore you I have sometimes an idea of sending you a history of your House, from the time of Elizabeth to the present day, to show you what you have belong'd to. But believe me, Dst Hart, when I tell you I *do* expect you to surpass them all, all except your dear father. He has a mind of most uncommon endowments, a rectitude few others could boast. Mr Fox and the finest men of the time look up to his judgment and sense. Dear Hart, banish but indolence, and add but a little activity to this character of your dear father, and you will bring him back with the only thing he wanted—*power to conquer idle habits, and to make the virtues that endear'd him to his friends of use to his country.*

◆

EPITAPH

And to God she offered
her deep contrition
And the sorrows of her life,
And her presumptuous hope
That the all good long suffering and all seeing Power,
Who best could know the extent of her errors,
Would, although dreadful in his judgements,
Compassionate and appreciate
Her repentance.

'I do no injury by not loving'

KATHERINE AUSTEN,
A YOUNG WIDOW OF LONDON

◆

BY BARBARA J. TODD

I first came to know Katherine Austen, a young widow who lived in Restoration London, by reading her manuscript journal in the British Library. In the small notebook of 114 pages, written mostly between 1664 and 1666, Austen recorded her poetry, notes on her reading, interpretations of her dreams, drafts of important letters and other personal records, as well as short essays of meditation and prayer. This volume is the only one that survives from the many similar notebooks Austen wrote, some of which she refers to here.

Although some passages, particularly her poems, were carefully transcribed from other notebooks, most entries were written in the heat of the moment: a few fragmentary lines, at most a couple of pages. Her handwriting was bold and vigorous; her punctuation and spelling haphazard. The fragmented spontaneity of her writing attracted me, because it offered direct insight into the mind of a woman grappling with her own personal crises during a turbulent time in English history. Katherine Austen's emotional responses to her experience, rather than the literary quality of her text, made this a fascinating manuscript. But because Austen's writings were never polished for publication, they badly needed to be illuminated by further research to be fully understood.[1]

So I began to reconstruct Austen's biography from records in other archives. When she started this notebook she was a thirty-five-

You all my three deare children ; That the Blessings
descended to you from the integrity and worthines of
all yor predecessors be a Blessing to discend in channells
to yor children ; and to many generations: And if
you doe yor parts by leading a commendable and use-
full lifes. and that you set vertuous Exsamples. God
will to every generation continue his favour who
is the ffountaine of all Blessings and happy Contint-
ment here, and. who has better blessings to crowne
our low and weake Endeavours with. Which that
to all you and yours may obtaine is the Unfained
prayers. and blessing of yor affectionate Mother.

Aug 28: 1665:   *Katherine Austen*

in goeing to Essex ye
28th Aug: the day be-
fore I went there
there was dead yt weeke
before I went.
900 :

Heavens goodnes was my ready Stay.
May not that kindnes goe away.
Thy former Conduct now appeare
In this mournfull Dying yeare.
Alas my Lord thy Dredfull hand
What potentate that can withstand
And whether can I goe or fly.
But thy Severity is nigh
Tis inward my Lord yet I have found
Th'effectes of mercy to abound
Those now I supplicate may attend
To the last periode of my end /

A page from Katherine Austen's journal.

year-old widow with three young children. Her father, Robert
Wilson, was a successful cloth dealer who died young. Records of
his estate filed in the orphans' office of the City of London show
that Katherine's mother managed the estate and brought up her
seven children. When Katherine married in 1645 at the young age
of seventeen, she had a dowry of more than £2,000. Thus, while she
was not noble, nor even a member of the gentry, she was well-to-
do by contemporary standards. There is no record of her education;
she may have attended one of the fashionable girls' schools patron-
ized by London merchants, or she may have been taught privately
at home. But like most women of her time, her schooling was haphazard and largely limited to preparing her for her calling as a wife
and mother. Her journal often reflects a tension between her intellectual strivings to rise above the frustrations of her limited education and the commonplaces that stocked her mind.

She married Thomas Austen, also the child of a successful
London merchant. Like many families in their position, the Austens
were attempting to move up the social ladder, to advance from
being merchants to living as landed gentry. Young Thomas had been
sent to Oxford University to obtain the intellectual polish of a gentleman. Through his sometimes shady transactions, Thomas's father
had also begun to acquire country estates around London, including a manor in then-rural Highbury, sometimes using methods that
later led to legal problems.

Tragedy derailed all these plans. In 1658 Katherine's young husband died, and at almost the same time, so did both his father and
younger brother. Suddenly at age thirty she was head of the family,
with the responsibility of raising and educating her daughter and
two young sons, managing the family properties and confronting
the legal problems arising from her father-in-law's property deals as
well as a disagreement with her sister-in-law over Thomas's brother's will. All these problems preoccupied her in the years when she
was writing this little notebook.

Other public and personal emotional crises marked these years. Katherine had lived through the Civil War and the political upheavals after Charles I was executed; now in 1665 there was war against the Dutch and in August and September bubonic plague killed thousands of Londoners (the great fire of September 1666 occurred only a month after regular entries in this volume of her journal stopped). Austen's little family emerged unscathed from all these public disasters. At the same time she was also passing through a personal emotional crisis. Seven years after the death of her husband, she was considering remarrying. Her suitor was a Scottish physician named Alexander Callendar. She recorded some of their conversations in her journal and also used its pages to debate the pros and cons of remarriage. She had apparently already decided against marrying again when Callendar died in October 1665, probably a plague victim.

Austen lived as a widow for the rest of her life (she died in 1683 in her fifties) devoting herself to her business affairs (for example, she invested in the East India Company), to managing the family property (she successfully defended the family estates in the law courts and against a private bill in parliament to take away the estate at Highbury), to establishing her children and to practising a spiritual life through prayer and meditations. She arranged good marriages for her elder son and daughter, and ultimately the family did achieve the transition to gentility; her grandson was a baronet and Member of Parliament.

Yet to judge from her writings, Katherine Austen would have been ambivalent about celebrating such success. To work for the advancement of her family was the duty of a person of her class. She expressed great anger and resentment at those who sought to deprive her and her children ('a poor widow and orphans') of their rights. Yet she also was constantly aware of God's judgement on her, and of the fragility of her dependency and faith. Austen's frustration with the handicaps of being female in a male-dominated world resonates with the experience of any twentieth-century working woman, but her pious spiritual framework for analysing and confronting these problems is utterly foreign to most twentieth-century secular readers. Her journal thus provides a remarkable insight into the mind of a woman whose problems are familiar but whose means for understanding the crises of her life are those of another age. She was like us, and yet so unlike us. That is the fascination of this text.

The little notebook reveals many specific aspects of Austen's life. Her sense of family and kinship appears in her worries about the bad habits that her son was acquiring at Oxford and in the letters she wrote to each of the three children reminding them of their duties as individuals and as family members. Her reflections on honour were intertwined with her sense of family. She was also particularly fond of her sister, Lady Mary Ashe, and wrote a sad little poem in mourning when Mary's small daughter died. Lives of children were fragile in Austen's world. So too were those of adults; at one point Austen stopped to take account of all the relations and friends who had recently died.

Yet she was also an active, public woman. She was concerned about the profitability of twelve new houses she was building near Covent Garden as investment properties. Managing other estates constantly claimed her attention as well. But it was the trouble over the manor at Highbury and a legal suit with her sister-in-law over the title to an inn called the Red Lion on Fleet Street that distressed her most. A private bill had been introduced in Parliament to take Highbury away from the Austens. Katherine hired lawyers and also attended the committee hearings herself.

To help herself through these crises she also relied on the consolation of analysing her dreams and recording examples of predictive visions and other cases of prophetic foreknowledge that she discovered in reading or conversation. Such entries suggest some of the books she had either read or was familiar with. Her notebook also served as the place where she recorded poems, prayers, sermons and devotions written by others. While I have not been able to trace the sources all of these entries, these items show an interest in history and current affairs. She refers to sermons by John Donne, Raleigh's *History of England* and Isaak Walton's *Lives*; she found inspiration in Thomas Fuller's account of the life and achievement of Hildegarde of Bingen. Generally, though, her reading seems to have been limited to fairly commonplace devotional writings.

The most dominant theme of her journal is religious faith. Her prayers give the most intimate insight into her mind and heart. She sought solace and courage from God's support, but angry imprecations against her opponents also mark her writings about her legal problems. This passionate and outraged woman solicited God's aid in punishing her enemies. Prayer for her was a form of private politics. Her meditations also betray the tension between her ambition and her vulnerability as a woman.

Keeping such meditational notebooks was a fairly common practice amongst literate and pious people of both sexes in this period, both conservative Anglicans and radical Dissenters. All Christians were urged to spend some time each day in private prayer and meditation. A technique recommended to help to focus one's thoughts and discipline one's mind was the writing of meditational essays or prayers, something only possible, of course, for those with leisure, funds and private space. One was to think about some verse from the Scriptures, or an event that had occurred in one's life, or some scene one had observed (however brief or fleeting) and then to concentrate on how that subject could be interpreted to show God's will. Writing down the meditation helped concentration, and once completed, the little essay might be reread on another occasion, copied, edited, rewritten and improved during later sessions. The meditator might go back to make additions to notebooks created years before (as Austen did). This spiritual exercise gave women like Katherine Austen an opportunity to write analytically and reflectively, as well as to explore their ability to compose in admired literary genres such as poetry, brief essays and prayers.[2] They wrote for themselves with no intention to publish, yet the act of writing created the expectation of an audience. Even in this private note-book, Austen addresses the potential reader.

In their lifetimes, some women wrote dozens of such notebooks. Lady Anne Halket, for example, left more than a hundred volumes of manuscript writings when she died.[3] In all, I have been able to discover surviving manuscripts or printed versions of about thirty other meditational books written by seventeenth-century English women (mostly published after their authors died), but incidental references suggest that many other women wrote books that have since been lost. The discipline of this intellectual exercise was a daily part of the lives of far more English women than we have hitherto guessed. Though women were denied university education, the opportunity to practise the learned professions and to participate in public life as preachers or parliamentarians, these little notebooks testify not only to the spirituality of the women who wrote them, but also to the courage with which they pursued the life of the mind and the political engagement that society would seem other-wise to have denied to them.

NOTES

1. The following account is woven together from fragments of information found in dozens of sources. Three of the most important of these were the account of Robert Wilson's estate in the Orphans Finding Book and Account Book of Money Received for Orphans (Corporation of London Record Office Mss. 93C and 94A) and the wills of Thomas and Katherine Austen in the Public Record Office, PROB 11/285/338 and PROB 11/PROB 11/375/1).

2. A good place to start learning about this form of written meditation is Frank L. Huntley, *Bishop Joseph Hall and Protestant Meditation in Seventeenth-Century England*, (Binghamton, 1981). For another example by a woman see *The Meditations of Lady Elizabeth Delaval written between 1661 and 1671*, Douglas G. Greene, ed., *Publications of the Surtees Society*. CXC (1975).

3. A list is included in the biography published with her selected *Works*.

KATHERINE AUSTEN'S JOURNAL
1664-1666

ON FAMILY AND HONOUR

*Austen's personal identity melded piety, maternal care,
love of her dead husband, ambition and a strong sense of
personal and family honour. This entry, addressed to
herself, near the beginning of this volume is a typical
blending of personal experience and faith.*

Look what God Almighty does for thee and then thou wilt not
regard what men [do] against thee. And see in this time of loneli-
ness what a pretty cheerful companion I have [who] knows not
anything of the clouds and damps of melancholy that God's gracious goodness allows me, my little daughter. I can't but recite to
myself my former sweetness of life. How I had [a husband] that
rendered me all the love and all the affection a person could possibly oblige his friend with. And God was pleased to give a conclusion of it. Yet instead I have the favour and love of my most
merciful God. And I can ... persuade myself I ... still [am influ-
enced] by his desires for my perfection ... who bore that regard
[for me] when he was on earth.

*Like most seventeenth-century people, Austen lived in
the web of a large kinship connection, and sometimes she
used her journal to comment on the lives of her parents
and other kin.*

I observe what a long and healthy age my grandmother Rudd lived (above 80) and Mr Smith of Aldermanbury, 90, and Parson Wilson about 80. All lived in the city and did not love the country. Their diet was temperate, their exercise little, at softly pace [they] ever went, [they did] not put nature scarce ever in any violence by overstirring or heating which make a faintness often times and a decay ... I attribute the chief part of their long life to the quiet of their minds, never engaged in anything [that] disquieted or disordered that peace within them.

How was my own mother's strong nature worn out by too much stirring and walking, and the many cares and businesses which a great family gave occasions to her. That nature was spent which, in likelihood, ... retirement would have prolonged. The distractions of the times wherein she lived [*the Civil War*] gave her many discomposures ... Dear mother, thou hadst a great estate and a great burden too.

> *A few pages later she seems to have been inspired by some reading to reflect on her own personality.*

To attain a sweet nature.

The beginning of a gracious disposition is to be qualified with joy. The fruits of the spirit [are] joy, long suffering, gentleness, goodness. A cheerful disposition is the fittest to serve God and please him. Also the most acceptable for a comfortable society. Cheerfulness is ready to forgive errors, 'tis full of love and love can pardon a multitude. You may observe in some young persons who are of a cheerful nature, of what sweet complying tempers they are of. And when age comes with infirmities [such] that joys are unpleasant, what sour peevish dispositions arise in the temper of men and women.

> *This passage inserted later on a blank page of the journal, apparently an angry response to an insult, shows that Austen sometimes was far from attaining 'a sweet nature':*

Sir, if you had been a gentleman, as you pretend to, you would
have had civiler words in your mouth. I do not deserve that odious,
immodest character your rudeness was pleased to give me. Besides I
should be unwilling to call a woman of fourscore old. Ancient is
honourable; old is despicable. Old belongs to old shoes, old clothes,
not to myself. For indeed when I am come to the longest date and
age in this world I hope then to be as young as when I first came in
it [because I] shall be entered into a new spring [where I will not]
come within the compass of any [more] change or decay ... Surely
I have not deserved in my conversation among men his most abusive and scandalous speech: 'I ride in my coach while I dare to let
the way be so bad for them to walk'. Old goat. The rudest speech
not proceeding from a gentleman as he pretends but from a hinde, a
soughter [*a peasant*] ...

> *Austen's reflections on human nature are then followed by*
> *these thoughts on self-discipline:*

To spend time.
Consider how to spend my time, not trifling away but with
method, usefully and comfortably. And to weigh the hours of the
day, to divide them in several studies, employments, in devotion, in
soberness, in educating my children, in history, in a portion for
retirement. In seeking knowledge, 'tis observed the ignorant man is
compared to a beast. But he is far worse than a beast. Their nature is
to be ignorant. 'Tis man's fault if he be so.

> *In mid-spring 1665, the death of a distant relation drew*
> *Austen's thoughts to her own health and that of friends*
> *and family.*

The last week I attended a friend of mine (Cousin Birkenhead's
wife, Mr Prier's daughter) to her grave. And when I recollect my
distemper which began in February last about the beginning, and
continued 'til the middle of March, [when] a violent cold in my

head took away my hearing, my speech, my eyesight and vapours
flew up almost continually as deffed [*deafened?*] me in that manner
I had scarce the benefit of my understanding. This cold and illness,
[along] with troublesome business, yet more discomposed me that
I could not tell whether my [worries] had augmented my illness,
or my illness made my business so tedious to be endured ... I
sometimes had the persuasions I should die ... And yet the Lord
was pleased to let my glass run longer and give a final stop to this
sweet good woman adorned with the graces and true humble
virtues of a Christian and a wife. The original of her illness, only a
cold in her head, caused the same effects as fell to me in my head.
Yet death became in earnest to her and after 3 or 4 days the sickness was contracting at her outward senses. In 2 or 3 days more
great violent convulsions which deprived her of her life the 3rd of
April 1665. God hath spared me and my two sons, all three having
felt severe effects of the sharp winter. And how many gone, and
withered as grass, and their places know them no more. The 5th
March 1664 [*=1665*] my brother-in-law Sir Edward Cropley died
[*first husband of her sister Martha*]. The same month little infant
Rowland Walters [*a distant relation*]. And Sir Thomas Bide's eldest
son of 13 years [*Bide was a neighbour and father of her future son-in-
law*]. The 21 April Aunt Wilson aged 79 died, mother to Cousin
Samuel Wilson.

*Then a few pages later her own birthday drew her thoughts
again to the passage of time.*

See Meditation in parchment book p. 73 on my 36th years. This
on my 37th, April 30th 1665 being Sabbath day.

God Almighty hath been pleased to add another year to my life
and made my 36 now thirty seven years. We know time passed
looks like the arrow that is flown, like the similitudes of swiftness
frequently recounted. And though my years are gone and I never
more recall a day back again, much more a year, yet o my soul
every day resolve with the psalmist to bless thee (O God). And

every year for this patient forbearance of me, for thy bounty, for thy tender providence over me. Therefore will I praise thy name for ever and ever.

> *Austen employed a variety of techniques in her medita-*
> *tions. Here she uses a common method of stating and then*
> *discussing a philosophical commonplace to analyse the*
> *meanings of financial and personal honour for herself and*
> *her family. Here honour connotes both the public status of*
> *a title and the private ethic of self-respect.*

Of honour and contraries.

Contraries and transcendants [*that is, obstacles and successes*] have a relation, though by opposition one to another.... The success of two thousand pounds has been the growth of most of my fortune. So I desire never to find the contrary ... by ... contracting a great debt ... [which] will eat and devour up a bigger estate then I have.

If I could have a fortune [that] would entice a person of honour [*that is, attract a titled husband*], yet I am not so in love with it [as] to be ready to part with [a fortune] and know for what extravagance it was sold.

I esteem honour not worth anything, unless it be well guarded with wealth, [lest] it ravel ... out to a degree far meaner than yeomanry is. So ... the fortune I judge [is] the real honour, and [a] title is the ornament, the embellishing of that fortune, which makes it look a little brighter to dark common eyes.

And if the costliness and splendor of my title eats up my estate, I shall rather [divest] myself of it ... than degrade me of my supportation [*that is, my self support*], or contrive unworthy detainings of any person's money, whereby I [would be] made most really contemptible. True honour consists not so much in those preferments and titles of the world, which for the most part are vain like itself, but in holy wisdom, gravity and constancy....

Perhaps I may change my condition [*and marry*] after I have answered some designs. Then shall I not aim at honour ... 'tis costly to maintain honour in all its circumstances; nay and 'tis scarce honour if punctilios is not kept up.... Neither is it riches I want.... 'Tis a person, whose soul and heart may be fit for me is the chief riches to be valued. Yet ... [it] hath a reflection of disrepute when women's inclinations are steered all by love. A rich woman must not marry with a person of mean fortune.

Surely mediocrity is the happiest condition we can obtain. And yet ... the lazy man comes not near it, and the active man stays not at it but climbs far beyond it, 'til he paces all the degrees from competency to superfluities. And from thence ambition tempts him with titles and eminency. And yet he may be as happy by a sweet peace without going up those additional steps which creates obligations &c.

> *Letters to her children which Austen drafted or copied in her notebook reveal more about how she saw honour as imposing obligations. The first letter is to her son Thomas, who was attending Balliol College, Oxford. A college tradition allowed students of his standing not to remove their hats in respect of others. This becomes the focus of a letter expressing some of Austen's personal values.*

To my Son TA:
A fellow of a college is made up of pride and unmannerliness ... and they that are fellow commoners [*as a wealthy student her son qualified for this more privileged student standing*] learn those ill habits. I repent ... of nothing more [than having] made you one ...

What makes noble men ... so extremely civil but being used ... to receiving a great respect [from all men] by observance and keeping their hats off in their presence? ... Civility and good breeding obliges the same answerable return [*that is, noble men take off their hats in response*]. As the Lord Manchester to Cousin TR [*Thomas Rudd?*] put off his hat all the time he [*Rudd*] had business to my Lord.

And truly, in my observation, this very rude fashion creates [an] abundance of pride in colleges ... And certainly ... the ill-breeding

and unaccomplishments in colleges [forces] gentlemen of quality to
send their sons to travel to learn civility and sweetness of deportment, [but] ... the early habit of pride and surliness and stoutness of
carriage they hardly ever forget ... while they live.... This custom,
in my weak opinion, may be [described] as the introduction to
rudeness, to lofty and conceited carriage, and which renders yourself
in your own esteem far better than your correspondent.

Tom: what ere the fashion is I would have your demeanour
otherwise. And though you may go scot free, hat free, be not so
rude in your carriage, but if a beggar puts off his hat, give the
like....

Be conversant in Civil Law. I have heard say it will fit you for
Common Law and is the foundation of law by so much reason in
it....

There is nothing I adore more in this world than ingenuity. And
an ingenious spirit is seen in all things. What is ingenuity? I take it
to be dexterity and aptness to undertake all things readily, with life
and apprehension, with judgement and solidity, as suits with the
undertaking. [As] for the proper derivation of the word, I am not a
scholar to know from whence it comes.

*Another letter draws a lesson from a specific example of the
costs of inheriting prestigious properties.*

To my children:
Let the example following divert your wishes and your [envy] at
the estates of friends. Your [great] Uncle Field had an estate of 800£
per annum and no children so that your father's mother and her sister Mrs Duffield had expectation of his estate to come to their children. When he died he left to [his] sister's younger son an estate of
reversion after his wife ... Yet my observation took notice that if he
had not left him anything it would [have] been better. First 2200£
it cost the widow's life [*that is, to buy out the reversion*] and so much
in finishing it, that had the purchase and finishing money been laid
out on any new purchase would have come to as much....

Suspend all craving and expectation. Go on in your own way of industry. [Be] the raiser of your fortune and leave the rest to God and he will do better than your own projects can.

As she prepared to leave London to escape the plague in
August 1665, Austen wrote these letters to her children,
to guide them should she die.

To my son Thomas if he lives to enjoy the blessing of his estate.

Dear son. Now you come to possess a comfortable estate. Think not that you must entertain and welcome it with the thoughts that it is flung upon you by the hands of fortune. For if you have no farther considerations, fortune will put on a pair of wings and fly from you just as the Goddess Fortune in old Rome and their other gods who could fly away to their disadvantage and transfer their favours to others.

You have a further duty: ... recollection and gratitude. You are not to think [that] though your father and grandfather [*that is, Thomas Austen*] are out of sight and out of your knowledge that your respects are cancelled. You must know an honour and duty is to be performed to the ashes of your most worthy father from whence your being sprung, and who did surpass conferring nature to you while he was with you by an ardent affection for your education. Also you are to pay a gratitude to the memory of your honour'd grandfather whose industry and just qualifications provided a fair possession. And ... to the former predecessors who brought a blessing to him, and from them all derived prosperity to you.

One part of duty is performed by a civil prudence, by a free charity and by an industrious [care]. That you may rather commendably augment than riotously or carelessly impoverish or diminish their estates descended to you. And 'tis easier and with less pains to spin the web out longer than to ravel it out. I say with less pains since where [there] is prodigality and vicious demeanour [there] is more study to fling an estate away than there is prudence to array and manage it with virtue, and usefulness to all the

intentions and purposes of nature, liberality and reputation. There is
more trouble to provide for pleasure because there is so great dissat-
isfaction in the last intermission of pleasure as it must be carried on
with more solicitation to create that vanity and keep it to the
height.

And we may observe to keep up those virtues of liberality and to
be useful and noble, to serve oneself and others too, and to arrive at
honour is by way of augmentation and enlargement of our patrimony which enables [us] to perform any lawful designment.

To my son Robert Austen.

This lesson is related to you. To revere your predecessors in your
heart. Nor can I be persuaded [that such reverence goes unnoticed]
or goes without a blessing ... We do receive [a great deal] by a rev-
erend memorial and respectful regard. And you are to look back to
the springs of your fortune. And though they have glided by your
worthy father and grandfather Austen, yet for as much as your estate
came particularly from my portion from my good father, your
grandfather Robert Wilson, and my unparalleled father in law
Alderman Highlord [*her mother's second husband*] 'tis fit you pay a
homage to their memory and merit. This is practised by imitation of
their virtues, by enjoying your blessings, by thankfulness to God that
blessed you with a good possession [through their] virtuous honesty
and praiseworthy industry. It may be a precedent to command the
same good endeavours and fair qualities in you. And if they
obtained it by their own faculty of industry (assisted by God's blessing) what may you then do by a ready help and supply from two
foundations.

I dictate this lesson to you of prudence since I know it is so
acceptable to our great Patron. And its contrary, careless profuseness,
[is] the original of all the unhappiness that attends on ourselves and
posterity in this world.

To my daughter Anne Austen

Nor are you my daughter to [neglect] this duty. Look you with honour on those predecessors mentioned and take along with you your grandmothers. Have your grandmother (Anne) Austen's virtue and goodness. Yet may you be defended from the passion of her melancholy and bear with more courage the encounters of endured separations which must necessarily attend us. Her too great love occasioned much unhappiness to her by it. And remember my dear mother, your grandmother (Katherine Wilson Highlord). Take industry from her and me. And as I have practised virtue and employment (I hope to be useful in my life) from my dear mother, be you an example and pattern to your children.

And in this I shall conclude to you all, my three dear children, my wishes that the blessings descended to you from the integrity and worthiness of all your predecessors be a blessing to descend in channels to your children, and to many generations. And if you do your parts by leading commendable and useful lives and that [by setting] virtuous examples, God will to every generation continue his favour, [for He] is the fountain of all blessings and happy contentment here, and [He] has better blessings to crown our low and weak endeavours ... [That] all you and yours may obtain [His favour] is the unfeigned prayer and blessing of your affectionate mother, Katherine Austen.

COURTSHIP AND CONSIDERATION
OF REMARRIAGE

In addition to her financial affairs, the possibility of remarriage preoccupied Austen at this time. Provisions in her husband's will had made it problematic for her to consider remarrying earlier, but by early 1665 those obligations were met, and she had met a possible suitor. Intermittent entries over the next six months trace the courtship.

In Answer to one [who asked] why not marry to ease me of my burdens.

O no, cousin, marriage should be peaceable and not strewed with thorns and encumbrances. I do not know what regrets might have been [thereby]. This [is] sufficient: I am able to bear with patience myself the loss of an estate because [of] bigger afflictions. And if my children should find loss in their estate by God's blessing [I] should be able to make a supply to them in their great disappointments, which I could never do by engaging myself away from them....

A few months later as plague ravaged London in September 1665 she was being courted by the physician Alexander Callendar:

O my God that has kept me all my lifetime, keep and defend me in this temptation now, when a person of a most subtle insinuation, of a most complying temper, of frequent opportunities seeks ... to take my affection by acts of readiness and assistances to me, and by his helpful offices of preservation to my health in the time of this great danger, does by all ways ... [dive] into my temper and inclination ...

I bless God I early see at what all his addresses and winning flattering discourses tend to. O God, do thou shield me as with a garment, and give me a cautious prudence to behave and acquit myself that I may not do a dishonourable folly to sully and disparage the fair prosperities of my life.

May my carriage (in this intervene) be watchful, resolute, and yet not contemptuous or ungrateful. But if he does oblige me by kind offices such as a friend may receive that I may return civility and a fair requital and not give so great a satisfaction as the reward of my self, and all my estate, for that which I am in a capacity civilly to requite by a lesser reward.

Most unhappy women, how many ... snares and trains [are] laid for you. I no more wonder how soon you are won to another affection ... [You] should design yourselves with the most discretion you can, to prevent the dangers [that] may unworthily surprise you in the race of a long widowhood.

My retreat is to fly to my ever watchful Guardian in heaven. And who can be safe without that special aid, which I depend on in all my surprisements and [which] will not leave me if I go not from that father of my spiritual and temporal conduct.

> *A few days later she was still convincing herself why she should not remarry, and then over the next series of entries recounts moments of Callendar's courtship.*

We must not [weaken] and consent to a dishonourable marriage and then lay it upon the appointment of heaven ... Not but that there may be singular virtue in a person of a low fortune. There may be also the same in one of a considerable. And I think it is a great folly ... to cast myself and a future issue into meanness when I may rise to [something] better. When fond affection and deluded judgement [are] thus ensnared into error, the unhappiness I must own as the contriver and carver of and not lay it on destiny (for we must know if we will consent to unhappy choices destiny will not contradict it). And we must sit down under the burden of that grievance [that] our own weak choice makes. Yet if we are in the care of God, [that, along with] our endeavours, will prevent our unhappiness.

The best way is not to [dwell on] the temptation which may insinuate into a weakness of consent and bring an undervaluing alteration of life.

Now [some say that] ... extraordinary virtues and endowments do [inspire] affections without relation to fortune and 'tis not so mean a thing [for those qualities] that does make [someone] be beloved. This answered, if there is such a thing as virtue to be loved for itself, let my Amoret entertain me as his friend, and not vitiate a noble friendship with interest, or any other respect but pure amity. Yet certainly because it is rare and scarce such a thing ... to be esteemed for itself (especially in single men and single women)....
Nor can I believe when they say that men had rather be in the society of women. And women loves better that of men.

No I [am persuaded] by a comparison not to give credit to
words: the King courts the city and loves it because it is rich ... [A]
rich wise woman is loved and if she does not love again, it is no
matter if she is not wise and rich.

For my part I do no injury to none by not loving. But if I do
[love], I may do real injuries where I am already engaged—to my
deceased friend's posterity.

As for my body it can be enjoyed but by one. And I hope it is
the worst part of me and that ... every servant maid and country
wench may excel mine, and can give the same satisfaction as mine.
But [where] my desire is should far excel my body is [with] my
soul, and [its] virtues and qualities ... And this I think may be useful
to more than one ... person. And if anything in me is to be loved I
hope 'tis my mind. And that I deny not a friendly correspondence
to you nor any beside. Thus all my friends may partake of me and
enjoy me and be married in the dearnesses and usefulness and ben-
efits of friendship. And more, then one can be satisfied with those
lawful intimacies of friendship and correspondences, of lawful public
safe conferences, which is the better part of me and which true
virtue should most affect. And thus I may be partaker of the noble-
ness of your parts by an open and free amity.

And thus that person which pretends so great affection to me
may be satisfied with an honest conversation and such lawful
allowed conferencies.

*Nevertheless, when Austen left London to go to Essex to
escape the plague, Callendar went with her. She recorded
their earnest conversations and then his sudden death:*

... He had many arguments to prove the papists had not idolatry
by their pictures. This he said Monsieur Amaruth [*a French protestant
theologian*] did prove in a book he set out wherein he shows the
idolatry of several nations as the Ancient Egyptians to be perfect
idolatry but of the papists not to be such. I answered divers things
to it and though at last I did not disapprove according as it might be

the having a picture of Christ or of Saints. Yet let Mr Amaruth say
what he pleased, I must condemn the Romanists of superstitious
and idolatrous adoring ...

He then said to me and protested if I was a ... beggar woman ...
I would have him, he would have me, and he would discourse with
me all day. For he never talked with me but [he] learned something
[from] me. I told him he was mistaken, and if I was [a beggar
woman], he would not.

For my part I declined all things [that] might give him a vain
encouragement and told him I was, like Penelope, always employed.
Aye, says he, her lovers could not abide her for it.

... He said, you would not take pity if one should grow
distracted for you. There is no fear of that, said I. Then as he took
me by the hand, he said what a hand was there to be adored. I
answered him [by] looking upon a tuft of grass which had growing in it a yellow flower, that that spear of grass was fitter to be
adored than my hand. Aye alas, says he, we are all but grass, but
shadows. And whenever we see the grass we are to adore the
Creator in it.

I think at that time he was not very well for afterwards he said
that on that evening he first began to feel his head ache which grew
for 4 days very painful so that eleven days after he ended his life on
the 7th of October 1665 at Tillingham in Essex....

... And ... on the last night he had in this world, [he] did
express how he had passed through many checks of fortune. It is
supposed [they] made some impressions on his mind, together with
late apprehensions at the place where he went with me to be freed
from the danger of the pest, and there he took notice of night birds,
of screech owls as he concluded one of the house would die.
[When] his sickness did increase my own fears suggested his end
was nigh and revolved to me a dream in its full meaning [*she refers to
her Book K where this is recorded*].

And ... that place and room ... was the very same fashion and
situation as I saw in my dream. The gravestone I bought in such a
corner was represented as Tillingham church stands and that place

where he was buried. And surely his worth and merit deserves to have a memorial of stone infixed over his grave, he lying buried in such a remote place from his friends.

> *Interwoven with these personal reflections are passages reflecting Austen's concerns as a property owner. She faced several legal and financial crises: a dispute with her sister-in-law over the Red Lion, a suit by a neighbour, a 'cash-flow' problem arising in part from a lack of return on her investment in new buildings in her property in Swan Lane near Covent Garden. Most important was the problem of the estate at Highbury, acquired by her father-in-law in the 1620s as part of a settlement of debts owed by the crown. Austen and her children faced two barriers to actually enjoying the profits of the estate. First, it had been under a long lease to another holder, and they did not actually enter possession until late in 1665. Second, and more serious, a group of creditors of a former holder of the estate were moving in Parliament to have the newly restored monarch Charles II reclaim the estate to settle their claims. Austen attended the committee hearings on the bill, and she was aware as well that the matter would be discussed in the Privy Council. Charles II might have taken prerogative action to seize the estate, and in her reflections on that possibility Austen links her own welfare to her political perspective on the Interregnum and the Restoration, which she, like all but the most convinced republicans, had welcomed.*
>
> *The framework in which she discussed these problems is drawn from the biblical language of retribution, based primarily on the angry discourse of the Psalms (a common source for such Protestant meditational writing). In counterpoint with Christian forgiveness, Austen felt obliged to express self-dramatizing anguish, titanic anger, and, occasionally, an attempt to find reassurance in prophetic*

interpretations of her dreams. Her poetry (here on attend-
ing Parliament and the estate at Highbury) often shows
her at her most intellectually pretentious. Like many self-
educated people her mind was stocked with a large fund
of philosophical commonplaces. Yet her striving as a
woman to express herself in the elite language of antique
pastoral poetics is moving evidence of the consequences of
limited education for a woman of intelligence and intellec-
tual aspirations.

Surely my God is preparing for me halcyon days, [because] days of trouble and molestation I have found from men who consider not afflicted widows. They take advantage of them who [have] little help and give frequent occasion of more disturbance. My God if it be thy will to consign me quiet and repose, if not in this life, I am sure in another, for thy promise has assured it. In thee there is peace to be comforted, though in the world [there is] trouble. And if I must taste of every variety of trouble in almost every concernment, and if my neighbours must dart envy and unkindness to me, circumventions and injuries, my God has strengthened me to this day.

A few days later she addressed this reflection to the cur-
rent holder of the lease of Highbury (also known as
Newington Barrow).

My Lord when the King had this estate in his interest it was of such a trivial value as he judged it not considerable at all, therefore parted with it. In earnest Sir, six and thirty years to come [*apparently the number of years left to run on the lease when Thomas Austen senior first acquired the estate*] is the age of a man, nor does a man live a man longer than that time, [since during] his first and his last time ... he acts the part of two children. And the next stage after his first childhood ... he is guided by irregular passions and desires, by folly and want of an experienced judgement to guide and command himself. And thus he runs in his ungoverned time to one vice or another

[so that] he can hardly redeem himself from ruin, either he is the
bondman of a usurer or of his tyrant appetite taken in the fetters of
a ruinating love. So that 'til he has relinquished his vice and makes
use of that refined faculty, reason, he is no man ...

Upon Courtiers at the Committee of Parliament striving for
Highbury the 14th February that I was there:

> Wise Solomon he tells me true
> There is a time for all things due
> A time to spare, a time to spend
> A time to Borrow, time to lend
> A time of Trouble, time of rest
> A time there is to be oppressed.
> Such is this time now men of power
> Do seek our welfare to devour
> Confederated in a League
> By an unjust and Dire intrigue.
> Envy thou base encroaching weed
> Never did any Noble deed.
> We cannot be secure for thee
> O thou most treacherous quality.
> No time in this same world secure
> Alive nor dead, a hold have sure.
> A shovel throws us from our grave
> As envy plucks from what we have.
> 'Tis better far on Heaven to place
> Where we are freed from envies chase
> No thief, no supplantation can
> Despoil what is the best of man
> Nor of thy favour most great Lord
> In our huge straits does aid afford.
> ....
> Men never think their wives may be
> Necessitate by misery

Or their children be a prey
When themselves are gone away.
I hot resented widows' tears
Before I was distressed with fears.
This retribution do I find
To meet with all the world unkind.
My sin forgive, let pity flow
And comfort unto sad hearts show.
Most gracious Heaven relieve sad hearts,
Be healing Balsam in their smarts.
O heaven send down thy full relief
Who are the help of all in chief.

My dream on 2nd of January [*entry written mid February, 1665*]
I dreamed I was going to a wedding and took my leave of my
mother. Then I went up a high pair of stairs and came into a room
where was a long table. [In] the middle of the upper end sat my
husband ... discoursing with a gentleman in a gown sitting at the
side of the table. I looked upon them and went down. As I went
down a few steps I saw my husband again. I kissed him and asked
him how he could come down before me since I left him sitting.
He told me by a back stairs. So down I went. And then I forgetting
my muff I went up the back stairs for it. But I had not gone up
above 8 [*inserted:* 9] or 9 [*inserted:* 10] steps but I waked.

This ran in my mind divers days afterwards and I concluded the
first pair of stairs signified to me to the end of January and the second was so many days in February and then something would fall
out to me. And indeed I was troubled that some unhappy adventure
would come in as I dreaded every day wishing February out. It
came to pass that on the 9th of February I was appointed to be that
day at the coming of parliament. And when I came into the room it
was the same as I saw in my dream, the situation of the room the
same with the table. And as soon as I cast my eye on Sir John
Birkenhead [*who was apparently acting as her agent in this affair*] I was
confident he was the very same man I saw my husband with.

This business was a wedding, for it was a contract, a confederacy to take away our estate. And I shall no more be of that opinion generally observed in dreams that a wedding foretells a burying and a burying a wedding. But that it is danger of conspiracy against one as this was to us....

[*inserted later*] By my muff going for it I was to be lapped warm; as it [happens, I] went in muff and velvet hood and mantle.

It proved a very troublesome time to me, for I was sick of an exceeding cold in my head [that] made me to be almost deaf and dumb and going to West[minster] about 6 times. I was exceeding ill and more unfit to contest [in] such a business than ever I had been before, God having continued my health always before. [Now] it was a huge burden. And how subtly carried they their design by resolving [that] the committee they chose should make what report they pleased to the parliament.

The 11 of Feb. My son was very ill [that I feared] he was in a consumption, and very dangerous by a cake of phlegm backed at his stomach. That day also was discovered to me what potent trains was laid to get his estate. And my own faintness and weakness became insupportable.

My need: If the Lord does not help me I shall be like to them that go down to the pit. This day that I have fears of the loss of my son, of the loss of ~~my~~ his land.

Of New Barrow [*Highbury*] hazard, 1665.

If there is such a power [as] can take away that which the laws of the land does affirm to us, I know no other remedy than to prepare myself to work for my living, for I must expect all that I have may be gone. And I bless God I shall be able to do it. They cannot take away the peace and content of my mind and that disposition to dispose of my time in a peaceable contentment. God's care has been over me, and it will be over me still, I trust.

How many enemies have I to contest with all, and how many parties to satisfy and to behave myself obliging to. Direct me my God....

Shall it be that my lord and king's [return] must prove a fatal blast to our estate? It cannot be. Yet if we are condemned by his clear judgement (and not by the violence of our craving Adversaries [*in Parliament*]) I submit. Since he is returned in peace I [will] sacrifice life and fortune, and let that blessing on a dying nation take all that I can offer.

Fortune, do thy worst, I am not in thy power, not in the hands of ... thy blind lottery that cannot destine any thing to the virtuous. No, I am in the hands of an especial providence which differs as much from thy gifts as virtue does from vice, as truth from falsehood. This shall truly satisfy me, [since] what I have did come by the blessing of God, so what may be lost comes by his permission too. I shall not murmur nor procure curses whoever is possessor of what was ours that a blast and caterpillar may devour it. 'Tis sufficient [that] he wrongs the fatherless, the widows, and oppresses innocent persons. Heaven has made laws from the world's creation and since that time ... no true prosperity is entailed to unjust attainments. I may be sure that a little which the righteous has is better than the proud revenues of usurpers.

O Heaven give me thy especial grace [that] whatever my condition is I may demean myself with sobriety and patience. I may see what thou has bountifully bestowed on me may retard all unevenness of spirit, may vanquish that unquiet temper of revenge and molestation, may conquer all weaknesses of passion, all clamours of discontent and the frailty of my sex....

On that day Highbury came out of lease, Michaelmas [*September*]: 1665 [*as plague raged in London*]

Am I the person [who is] to reap the first fruits of that long expectation, and enter into those pleasant fields of a fair inheritance? And that it should be appointed for my children, this is a blessing I know not how to receive. Yet let me and mine ever remember that we receive our prosperity and enter into a large revenue through the jaws of death, and by the heaps of mortality. That we may be

instructed always to be ready to part from it, as readily as we do
receive it and not to set up a rest in a earthly paradise. Aye, and let
the name bear the same remembrance. Highbury: to bury those that
are mounted never so high in this world.

> Is't true indeed, to me and mine
> That many Blessings richly shine
> On the frail stock of flesh and blood?
> 'Tis more than can be understood.
> We exalted and made high
> Others in their Anguish lie;
> We accessions of this world
> They in penury are hurl'd.
> Beyond my apprehension comes
> Our favours in the largest sums.
> Yet one thing we must sure to know:
> By engagements more do owe
> Unto Heaven and one another,
> To our God, and our poor Brother.

On the situation of Highbury.

> So fairly mounted in a fertile soil
> Affords the dweller pleasure without Toil.
> Th' adjacent prospects gives so sweet [*inserted:* rare] a sight
> That Nature did resolve to frame delight
> On this fair Hill, and with a bounteous load
> Produce rich Burthens, making the abode
> As full of joy, as where fat valleys smile,
> And greater far, here sickness doth exile.
> 'Tis an unhappy fate to paint that place
> By my unpolished Lines, with so bad grace.
> Amidst its beauty, if a stream did rise
> To clear my muddy brain and misty eyes
> And find a Helicon [*a horn like a tuba*] t'enlarge my muse,
> Then I no better place than this would choose.
> In such a Laver and on this bright Hill

I wish Parnassus to adorn my quill.

Early in 1666 Austen engaged in some long-term reflec-
tions on her financial success, only to discover just a few
weeks later that in fact her affairs seem to be in crisis.

When I deduct the legacy my dear mother left me (at her
decease) and sever it from my husband's estate, I have added to our
estate by God's great blessing upon me these seven years of my widowhood such another estate as was left to me and my children.

And if we inherit Highbury is as much as any one of those two parts.
I do reckon our estate is 3 parts;

>First what my husband left
>
>2nd what by God's extraordinary blessing added [*that is,*
>*by Austen herself*]
>
>3rd that long expectation the discourse of many, the
>interruption of more [*that is, Highbury and other future*
>*inheritances*]

And that so much should come in my possession, O my God,
what am I to receive so much. And that by such plentiful acquisitions our God should please to free me and mine from a great
many of those huge miseries of want which do afflict the most of
mankind. Yet our God pleases to mingle some bitternesses in my
comforts. Grant Lord they may be advantages to me of wisdom and
piety to draw me from the love and desire of this world to the pursuit of the divine and spiritual felicities [that] will last forever.

MARCH 20 [1666]

Our estate is sunk now almost to half [of what] it was, which
seems to be a paradox at this time [when] it appears to the eye of the
world to be quite as much again, if not twice more. Now let me do
as the merchant to save his credit and to promote his adventure. Let
me borrow too and keep up my repute and freely pay the encum-
bents [encumbrances?] and taxes and debts I [have] engaged ...

And still I am attended with law suits ... These make up to me a

triple tax. Now that the taxes by appointment are doubled, my
molestations are trebled too. How I shall come off of all? Time must
tell the narration whether good or bad.

And now must I reckon up my error that I have been mistaken
in my account, and calculated wrong by measuring that Highbury
and the Swan would arrive both together in their profits at
Michaelmas last. 'Tis true then my buildings were most of them finished and the other out of lease. Yet accidents and general troubles
and the unseasonable former year of drought and mortality have
gave an interruption, so that at this time instead of profit they are a
Hydra, a cormorant of a double head [which] devours all I can procure (and make me feel the charge of [Thomas' fees at] Oxford and
necessary things more pinching). 40£ in a [month?] is paid taxes for
Highbury; 33£ fee farm and to fit it up by gates and fences &c.

[*inserted later:* There is nothing but has interruptions and these little things may blow away]

O my God you have helped your servant through infinite many
plunges and obstacles formerly, and still there does grow more, and
more will arise when this world is strewed with thorns and thistles,
with ruggedness and trouble.

Lord let me never [try to] determine when my tumults, when
my crosses, when my disappointments shall cease. But inform myself
to wait thy leisure to learn what my duty is, my part of the
covenant that is the condition for me to perform of resignation and
obedience. Not to place my expectation on the promised part, for I
know not thy pleasure whether the full performance of it may not
be respited, 'til that time when I may be sure by the merits of my
saviour no interruption shall ever come ...

O that heaven would direct me what I should do, whether I shall
glorify his name by a contemplative private life or by an active public
life. Direct thy servant in what may be conducing to thy praise and
not to me, O Lord, but to thy name by the glory of my whole life ...

'Never was any woman like her'

MARY FRITH, COMMONLY CALLED MAL CUTPURSE

◆

BY VALERIE FRITH

The type of book that we call 'true crime' was just as popular two and three hundred years ago as it is today and probably for much the same reasons. These stories offer inside knowledge of how criminals operate, which makes the reader feel a little less of a rube. And their simple, predictable plot-line, which always culminates in a day of reckoning, is amenable to a beguilingly infinite number of variations: as many, it would seem, as there are individuals to be led into a life of crime.

Historians refer to these confessional accounts as criminal biography, and in the annals of that munificent genre, few volumes rival *The Life and Death of Mrs Mary Frith, Commonly Called Mal Cutpurse*. Long before *The Life and Death* was published in 1662, Mal Cutpurse had been celebrated in literature, most notably in 1610, when she just twenty-seven, as the heroine of Middleton and Dekker's play, *The Roaring Girl*. She was a legend in her own time: a self-confessed bawd and fence, she was the acknowledged 'governess' of the London underworld. Though she was known as Mal (or 'Moll') Cutpurse, Mary Frith tirelessly insisted that she had never been a pickpocket: only a dealer in the proceeds and a runner of the practitioners, a Fagin.

How did Mary Frith, whose criminal activities dictated a life of concealment, become a conspicuous, universally recognized figure

MOLL CUT = PURSE.

See here the Prefideffe o'th pilfring Trade
Mercuryes second Venus's onely May'd
Doublet and breeches in a Un'form dreffe
The female Humurrift a Kickfhaw meffe
Here no attraction that your fancy greets
But if her FEATURES pleafe not read her FEATS

Publ: by W. Richardson. Caftle Street. Leicester Fields.

Illustration from *The Life and Death of Mrs. Mary Frith*,
W. Richardson, 1662.

in the streets of London? By her 'habit and manners'. As one observer put it, there 'never was any women like her in her clothes'. Though she was sometimes described as a 'hermaphrodite', other times as a 'prodigy' or a freak of nature, she was no mere cross-dresser (which would have made her rare but hardly unique). Mary Frith's 'habit and manners' were a crossover: her 'habit' [dress] was always a combination of male and female attire—hats, shoes, shirts, breeches—with the one constant being her doublet, to which she was very much attached. She mourned when her final illness forced her to give up her doublet for a shawl.

Susan Brownmiller's *Femininity*, published in 1982, almost four centuries after Mary Frith's heyday, tackled the question of how society constructs gender through chapters that declare themselves baldly in the table of contents: Shoes, Hair, etc. *The Life and Death of Mary Frith* puts flesh and bones on Brownmiller's analysis.

Like all 'true crime' stories of that day, Mary Frith's memoirs came with a preface, an introduction and assorted other editorial interventions designed to ensure that the moral lessons to be learnt from the reprobate's life were clear and that the requisite penitential paragraphs appear near, if not right at the end.

Prefaces and introductions had to serve a dual purpose: to entice the bookstall browser and to satisfy the censor that the book was a cautionary tale; that it would serve as an agent of social control. The Preface and Introduction to *The Life and Death of Mary Frith* legitimized its publication by arguing that her memoirs would reinforce gender conformity not only by illustrating the spiritual and circumstantial decay that androgynous 'habit and manners' bring in their train, but also by warning that the repudiation of gendered apparel may be taken to signify seditious commentary on the social order.

Clothes may not make the man, but in a deeper and more dismaying sense, they do make the women, as Mary Frith and Susan Brownmiller, across their appointed centuries, attest. The passages I

have selected from *The Life and Death of Mary Frith* are taken from
the admonitory Preface and Introduction, as well as from the first-
person narrative of the memoir itself, which, though it shows signs
of further editorial incursion, at least aims for a convincing autobiographical voice. By focusing on Mary Frith's 'habit and manners',
I suspect that I may have given an inadequate sense of the whole,
which abounds with anecdotes sufficiently detailed to constitute a
crash course for the criminally inclined. At other times, the criminal
underworld that Mal depicts seems implausibly complex and cant-
laden. One wonders if this malign Atlantis is a fabrication of Mal's
own sentimental exaggerations or if the editorial hand is here, too,
sensationalizing the material, the better to satisfy the reader's
appetites and the censor's, too, by rendering crime as the mirror
image of legitimate society, a world turned upside down, a constant
threat demanding constant vigilance, if peace and prosperity are to
be maintained.

Reading early modern criminal biographies always raises questions like these, but *The Life and Death of Mary Frith* also raises
questions of its own about the mechanics of gender ideology and
about how individuals construe the gender that society constructs
for them, if indeed it does.

FROM *THE LIFE AND DEATH*
OF *MRS MARY FRITH,*
COMMONLY CALLED MAL CUTPURSE
1662

The story opens with a preface that promises an account straight from 'the oracle of felony, whose deep diving secrets are offered to the world entire'. But the editorial voice in the preface proceeds directly to the question of Mal's 'ambiguous' clothing and manners. Among the explanations that have been offered, some took her simply for a 'prodigy of the times she lived in ...'

One might as easily have guessed there were some capriccios in the state (which appeared afterwards in the jealousies, whimsies, and odd conceits of the whole mass of the multitude) by [Mal] and others [of] her contemporaries, [with their] odd and fanatic and unheard of tenor and manner of life ...

This it is which indeed makes her remarkable (and may we never see her successor or such a mad Cassandra) beyond all other considerations ... nothing appertaining to her being to be matched throughout the whole course of history or romance; so unlike herself, and of so difficult a mixture, that it is no wonder she was like nobody, nor could be sorted by any comparison or suited with any antic companion.

She was the living description and [portrait] of ... schism and separation, her doublet and petticoat understanding one another no better than Presbytery and Independency [*factions in the English civil wars*] ...

ILDIEFIH

So much may suffice for her person; there is something due to be said of her practice ...

Know you, therefore, O all you pickpockets, lifers, heavers, rumpads, bawds, &c., that ... we have prosecuted the discovery of all those arts and artifices for which your governess was famous, and your government under her discipline no less reputable for its due regulation. Read, therefore, if you can spare time from your business, the sad decays of your trade in the loss of this monopolizing improver thereof, and begin hereafter to thieve with discretion and judgement, that your incomes be weighed and balanced with the issues ...

There is a word due also to the venerable matrons that [traffic] in petticoats [i.e. prostitution] be not you so impudently immodest and shameless in your profession [that you] debauch [the] unwary and unarmed ... [be] assured [that] Mal was no such open and common offender in this kind, but was very heedful where she laid her baits and temptations, though her bribes were high and those that employed her very potent, who yet would descend to the lures of poor and naked beauty: such she most generously scorned to betray, if they had magnanimity to resist. The town abounds with you, and therefore this caution from so great an example, to which you owe respect and observance, may be very necessarily and civilly welcome.

Her other more indifferent pranks and feats will be good diversion to the honest and ingenious, and to him they are commended ... [but] it was impossible to make one piece of so various a subject as she was both to herself and others, being forced to take her as we found her, though at disadvantage; which we pray you to consider and accept of this endeavor as it is.

> *To further prepare the reader for Mary Frith's memoirs, a lengthy introduction follows the preface. Here the editorial voice opens by declaiming that 'many strong and sufficient reasons' justify recording 'this woman's history':*

... partly ... the strangeness and newness of the subject, and her unparalleled practices and courses, and manner of life and livelihood

244

(which in their time were the talk and discourse of the town, and therefore may not be unworthy of a reducing them to memory), and partly out of a pleasant officiousness to the public good, which has been advantaged (according to information) by such kind of essays.

But the introduction does not pursue any of these fascinating details. Instead, it proceeds directly to the question of Mal's 'being an hermaphrodite in manners as well as in habit [dress]', and Mal's 'habit' is the introduction's sole preoccupation thereafter.

She was indeed a perfect ambidexter, being mistress of that thriving art: no doubt Mercury was lord of the ascendant at her birth, and with his influences did so endow her that from her very cradle she gave signs of a very towardly and pregnant wench, manifested by several petty stratagems and designs as oft as occasion and opportunity presented, at her neighbours' as well as at home.

She was born Anno Domini 1589, in Barbican, at the upper end of Aldersgate Street (a very ancient street, and probably of as ancient a house, and thence she may challenge gentility)....

I do not find that any remarkable thing happened at her nativity, such as the flattering soothsayers pretend in eclipses and other the like motions above, or tides, and whales, and great fires, adjusted and timed to the genitures of great statesmen: though for a she-politic, she be not much inferior to Pope Joan*; for she was in her time the great cabal and oracle of the mystery of diving into pockets, and was very well read and skilled in [prostitution] too, among the great ones.

She was born of honest parentage, her father being by his trade a shoemaker living in good esteem and repute in the world and in love and friendly familiarity with his neighbours, a fair and square-conditioned man, that loved a good fellow next to himself, which made his issue be so sociable: we do not here dispute the company, for she kept all sorts.

Both of her parents were very tender of this daughter, but especially

* A woman who, according to folklore, dressed as a man and became Pope.

the mother, according to the tenderness of that sex, which is naturally more indulgent than the male; most affectionate she was to her in her infancy, most careful of her in youth, manifested especially in her education, which was the stricter and diligentlier attended by reason of her boisterous and masculine spirit, which then showed itself, and soon after became predominant above all breeding and instruction.

A very tomrig [*tomboy*] or rumpscuttle she was, and delighted and sported only in boys' play and pastime, not minding or companying with the girls. Many a bang and blow this hoiting procured her, but she was not so to be tamed or taken off from her rude inclinations. She could not endure that sedentary life of sewing or stitching. A sampler was as grievous as a winding-sheet. Her needle, bodkin and thimble she could not think on quietly; [she wished] them changed into sword and dagger for a bout at cudgels. For any such exercise, who but she! ... She would not fail ... to be a busy spectator; so that she was very well known by most of the rougher sort of people thereabouts when she was yet very young and little.

Her headgear and handkerchief (or what the fashion of those times were for girls to be dressed in) was alike tedious to her, wearing them as handsomely as a dog would a doublet, and so cleanly that the driven pothooks would have blushed at the comparison, and always standing the Bear Garden way, or some other rabble-rout assemblies.

This perplexed her friends, who had only this proverb favourable to their hope, that an unhappy girl may make a good woman. But they lived not to the length of that expectation, dying in her minority, and leaving her to the swing and sway of her own unruly temper and disposition.

She would fight with boys, and courageously beat them, run, jump, leap or hop with any of them or any other play whatsoever: in this she delighted, this was all she cared for. And had she not very young ... been taught to read perfectly, she might well through her ... addiction to this loose and licentious sporting have forgotten and blotted out any easy impression. But this learning stood her much in stead afterwards ...

I have thus traced her from her originals [*antecedents*] to show in what proportions she differed from and approached to them, and that neither the derivations of the same blood, the assimilation and resemblance of parts, can conform the mind and the faculties thereof or [endow] it with the like qualities, but that there is a prevalent power of our stars which overrules all, and resists and subdues the additional and auxiliary strength and reserves of education and this I have said to be Mercury in conjunction with, or rather in the house of, Venus at her nativity.

This planet Mercury you must know (if you have not well studied [astrology]) is of a thievish, cheating, deceitful influence, which is not so powerful in citizens' shops, warehouses, bargains and sales, merchandizing and bartering. Nevertheless some little finger it has as with a ray to point at them, so that seldom but some cozenage or lying at the least intervenes in those affairs. In great fairs and markets this planet operates exceedingly, but it violently rages in great throngs and concourses of people at any great show, pomp or solemnity, as coronations, my Lord Mayor's Day, and the like, where it does so whet and set such an edge on the knives and cutting instruments, so quicken and expedite their fingers ... that it were impossible to be done without the connivance of this star, under the position whereof Turnmill Street [*a dangerous part of town*] is directly fixed.

For the other of Venus, most men and women know without teaching what are her properties. She has dominion over all whores, bawds, pimps &c., and joined with Mercury, over all trapanners and hectors. She has indeed a more general influence than all the other six put together, for no place nor person is exempted from it, invading alike both sacred and profane nunneries and monasteries as well as the common places of prostitution, Cheapside and Cornhill as well as Bloomsbury or Covent Garden.

Under these benevolent and kind stars she grew up to some maturity of years, seasoned all along with such rudiments as these, to be put in use as soon as occasion should present; she was now a lusty and sturdy wench, fit to put out to service, having not a competency of her own left her by friends to maintain her of herself. But this went against the grain and the hair, as we use to say: she was too great a libertine and lived too much in common to be enclosed in the limits of a private domestic life.

A quarterstaff was fitter to her hand than a distaff, stave and tail instead of spinning and reeling. She would go to the alehouse when she had made shift for some little stock, and spend her penny, and come into anyone's company, and club another 'til she had any left, and then she was fit for any enterprise.

She could not endure the bakehouse, not that magpie chat of the wenches; she was not for mincing obscenity, but would talk freely whatever came uppermost; a spice she had even then of profane dissolute language, which in her old days amounted to downright swearing, which was in her not so malicious as customary.

Washing, wringing and starching were as welcome as fasting days unto her; ... but above all she had a natural abhorrence to the tending of children, to whom she ever had an [aversion] in her mind equal to the sterility and barrenness in her womb, never being made a mother to our best information.

At this age we spoke of before, she was not much taxed with any looseness or debauchery ... Whether the virility and manliness of her face and aspect [put] off any man's desires that way (which may be very rational and probable), or that besides her uncompliable and rougher temper of body and mind also, which in the female sex is usually persuasive and winning, not daring or peremptory (though her disposition can hardly find a suitable term for an indifferent expression of the manage of her life), she herself also from the more importunate and prevailing sway of her inclinations, which were masculine and robust, could not intend those venereal impurities and pleasures ... [stronger] meats are more palatable and nutritive to strong bodies than *quelque choses* and things of variety, which may perchance move an appetite, provoke a longing, but are easily refrained from by any considerate good fellow that knows what is the lastingest friend to good drink and good company: her motto.

She could not but know, moreover (for I suppose her of a very competent discretion and sagacity of mind as well as maturity and suitable growth at those years), that such prostitutions were the most unsatisfactory, that like an accidental scuffle or broil might end in danger, but never in love, to which she was no way so happily formed, nor was [she] so much a woman as vainly to expect it.

Several romances there are of many knights who carried their ladies away in disguise from their parents and native countries, most commonly in the habits of a page or some such manservant. Certainly it must be a stupified and far advanced affection which can admire, or fancy, or but admit the view of so unnatural a shape, the reverse of sexes in the most famed beauties, and to whose excellencies and lustre the world were devoted.... What an uncomely mantle is that heap of waters which covers the ground, and deluges and invades the dry land? That which so much offends us in the boisterousness of the elements cannot but be disgustful to mankind in the immodesty of either sex's attire and dress.

Hercules, Nero and Sardanapulus, how are they laughed at and exploded for their effeminacy and degenerated dissoluteness in this extravagant debauchery? The first is portrayed with a distaff in his hand, the other recorded to be married as a wife and all the conjugal and matrimonial rites performed at the solemnity of the marriage, the other lacks the luxury of a pen as loose as his female riots to describe them. These were all monsters or monster killers, and have no parallels either in old or modern histories 'til such time as our Mal Cutpurse approached this example; but her heroic impudence has quite undone every romance, for never was any woman ... like her in her clothes.

Generally we are so much acquainted with ourselves, and so often do dislike the effect of too much familiarity, that though we cannot alter the inside, yet we diversify the outside with all the borrowed pomp of art in our habits. No doubt Mal's converse with herself (whose disinviting eyes and look sank inwards to her breast when they could have no regard abroad) informed her of her defects, and that she was not made for the pleasure or delight of man. And therefore since she could not be honoured with him she would be honoured by him that garb and manner of raiment he wore ... [some] wenches have been got with child [by] only shaking of the breeches.

Whereof having no great hopes, she resolved to usurp and invade the doublet, and vie and brave [that] manhood, which she could not tempt nor allure.

I have [drawn attention to the doublet] because it was the chief remark of her life, as beginning and ending it; for from the first entrance into a competency of age she would wear it, and to her dying day she would not leave it off 'til the infirmity and weakness of nature [that] had brought her abed to her last travail, changed it for a waistcoat and her petticoats for a winding sheet.

These were no amiable or obliging vests. They wanted of a mutual correspondence and agreement with themselves, so unlikely were they to beget it abroad and from others. They served properly as a fit covering, not any disguise [for] her (according to the primitive inventions of apparel), wherein every man might see the true dimensions and proportions of body, only hers showed the mind too.

So that by this odd dress it came that no man can say or affirm that ever she had a sweetheart, or any such fond thing to dally with her. A good mastiff was the only thing she then affected and joyed in, in whose fawnings and familiarity she took as much delight as the proudest [woman] ever gloried in the courtship, admiration, attraction and flatteries of her adored beauty. She was not wooed nor solicited by any man, and therefore she was honest, though still in a reserved obedience and future service, either personally or by proxy to Venus.

Her nuptials and wedding grew to be such a proverb … that is to say, as much design of love in one as in the other: [the only] matches she ever intended [were] at bearbaiting, whose pastimes afforded not leisure or admittance to the weak recreations and impertinencies of lust.

She never had the green sickness, that epidemical disease of maidens after they have once passed their puberty; she never ate lime, oatmeal, coals or suchlike trash, nor never changed complexion; a great felicity for her vocation afterwards that was not to be afraid nor ashamed of anything, neither to wax pale or to blush.

No sighs or dejected looks or melancholy clouded her vigorous spirit or suppressed her joviality in the retired thoughts and despair of a husband; she was troubled with none of those longings which poor maidens are subject to. She had a power and strength (if not the will) to command her own pleasure of any person of reasonable ability of body, and therefore she needed not whine for it was long as she was able to beat a fellow to a compliance without the unnecessary trouble of entreaties. Nor in all her lifetime was it ever known that by mere request, and precariously, she ever designed or obtained any favour whatsoever, but by a strong hand carried and performed all her enterprises.

She made much of for awhile—and was very often in company—with a shoemaker (a profession, for her father's sake, she always favoured), to whose expenses she contributed all she could wrap and run ... until she found the fellow made an absolute prey of her friendship and squandered away the money she with difficulty enough provided.

This and some such other like [hucksters] to which a freeness of nature subjected her, not only [put] her off the consideration or thought of wedlock, but reduced her to some ... way she might maintain herself single.

She cast about therefore what course of life she should betake herself to, and long she was not in the determination, choosing that which was the most easy, and by a good management would prove also the most profitable, called living by the quick.

> *Mal's memoirs do not turn out to be the book that the introduction prepared the reader for. At the outset Mal declares that she'll skip over her childhood and her 'originals'.*

I will not therefore [describe] my childish ignorance and those extravagant sallies of an undisciplined wench ... for it is no matter to know how I grew up to this, since I have laid it as a maxim that it was my fate not me. I do more wonder at myself than others can do, and dare assure them that nature does sometimes disport herself not only in the careless nativities of dwarves, changelings, and such naturals, but also in her more considerate productions; for I am confident I can boast of as much ... in acquisitions, revenges, dissemblings, &c., as any of the grandees of the world, if proportionably considered.

I was hardly twenty, from whence I date myself, when viewing the manners and customs of the age, I [saw] myself so wholly distempered and so estranged from [society] as if I had been born and bred in the Antipodes ...

> *Unlike the editorial voice of the Introduction, then, Mal's own voice discounts her youth and 'dates' herself from the age of twenty instead. Nor does Mal's own account reflect the Introduction's preoccupation with her androgynous 'habit and manners'. She devotes very little space to explaining her attire. Instead she opens by recounting, over the course of six or seven pages, her induction into the life of crime and the skills that helped her survive there. Only when she comes to the point in her story where she was arrested for 'unseasonable and suspicious walking' does the question of her clothing even arise: 'the strange manner of my life' that 'aggravates the offense'. But she quickly moves on to how she outsmarted the constable, William Wall, who, in revenge, cast himself as her nemesis thereafter.*
>
> *It is not until midway through her memoirs that Mal takes up the question of her 'habit and manners': when she stands accused (in the Court of Arches) of 'wearing indecent and manly apparel'.*

While I thus reigned, free from the danger of the common law, an adversary of mine, [arranged to have me ordered] to appear in the Court of the Arches, where [there] was an accusation against me for wearing indecent and manly apparel. I was advised ... to demur to the jurisdiction of the court, as for a crime, if such, not cognizable there or elsewhere; but he did it to spin out my cause and get my money. For in the [end] I was sentenced there to stand and do penance in a white sheet at St. Paul's Cross during morning sermon on a Sunday.

They might as soon have shamed a black dog as me with any kind of such punishment ... [For] a half penny I would have travelled to all the market towns in England [dressed as I was], and been as proud of it as that citizen who rode down to his friends in his livery gown and hood, or that parson who being enjoined to wear the surplice contrary to his will, when he had once put it on wore it constantly in his own and other towns, while he was complained of for abusing that decent ministerial garment. I am sure there were some few who had no cause to be merry or sport themselves at the sight, for my emissaries were very busy without any regard to the sacredness of the place, but in revenge of this disgrace [imposed on] me, spoiled a good many [of the spectators'] clothes by cutting of part of their cloaks and gowns and sending them home as naked behind as an ape's tail....

I did not say as much, whatever I thought, when my penance was over; but ... dealing with me [this way] was ... so far from reclaiming me to the sobriety of decent apparel, that I was [even more] offended with it ... I could by no means endure at any time the finical and modish excesses of attire into which women were then, as in all ages, very curious, to the wasting and impoverishing [of] their husbands, beyond what they are able to afford towards such lavish and prodigal gallantry.

There was a pleasant story I used to prate of, of a neighbour of mine that was given this way.... Her husband liking and not liking the riches and gaudery of her clothes, by way of [being] droll accosted her in this manner: 'Sweetheart', quoth he, 'you are very fine, but you never think of the [cost]. There is never a time I have anything to do with you but it stands me in a crown towards this superfluity.' 'Husband', replied the dame, 'it is your own fault that you pay so dear, for if you would do it oftener, it would not be above a groat a time ... I would rather take my money in such quids and parcels than in sums and in gross, provided the coin be as current, neither clipped, washed, nor counterfeit.'

The rest of her memoirs Mal devotes to her 'pranks and

*devices', and to illustrating her claim that 'I was always a
good fellow'. She ties her own declining fortunes to those
of her fellow Royalists as she sums up her life:*

My trade I am sure was wholly at an end, and my money gone ...
[The] Cavaliers, my friends, were so needy, [that] I was glad to stay at
home and play at tick tack for drink with one of my companions and
bemoan my decayed fortune.

Having run this race, and seeing all things grow every day worse
and worse by the desperate evil of the times, I became weary of them
and myself ... so that I wholly relinquished all converse or commerce,
betaking myself to a sedentary life and to reading. [Whereas] before,
... I was well versed in tale books and romances and the histories of
the seven champions, and the like fopperies ... now I considered that
I had an account of my time to make by spending it in more serious
writings and contemplations.

He runs long, we use to say, that never turns: it was therefore high
time for me of thinking of the way by which I should turn, and that
presently offered itself to me. For being grown crazy in my body and
discontented in my mind, I yielded to the next distemper that
approached me, which by my bustling and active spirit I had kept off
a good while from seizing me. It was a dropsy, a disease whose cause
you will easily guess from my past life, but it had such strange and ter-
rible symptoms that I thought I was possessed and that the devil was
got within my doublet.

For what all the ecclesiastical quirks with their canons and injunc-
tions could not do, this boisterous malady soon effected. I was forced
to leave off [my doublet] and do penance again in a blanket, a habit
distant from the Irish rug and the Scotch plaid, their national vests for
women of quality, whom my scoffing neighbours said I did very
much resemble. As for my belly, from a withered, dried and wrinkled
piece of skin, it was grown the tightest, roundest globe of flesh that
ever any beauteous young lady strutted with, to the ostentation of her
fertility and the generosity of her nature. I must tell you I could not
but [pride] myself [on] it, and [I] thought nature had reserved that

kindness for me at the last, insomuch that I could have almost been impregnated (as Spanish jennets are said to be begotten by the wind) with my own fancy and imagination. My conceit proving the same with conception, and to please and maintain me in this delusion, a woman of my age then living in London was brought to bed of a son, which was very certainly true. And an old parson in the north, one Mr Vivan, of near a hundred years old, was juvenilized again, and his age renewed as to all his senses [as] he enjoyed [them] before at fifty. But these were signal miracles and presages of a revolution in the state ... and this of mine the certain forerunner of my dissolution: for there was no blood that was generative in my belly, but only that destructive of the grape, which by my excesses was now turned into water, so that the tympanied skin thereof sounded like a conduit door.

I cannot further anatomize my body, for I dared not look on my legs ... they did so [resemble] a bull or bear's, and my head so wrapped up with cloths that I looked like Mother Shipton* ... [With] all the looking glasses my house was furnished with for ornaments, I had never a one big enough to see it altogether and at once. But myself was indeed the best mirror to my self; for every afflicted part and member of me did represent and point out the wickedness every one of them had been instrumental in, so that I could not but acknowledge the justice of my punishment. My hands indeed escaped this vengeance, and I think they were the most innocent; for I never actually or instrumentally cut any man's purse, though I have often restored it; but oh my plotting, matchmaking head in those sorceries of lust I practised! The lewdness and bastardies that ensued, and those frequent trottings and runnings up and down to facilitate and bring about those debaucheries! These I cannot but acknowledge were indicated to me so plainly that I was forced to take notice of them. And I hope with a real penance and true grief to deplore my condition and former course of life [which] I had so profanely and wickedly led.

As an advantage thereto, this disease lingered with me a long

---

* A legendary witch and miscreant.

time, which I had solitude enough to improve, all people but some of my old and nearest acquaintance forsaking me. I will not boast of my conversion lest I encourage other vile people to persist in their sins to the last, but I dare assure the world I never lived a happy moment in it 'til I was leaving of it, and so I bid it adieu this threescore and fourteenth year of my age.

It may be expected I should have made a will. Let the reader therefore understand that of fifteen hundred pounds which I had of my own in good gold, which some of my neighbours can bear witness to have seen, out of my kindheartedness to my old friends the distressed Cavaliers, [after helping them] I had not a hundred pounds to command, which I thought too small a sum to give to charitable uses (as to build an hospital, &c.), it being no way proportionable to my unjust gains, as they were everywhere esteemed....

Yet to preserve something of my memory, and not leave it to the courtesy of an executor, I anticipated my funeral expenses, for it being the fashion of the times to give rings, to the undoing of the [jewellers], who live altogether by the dead and the new born, I distributed some that I had by me (but of far greater value than your pitiful hollow ware of six of seven shillings apiece that a juggler would scorn to show tricks with) among my chief companions and friends.

These rings (like princes' jewels) were notable ones, and had their particular names [like] the Bartholomew, the Ludgate, the Exchange, &c., deriving their appellations from the places they were taken in. They needed no admonition of a death's head, for they were the wages and monument of their thieving masters, who were interred at Tyburn; and I trust my said friends will wear them both for my sake and theirs.

In short, for my breath fails me, I did make no will at all, because ... if I had had my desert, I should have had an executioner instead of an executor.... But remember me to [*the constable*], and tell him he will not need my legacy, for my divining spirit tells me there's a glut coming which will make him happy and rich, if he knows how to use it.

I have also already disposed of thirty pounds of [the] one hundred pounds I have by me to my maids, and have charged them to [use] it the best way they can. That and some of my arts which they have had time to [become] expert in will be beyond the advantage of their spinning and reeling, and will ... keep them in repair, and promote them to weavers, shoemakers, and tailors.

The rest of my estate in money, movables and household goods, my kinsman Frith, a maker of a ship, dwelling at Redriff, will lay claim to, as next of kin, whom I advise not to make any adventures therewith, but stay at home and be drunk, rather than to be drowned with them.

Let me be lain in my grave on my belly, with my breech upwards, as well for a lucky resurrection at doomsday, as because I am unworthy to look upwards. And ... as I have, in my life, been preposterous, so I may be in my death. I expect not nor will I purchase a funeral commendation, but if Mr H—— be squeamish and will not preach, let the sexton mumble two or three dusty, clayey words and put me in, and there's an end.

FINIS

CONTRIBUTORS' NOTES

DONNA T. ANDREW teaches British history and women's history at the University of Guelph. She has published two books, *Philanthropy and Police: London Charity in the Eighteenth Century* (Princeton University Press, 1989) and *London Debating Societies 1776-1799* (London Record Society, 1994). A piece entitled 'Popular Culture and Public Debate: London 1780' will appear in *Historical Journal* early in 1996.

JOHN BEATTIE is a professor of History at the University of Toronto. He has published *The English Court in the Reign of George I* (Cambridge University Press, 1967) and *Crime and the Courts in England, 1660-1800* (Princeton University Press, 1986). He is currently writing a book on crime, policing and punishment in London, 1660-1750.

PHYLLIS DEUTSCH has taught modern European, British and women's history at the University of Pennsylvania, New York University, Columbia University and the New School for Social Research. Her most recent publication, 'Moral Trespass in Georgian London: Gaming, Gender and Electoral Politics in the Age of George III,' will appear in *Historical Journal* in spring 1996.

VALERIE FRITH currently teaches at the University of Guelph as an SSHRC Postdoctoral Fellow. She is the author of the forthcoming *The Double Claim: Liberty and the Press in England 1695-1792.*

PAULA M. HUMFREY is a doctoral candidate in History at the University of Toronto. Her thesis, in progress, is *'Everybody's Business is Nobody's': Domestic Service for Women in Defoe's Metropolis.*

MARGARET R. HUNT is Associate Professor of History and Women's and Gender Studies at Amherst College. She is the author of *The Middling Sort: Commerce, Gender and the Family in England, 1680-1780* (University of California Press, 1996), and of a number of articles on women, the family, sexuality and culture in late seventeenth and eighteenth-century England.

ALLYSON N. MAY is a doctoral candidate at the University of Toronto. Her thesis is entitled *The Old Bailey Bar, 1783-1834.*

SARA HELLER MENDELSON teaches in the Arts and Science Program at McMaster University. She is author of *The Mental World of Stuart Women: Three Studies.* Her joint book with Dr. Patricia Crawford, *Women in Early Modern England, 1550-1720,* is forthcoming with Oxford University Press.

ANN B. SHTEIR is Associate Professor of Humanities and Director of the Graduate Program in Women's Studies, York University. She is author of *Flora's English Daughters: Women and the Culture of Botany, 1760-1860* (Johns Hopkins University Press, 1996), and editor of Priscilla Wakefield's *Mental Improvement, or the Beauties and Wonders of Nature and Art* (Colleague Press, 1995). She is guest editor of an issue on 'Women and Science' for the journal *Women's Writing: The Elizabethan to Victorian Period* (vol. 2, no. 2, 1995).

HILDA L. SMITH, an Associate Professor of History at the University of Cincinnati, has a dual interest in the fields of women's history and the intellectual and social development of seventeenth-century England. She has published *Reason's Disciples: Seventeenth-Century English Feminists* (University of Illinois Press, 1982), and co-authored with Susan Cardinale *Women and the Literature of the Seventeenth Century: An Annotated Bibliography based on Wing's Short-Title Catalogue* (Greenwood Press, 1990). She is completing a monograph, *'All Men and Both Sexes': False Universals of Human Experience.*

BARBARA J. TODD is Associate Professor of History at the University of Toronto. She teaches British history and the history of women and gender in early modern Europe. Recent publications focus on aspects of widows' lives (see e.g. 'Demographic Determinism and Female Agency: Remarriage Reconsidered ... Again,' *Continuity and Change IX*, [1994] 421-450). Her current projects include a biography of Katherine Austen and a study of how English women used their wealth as investors and benefactors during the late seventeenth and early eighteenth centuries.

ACKNOWLEDGEMENTS

Disorderly Women in the Church Courts, Sarah Heller Mendelson. The source document is MS Chanter 866, Diocese of Exeter Depositions 1634–1640, held in the Devon Record Office. For permission to reproduce extracts, the author thanks the Devon Record Office and the Diocese of Exeter.

Infanticide Trials at the Old Bailey, Allyson N. May. The source documents are 'The Proceedings at the Sessions of the Peace and Oyer and Terminer, for the City of London and the County of Middlesex,' commonly known as the Old Bailey Sessions Papers. Extracts from these Crown Copyright records appear by permission of the Controller of Her Majesty's Stationery Office.

What the Servants Knew, Paula M. Humfrey. The source documents are session papers of the Court of Arches, Province of Canterbury. Extracts from these Crown Copyright records appear by permission of the Controller of Her Majesty's Stationery Office.

Wife-beating in the Eighteenth Century, Margaret R. Hunt. The source documents are held in the Greater London Record Office, Consistory Court of London (Matrimonial Causes), Spinkes v. Spinkes (1711). MS. DL/C/154 (Libels, Allegations and Sentences); MS. DL/C/632 (Depositions); MS. DL/C/42 (Acts of the Court). Extracts from these Crown Copyright records appear by permission of the Controller of Her Majesty's Stationery Office. Thanks to Valerie Frith for assisting in the transcriptions.

Women and Crime in Augustan London, John Beattie. The source documents are depositions and examinations taken by magistrates of the City of London, now held in the Sessions Papers in the Corporation of London Record Office. Extracts from these Crown Copyright records appear by permission of the Controller of Her Majesty's Stationery Office. The essay draws on material from John Beattie's essay 'Crime and Inequality in Eighteenth-Century London,' in *Crime and Inequality,* edited by John Hagan and Ruth D. Peterson, and used with the permission of the publishers, Stanford University Press. © 1995 by the Board of Trustees of the Leland Stanford Junior University.

Margaret Cavendish, Duchess of Newcastle, Hilda L. Smith. Excerpts are from the writings of Margaret Cavendish, Duchess of Newcastle, published in *Poems & Fancies* (1653) and *CCXI Sociable Letters* (London: Printed by W. Wilson, 1664)

Women in Botany, Ann B. Shteir. Excerpts are from *An Introduction to Botany* by Priscilla Wakefield (London: Harvey and Darton et. al, 1796).

Women's Debating Societies, Donna T. Andrew. Excerpts are from contemporary newspaper accounts, as noted in the text after each quotation.

Georgiana, Duchess of Devonshire, Phyllis Deutsch. Excerpts are from *Georgiana: Extracts from the Correspondence of Georgiana, Duchess of Devonshire,* edited by the Earl of Bessborough P.C., G.C.M.G. (London: John Murray Ltd.). Reprinted by permission of the publisher.

Katherine Austen, A Young Widow of London, Barbara J. Todd. Excerpts are from the manuscript edition of Katherine Austen's diary, held in the British Library [Add MS 4454]. Extracts are reprinted by permission of the British Library.

Mary Frith, Commonly Called Mal Cutpurse, Valerie Frith. Excerpts are from *The Life and Death of Mrs Mary Frith, Commonly Called Mal Cutpurse,* by Mary Frith (London: Printed by W. Gilbertson, 1662).